LIBRARY
NETWORK

MAINTAINING INFORMATION SYSTEMS IN ORGANIZATIONS

Editors

Richard Boland
University of Illinois at Urbana-Champaign

Rudy Hirschheim
University of Houston

Hirschheim: *Office Automation: A Social and Organizational Perspective*

Jarke: *Managers, Micros and Mainframes: Integrating Systems for End-Users*

Boland & Hirschheim: *Critical Issues in Information Systems Research*

Baskerville: *Designing Information Systems Security*

Schäfer: *Functional Analysis of Office Requirements: A Multiperspective Approach*

Mumford & MacDonald: *XSEL's Progress: The Continuing Journey of an Expert System*

Swanson & Beath: *Maintaining Information Systems in Organizations*

Friedman: *Computer Systems Development: History Organization and Implementation*

MAINTAINING INFORMATION SYSTEMS IN ORGANIZATIONS

E. Burton Swanson
Anderson Graduate School of Management
University of California, Los Angeles

AND

Cynthia Mathis Beath
Carlson School of Management
University of Minnesota

John Wiley
INFORMATION SYSTEMS SERIES

JOHN WILEY & SONS
Chichester · New York · Brisbane · Toronto · Singapore

Wiley Editorial Offices

John Wiley & Sons Ltd, Baffins Lane, Chichester,
West Sussex PO19 1UD, England

John Wiley & Sons, Inc., 605 Third Avenue,
New York, NY 10158-0012, USA

Jacaranda Wiley Ltd, GPO Box 859, Brisbane,
Queensland 4001, Australia

John Wiley & Sons (Canada) Ltd, 22 Worcester Road,
Rexdale, Ontario M9W 1L1, Canada

John Wiley & Sons (SEA) Pte Ltd, 37 Jalan Pemimpin #05-04,
Block B, Union Industrial Building, Singapore 2057

Library of Congress Cataloging-in-Publication Data:

Swanson, E. Burton.
Maintaining information systems in organizations/E. Burton Swanson and Cynthia M. Beath.
p. cm.—(John Wiley information systems series)
Bibliography: p.
Includes index.
ISBN 0 471 91969 1
1. Software maintenance—Management. 2. Data base management.
I. Beath, Cynthia Mathis II. Title. III. Series.
QA76.76.S64S93 1989 89-14630
005.74—dc20 CIP

British Library Cataloguing in Publication Data:

Swanson, Burton
Maintaining information systems in organizations.—(John Wiley information systems series).
1. Business firms. Information systems.
Management
I. Title II. Beath, Cynthia M.
658.4'038

ISBN 0 471 91969 1

Printed and bound in Great Britain by
Biddles Ltd, Guildford and King's Lynn

For Cheryl and Andrew

Contents

Series Foreword

In order for all types of organizations to succeed, they need to be able to process data and use information effectively. This has become especially true in today's rapidly changing environment. In conducting their day-to-day operations, organizations use information for functions such as planning, controlling, organizing, and decision making. Information, therefore, is unquestionably a critical resource in the operation of all organizations. Any means, mechanical or otherwise, which can help organizations process and manage information presents an opportunity they can ill afford to ignore.

The arrival of the computer and its use in data processing has been one of the most important organizational innovations in the past thirty years. The advent of computer-based data processing and information systems has led to organizations being able to cope with the vast quantities of information which they need to process and manage to survive. The field which has emerged to study this development is *information systems*(IS). It is a combination of two primary fields: computer science and management, with a host of supporting disciplines, e.g. psychology, sociology, statistics, political science, economics, philosophy, and mathematics. IS is concerned not only with the development of new information technologies but also with questions such as: how they can best be applied, how they should be managed, and what their wider implications are.

Partly because of the dynamic world in which we live (and the concomitant need to process more information), and partly because of the dramatic recent developments in information technology, e.g. personal computers, fourth-generation languages, relational databases, knowledge-based systems, and office automation, the relevance and importance of the field of information systems, and office automation, the relevance and importance of the field of information systems has become apparent. End users, who previously had little potential of becoming seriously involved and knowledgeable in information technology and systems, are now much more aware of and interested in the new technology. Individuals working in today's and tomorrow's organizations will be expected to have some understanding of and the ability to use the rapidly developing information technologies and systems. The dramatic increase in the availability and use of information technology, however, raises fundamental questions on the guiding of technological innovation, measuring organizational and managerial productivity, augmenting human intelligence, ensuring data integrity, and establishing strategic advantage. The expanded use of information systems also raises major challenges to the traditional forms of administration and authority, the right to privacy, the nature and form of work, and the limits of calculative rationality in modern organizations and society.

The Wiley Series on Information Systems has emerged to address these questions and challenges. It hopes to stimulate thought and discussion on the key role information systems play in the functioning of organizations and society, and how their role is likely to change in the future. This historical or evolutionary theme of the Series is important because considerable insight can be gained by attempting to understand the past. The Series will attempt to integrate both description—what has been done—with prescription—how best to develop and implement information systems.

The descriptive and historical aspect is considered vital because information systems of the past have not necessarily met with the success that was envisaged. Numerous writers postulate that a high proportion of systems are failures in one sense or another. Given their high cost of development and their importance to the day-to-day running of organizations, this situation must surely be unacceptable. Research into IS failure has concluded that the primary cause of failure is the lack of consideration given to the social and behavioural dimensions of IS. Far too much emphasis has been placed on their technical side. The result has been something of a shift in emphasis from a strictly technical conception of IS to one where it is recognized that information systems have behavioural consequences. But even this misses the mark. A growing number of researchers suggest that information systems are more appropriately conceived as social systems which rely, to a greater and greater extent, on new technology for their operation. It is this social orientation which is lacking in much of what is written about IS. The current volume, *Maintaining Information Systems in Organizations* by E. Burton Swanson and Cynthia Mathis Beath, exemplifies the theme of the series by presenting a rich empirical study of system maintenance as the interaction among technical, organizational and personnel issues over time. The twelve case studies they report and the conclusions they draw from them provide guidance to managers of information systems that links theory and practice in the best tradition of organizational studies.

The Series seeks to provide a forum for the serious discussion of IS. Although the primary perspective is a more social and behavioural one, alternative perspectives will also be included. This is based on the belief that no one perspective can be totally complete; added insight is possible through the adoption of multiple views. Relevant areas to be addressed in the Series include (but are not limited to): the theoretical development of information systems, their practical application, the foundations and evolution of information systems, and IS innovation. Subjects such as systems design, systems analysis methodologies, information systems planning and management, office automation, project management, decision support systems, end-user computing, and information systems and society are key concerns of the Series.

Rudy Hirschheim
Richard Boland

Preface

Information systems (IS) maintenance is a subject apparently lacking in glamor. At least, this has been our impression. As academics, we have often been questioned by practitioners as to our research interests. When we answer that maintenance is one of these, we sometimes notice a certain glazing of the eyes of our questioner. Evidently, in the current heady climate of 'strategic applications' for competitive advantage, a focus on the maintenance of currently installed systems appears unexciting, even retrograde, to some persons.

However, we confess to being rather fond of our subject. In contrast to more *avant-garde* topics, which are sometimes more anticipated than widely realized in practice, the world of IS maintenance is the everyday experience of the substantial majority of computer professionals. It is also a poorly illuminated world, one not well understood and appreciated by senior management or the consumers of the information services provided. It is thus deserving of increased attention and careful consideration.

This book is constructed from the results of a recent study, the focus of which is on comparative environments for IS maintenance and alternative strategies for management of the maintenance process, including alternative approaches to organization design, task definition and assignment, work technique, and policies for co-ordination and control. Field studies of twelve IS organizations were involved as part of the overall research effort.

From the field studies, a set of cases on IS maintenance has been developed. These cases serve as the basis for the book, and are incorporated within it in Chapters 4 through 7.

The book is designed to be readable both in whole and in part. The twelve cases, written so as to be self-contained, constitute the heart of the material, slices of systems life which we hope the practitioner will find genuine and appealing. Included with each case are several questions for discussion, designed to surface selected issues of particular interest. Certain of these questions reference other cases for comparison in the spirit of the study itself.

Around the cases we present our own interpretation of selected management issues in IS maintenance. Together with the cases, this material is grouped into Chapters 4 through 7 of the book. Chapter 4 places maintenance in its policy and strategy context; Chapter 5 examines the nature of the maintenance task itself; Chapter 6 concerns itself with the organization and management of maintenance; and Chapter 7 focuses upon building a maintenance staff. Each of these chapters begins with a discussion of the issues and concludes with cases and questions.

Chapter 8 ends the book with a look at the future for maintenance. Here we summarize in terms of the basic problems of maintenance and offer specific direction for management and further research.

The first three chapters introduce our study. Chapter 1 provides the motivation for the new view of maintenance proposed and includes several vignettes from the cases. Chapter 2 describes the background for the study and our research strategy and focus. It also comprises a section on our research methods, which may be skipped without loss of continuity by those not interested in such matters. Chapter 3 provides an overview of maintenance in the twelve organizations studied, which may be used to guide further reading.

Acknowledgements

As mentioned above, this book is a by-product of a field study of organizational alternatives for the management of application software maintenance. This field study was itself part of a larger project effort. A number of individuals were involved in this project, apart from ourselves. Professor Bennet P. Lientz of The Anderson Graduate School of Management (AGSM), UCLA, served as a co-director of the overall project (with Swanson). Apart from working on other aspects of the project, he and Harold G. Plain, an AGSM doctoral student, assisted with the data collection for the present study, and also contributed one of the twelve cases (West Coast High Tech Manufacturing).

Thomas Gosnell and Chung-Fern (Rebecca) Wu, both AGSM doctoral students, worked during the early phases of the study on the development of reference materials on software maintenance. Many of these references have found their way into this book.

Patricia C. Plessinger and Amy H. Sand, both MBA students at AGSM, made important contributions to later phases of the study. Plessinger assisted in the development of the United Food Stores case and in the establishment of the overall case database. Sand participated in the development of two cases, Big City State University and Metropolitan Gas Company, and added further to the reference materials collected.

Mary K. Lee, an AGSM doctoral student, helped in the final preparation of the book, locating several needed references in the Library and developing the Index. Michael Sachs, Wendy Jorgensen, and Merle Baluyut, members of the IS staff at AGSM, provided word-processing assistance.

Financial support of the research was provided by the Information Systems Research Program (ISRP) at AGSM, the MISSLE (Management of Information Systems Learning Environment) Project of AGSM funded under the IBM Corporation's Program of Support for Education in the Management of Information Systems, and the Carlson School of Management, University of Minnesota. Additional important support came through the efforts of R.K. and B.W., both of whom believed in the importance of our work, and to whom we offer our special thanks.

Lastly, the most important contributors to the present book were, of course, the many participants in the twelve organizations with whose co-operation the cases were developed. These individuals gave generously of their time and views during our numerous discussions. They shared with us their own theories of maintenance and it is from this collective wisdom that our best practical suggestions for managing maintenance arise. Because of confidentiality agreements, we cannot thank these observant, insightful, and creative individuals by name here. However, we do take this opportunity to thank them collectively for their assistance in our discoveries.

Chapter 1

INFORMATION SYSTEMS MAINTENANCE IN A NEW LIGHT

INTRODUCTION

H.B. manages Systems and Programming at Westcoast Refining & Marketing, heading a staff of 148 individuals responsible for business application software development. Among the functions served by 51 major installed systems are crude oil accounting, basic manufacturing, distribution, sales processing, sales reporting, payments and receivables, and financial accounting. Some months ago, upon assuming his current position, H.B. initiated a series of employee discussions on ways to effect organizational improvement. Five problems were identified as important enough to warrant task force efforts. Maintenance was one of these.

Now the Maintenance Task Force has submitted its first report, detailing 22 specific problems. Included among these are:

(1) Absence of a maintenance philosophy, a fundamental set of concepts and principles which governs the maintenance function;
(2) Inadequate planning for maintenance;
(3) Failure to define maintenance training requirements;
(4) Lack of systematic and periodic check-up of systems being maintained;
(5) Organization of maintenance within area of application;
(6) Tracking of maintenance activities;
(7) Lack of formal change control process;
(8) Lack of systems and programming knowledge of data-processing environment;
(9) Lack of recognition of maintenance function and its accomplishments; and
(10) Lack of systems and programming knowledge of business functions.

H.B. does not find the list surprising. 'About 90% of what has bubbled up was predictable,' he remarks.

Having compiled its problem list, the Maintenance Task Force will next generate, organize, and prioritize a set of proposed solutions. Ultimately, H.B. will reorganize maintenance within his department on the basis of the recommendations he receives.

Maintaining information systems in organizations is, as we see from this example, problematic for managers. That is, maintenance is a task which creates organizational stress and strain and demands management attention. It is also a very substantial task by many reports. 'Today, maintenance chews up 60% to

70% of MIS operating budgets. By 1990 it could hit 80%,' claims one recent report (Port, 1988). Over $30 billion per year was spent on maintenance, worldwide, in 1985, according to another (Martin and McClure, 1983). About 75 billion lines of code are estimated to be in use, worldwide. Much of this is used by the US Federal Government alone, according to Harrison (1987), who remarks, 'Possibly the only other number of significance counted in Washington these days requiring more zeroes than the total federal software inventory is the combination of the national debt and the trade deficit' (p. 81).

What is the nature of this maintenance task, such that it is associated with problems of the types listed by H.B.'s Task Force? Viewed very narrowly by some, maintenance consists of changes to operational software to eliminate 'bugs', those errors in a program that interfere with its correct functioning. Though such corrective, 'fix-it' work is clearly important, in this book we reject this narrow view. Corrective work accounts for a relatively small portion of the large budget percentages reported above (Lientz *et al.*, 1978), and reflects few of the actual problems of information systems maintenance, such as, for example, those reported by H.B.'s Task Force (Lientz and Swanson, 1980). We adopt instead an inclusive view, one which incorporates all task components involved in sustaining operational information systems within organizations. Such components include not only corrective aspects but adaptive and perfective ones as well, as we shall see. Moreover, maintenance involves changes to more than just the software, as has been emphasized by Edwards (1984).

Taking this inclusive view, this book seeks to illuminate in particular the organizational problems of IS maintenance. From this perspective, our concern is not so much with the individual practice of maintenance programming, involving such matters as how to debug programs, implement changes, and reconstruct documentation. Rather, it is with problems which managers face regarding maintenance. How should maintenance be planned? How should the maintenance staff be organized? What information is needed to manage maintenance? What tools should maintainers have? How can maintainers be motivated?

Here, in this first chapter, we provide an introduction. We begin by tracing the rise and growth of IS organizations, based on the in-house development of their application system portfolios. Limits to this growth are next encountered. Characteristic problems in system maintenance and development in the IS organization are sketched and the roots of these problems are identified. Finally, a glimpse of a new view of the maintenance task is offered, as is an introduction to the chapters to follow.

THE RISE AND GROWTH OF THE IS ORGANIZATION

It will be helpful to briefly recall the origins of IS organizations and their application software. (See also Bohl, 1980.)

The first business use of a computer is said to have taken place in 1954, the same year that IBM installed its first commercial computer and three years after Sperry Rand installed the first UNIVAC at the US Bureau of the Census. The first business applications were generally in commercial record keeping and accounting, which had heretofore been carried out largely by means of punched-card tabulating equipment. The first application software was typically written in machine or Assembler language. COBOL (COmmon Business Oriented Language) was introduced in 1959 and, with the support of the US government, soon became the dominant programming language for business applications.

Application software was thus originally developed 'in-house', for local use. Computer hardware and system software, consisting of compilers, control programs, and general-purpose utilities, were commercially available but application software was generally not. Applications, by their nature, tended to be more specific to the firm and its business. It was necessary to organize a local workforce for their development. Given the domain of these original applications, this workforce and the computer equipment it employed were typically located within the accounting department of the business.

Two jobs associated with application software development were soon defined, that of the programmer and that of the systems analyst. The programmer produced the software in the language of local choice, working from a specification provided by the systems analyst, who interpreted the business needs of organizational users. (The ideal language for a specification has, over the years, become the holy grail of the profession. For a formalist's view, see Goguen, 1986.)

From its accounting origins, the domain of business application software expanded greatly during the 1960s and 1970s, both within and among businesses, to eventually penetrate all aspects of industrial production and operations, as well as other common business functions such as marketing, finance, and personnel. Increasing numbers of programmers and systems analysts were employed, computing capacity continued to be enlarged, and the installed base of application software grew steadily. Accordingly, the information systems organization rose from its humble beginnings to become a major organizational function in its own right. Its executive frequently became a vice-president, or a 'chief information officer (CIO)'.

How far have we progressed since 1954? Boehm (1986), citing estimates of the professional programmer population to be 3.25 million worldwide as of 1984 with an annual growth rate of 7 per cent, projects a programmer population of 10 million by the year 2000. The great majority of this population will devote its efforts to application, as opposed to system, software, and it will devote its efforts to maintenance.

ENCOUNTERING THE LIMITS TO GROWTH

Historically, new system development has occupied the foreground of IS work and maintenance the background. This view, which still persists, is a direct consequence of the adolescent growth phase of the IS organization during the 1960s and into the 1970s.

Alarms began to be sounded in the early 1970s. Maintenance was likened in one memorable article to an 'iceberg', that is, something very large, submerged from sight, and dangerous to the course of the IS mission (Canning, 1972). Worse news followed. Research confirmed that, on average, maintenance consumed half of the total systems and programming budget (Lientz *et al.*, 1978).

Original emphasis had been on the development of new systems, but each system successfully implemented required continued care and feeding, i.e. maintenance, work which was not well understood, and which was also often interpreted as reflecting poorly on the quality of the original development. Like an unwanted stepchild, maintenance was therefore typically confined to upstairs quarters and not presented to honored guests such as top management, for example.

Of course, the stepchild continued to grow and become ever more difficult to provide for by simply adding more rooms upstairs. Keeping it from view became increasingly problematic. Eventually and predictably, the IS house could not continue to expand unchallenged, while new systems work queued indefinitely and impatiently at the front door. 'What is going on in there?' was the obvious and painful question finally asked.

Thus we arrived at the present state of affairs. The problems of maintenance must be faced. But what are they, exactly?

CHARACTERISTIC PROBLEMS IN MAINTENANCE

Managers face a number of problems in information systems maintenance. Many of these are of an organizational nature, involving issues of, for example, organization design, task definition and assignment, work technique, and policies for co-ordination and control. They are very much like those problems itemized for H.B. above.

In this section we focus briefly on situations in which such organizational problems arise. In doing so we identify a set of six relationships which, we argue, constitute the relational foundations of maintenance in that they provide the basis for its effective management. We summarize these relationships in terms of a Relational Foundations Model, shown in Figure 1.1. The six relationships involve three groups: the application systems, IS staff, and users. Within these groups, members are related to each other by means of (1) among-systems, (2) among-staff, and (3) among-users relationships. Further, between the groups, there are (4) systems–staff, (5) systems–user, and (6) staff–user relationships.

We will have much to say about these relational foundations throughout this book. Here we simply introduce the six relationships by means of a series of vignettes, drawn from the book's cases.

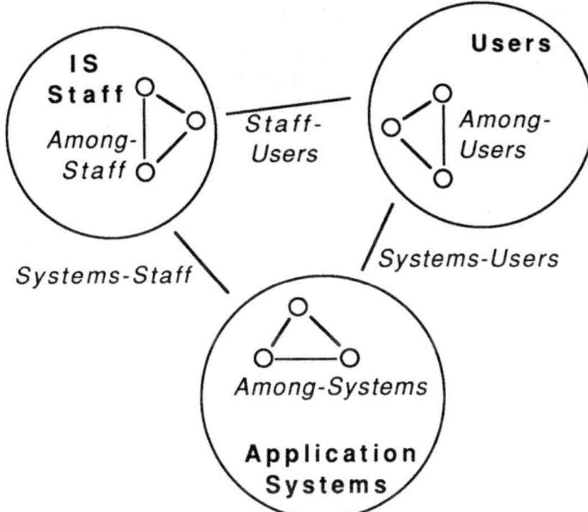

FIGURE 1.1 The Relational Foundations Model: six relationships in information system maintenance

Situation 1. The among-systems relationship
Management Information Systems (MIS) at United Food Stores oversees an applications portfolio of 33 major installed systems, 60 per cent of which are regarded as 'critical' to the business. From an annual budget of about $8 million for hardware, software, and people, an estimated 86 per cent is spent on operations and maintenance. G.E., manager of MIS, views his organization as a factory, where the strategic impact of existing applications is high while the strategic impact of new systems under development is comparatively low. 'Since we have a large application portfolio and can't be down for any length of time, we are in a position where software maintenance is a big issue for us . . . ,' says G.E., emphasizing the importance of day-to-day operational reliability. 'We have a policy here that we don't have the same problem twice.'

Maintenance policy at United Food Stores is seen to be based in part on distinguishing among systems in terms of their operational criticality, enabling management to give special emphasis to keeping certain systems up and running. This illustrates the among-systems relationship as a foundation for maintenance, and is but one example of the several dimensions on which similarities and differences among systems may be usefully established. Apart from operational criticality, systems also vary in terms of, for example, life-cycle phase, age, size, hardware and system software base, language, and application domain. They are further related in terms of their direct integration, through their shared data. All these dimensions have implications for maintenance policies and organization. For example, if a portfolio is aging, as indicated by the proportion of systems over ten years old, a policy to guide replacement may be sought. Similarly, should programming languages be observed to proliferate unnecessarily among systems, the need for an organizational standard may be signalled.

Such among-systems relationships and their implications for maintenance have not gone unnoticed by IS managers and researchers. However, five additional relationships are just as important.

Situation 2. The among-staff relationship
Nationwide Soft Drink organizes maintenance separately from new system development. F.H., manager of Production Systems Support (PSS), is concerned about the 'stigma of maintenance' and its effect upon his group. In contrast to development staff, many of whom have computer science degrees, PSS staff tend to be less technically educated. They also tend to work longer hours without additional compensation, and are on call by means of 'beepers' which summon them when problems occur. The main incentive in PSS is to 'move up' to development work. Over the last four years PSS staff turnover has been 100 per cent. However, K.R., manager of the Management Information Systems Department, is apparently content, remarking that 'PSS costs are relatively low. It functions well. It's responsive.'

At Nationwide Soft Drink, IS staff are of two classes, those qualified for new system development and those unqualified for it. Maintenance organization and policy follow directly from this among-staff distinction, which appears to have significant ramifications for staff morale. Other dimensions on which IS staff may be compared include, for example, length of organizational tenure, level of education, prior work experience, language knowledge, and career growth need strength. (See Couger and Colter, 1985.) All these dimensions have important implications for the management of information system maintenance. IS staff skills and motivation levels, for example, should be an important driver of maintenance policy. Schemes for rotating staff between maintenance and development may be concocted to ameliorate motivational problems identified, for instance. Similarly, policies for training maintainers, often sadly lacking, may be based on a thorough inventory of staff skills.

Situation 3. The among-users relationship
Systems Development at Integrated Information Technologies, Eastcoast Manufacturing Location, employs 266 individuals organized into five department groups according to area of application. Overall, 89 major installed systems serve an estimated 1300 'serious users'. Recently, a survey of these users revealed complaints about the current 'application backlog', work requested of IS but not yet undertaken. After some debate, IS has been instructed by top management to measure and report its progress in reducing this backlog. In the meantime, an effort to relieve the problem by means of an Information Center is viewed with some skepticism. Once users experience the ease with which they

can provide themselves with reports they may conclude 'If I can do this, you guys can probably do more,' laments one IS manager. Another sees the threat of end-user computing somewhat differently. 'We're the professionals,' he asserts, but (we have to contend with) 'the engineer who would do it all.'

A number of issues in the management of information system maintenance at Integrated Information Technologies may be identified, including those of expertise and professionalism on the part of IS staff and users. Focusing for the moment on users, we note that an among-users relationship is illustrated in terms of engineering education and training. A significant number of users at IIT are engineers who are well schooled in computing, and who are thus inclined to 'do it all'. Their expectations for information systems maintenance may be quite different from those of less sophisticated users; they may be very intolerant of poor service, for example. More generally, dimensions on which users of information systems may be compared include length of organizational tenure, level of education, computer skills, job expertise, and job satisfaction, among others. All these may be significant for the management of maintenance, although their implications have received little attention in the IS literature. Experienced users, for example, may be more able and willing than inexperienced ones to participate fully in maintenance planning. They may also be more able to assist in system re-installation efforts.

Situation 4. The systems–staff relationship
Information Resources (IR) at National Foods employs a staff of 46 individuals responsible for application systems development and maintenance. The current portfolio comprises 103 installed systems, serving users at NF headquarters and more than 100 other locations. For the most part, staff work either on new system development or on maintenance. Management is firm in its belief that development and maintenance appeal to different types of people and it hires accordingly. There is little mobility between the two groups. Maintainers are viewed as those who prefer working on multiple small problems, with quick feedback. 'They like the big in-basket, big out-basket,' remarks one manager. On the whole, separate maintenance is seen as a plus. However, the approach has prevailed over a period of relative organizational stability. 'That's changing now,' observes the manager, referring to a new dynamism in the business as well as new software tools and techniques available in the marketplace. Whether maintenance will continue to be separated is thus less certain.

National Foods organizes maintenance on the basis of matching staff to systems. In management's view, new systems in development are best worked on by one group while maintenance of installed systems is best carried out by another. Systems move from the first group to the second upon installation. Illustrated is the importance of the systems–staff relationship in the organization and management of maintenance. Here it may be observed that job assignment, in general, requires that staff be related in some equivalent way to the objects of their work. However, systems and staff may be significantly related in various ways. System age may be usefully related to length of tenure of staff, for example. Similarly, domain of system application may be linked to staff work experience and language knowledge and use related between staff and systems. Accordingly, policies for assigning maintenance responsibilities to staff may be shaped in one situation by technical skills and familiarity, while in another they may be based on staff knowledge of the business function and environment. We will have more to say about this in later chapters.

Situation 5. The systems–user relationship
The Technology Information Systems (TIS) Department at Advanced Technologies Manufacturing maintains 30 major installed systems in support of plant manufacturing. User knowledge of these systems is seen by TIS management to be a significant problem. 'The biggest chunk of maintenance is answering user questions,' remarks one manager. Fourteen of the systems maintained are more than ten years old; among these are systems which have been adopted by multiple-plant locations. Ten of the installed systems are considered 'leading-edge' applications in the sense of providing users with functions beyond those typically available elsewhere in the industry. Direct contact between TIS staff and users is reported to be frequent. Nevertheless, according to another manager, '[We are] still evolving to high user involvement, particularly in helping users understand what is involved in development.'

User knowledge of systems at Advanced Technologies Manufacturing illustrates the importance of the systems–user relationship in information system maintenance. System-specific user training, user involvement in system development, and accumulated experience with a user interface provide additional examples of this relationship. All are consequential for the organization and management of maintenance, in establishing policies for user training, for instance, or in deciding to refit older systems with a common user interface.

Situation 6. The staff–user relationship
Small City Manufacturing has recently formed a Manufacturing Information Services (MIS) Department, spun off from the large centralized IS Department which has, until now, served all functions of the business. Reflecting a new emphasis on decentralized profit responsibility within the company, MIS is responsible for development and maintenance of all systems directly supporting the manufacturing function. It is staffed both by programmers taken from the centralized IS department and by systems analysts who formerly worked in user

departments. All now work as programmer/analysts in an expanded role which combines computer and business expertise and necessitates widespread individual adjustment. Among former analysts are many with few programming skills and among former programmers are some not necessarily comfortable in face-to-face communication with users. 'Now you're going to have to talk to people who talk funny,' their manager warns them.

MIS at Small City Manufacturing illustrates a sixth type of relationship which is critical to the organization of maintenance, that between IS staff and users. In this particular instance the IS staff is reconstituted to draw upon the business analysis skills formerly within the user province. At the same time, the staff is brought under more direct user control, as it now reports directly to Manufacturing.

Prior job experience of IS staff and users also illustrates the significance of the relationship between the two groups. Here, the extent to which IS staff have prior experience as users, or users have prior experience as IS staff, has important ramifications for the organization of maintenance—for example, in establishing policies for co-ordination between IS and users. Where there is common experience, co-ordination is naturally facilitated; where there is non, more formal co-ordinating mechanisms may be needed.

In summary, organizational problems in information systems maintenance may be illuminated by focusing upon six types of relationships: (1) among-systems; (2) among-staff; (3) among-users; (4) systems–staff; (5) systems–user; and (6) staff–user. We summarize these in the Relational Foundations Model of Figure 1.1. As a technical note, for those readers who may be interested we also observe that the first three types of relationships form the bases for the second three. For example, systems–staff relationships are based on among-systems and among-staff ones. (Relating system age to staff service length is based on distinguishing among systems in terms of age and among staff in terms of service length.) Similarly, systems–user relationships are based on among-systems and among-user ones, and staff–user relationships on among-staff and among-users ones.

Of course, our illustrative vignettes merely scratch the surface of these relational foundations, which also serve as the basis for the research on which this book is based. In the next chapter we develop our ideas further, and restate them in the form of a Task Fit Hypothesis. Before doing so, however, we examine the roots of these problem situations in the nature of the application systems themselves.

ROOTS OF THE PROBLEMS

What are the roots of organizational problems in IS maintenance, and to what extent do they differ fundamentally from organizational problems of other types? We argue that the roots may be found in the nature of the systems themselves. It is here that the various tasks involved—those of design, development, implementation, operation, maintenance, and use—are based. Here the unique character of the organizational problems in maintenance may be identified.

Among the significant characteristics of information systems, four are of particular importance in terms of their organizational implications. Briefly, information systems pose particular organizational problems for maintenance in that:

(1) They embody and institutionalize organizational knowledge;
(2) They tend to grow and elaborate over time;
(3) They tend to be long-lived; and
(4) They tend to congregate and develop as families whose members are highly dependent upon one another.

Without doubt, the most important of the characteristics pertains to the role of information systems in the development and transmission of organizational knowledge. Simply put, information systems embody and institutionalize the knowledge of the organizations they serve. By their data, they establish those facts upon which organizational choices depend, and, just as importantly, they also dictate the linguistic forms, or data models, by which these facts are articulated. By their software, they incorporate further the organizational reasoning applied to facts in making inferences about organizational objects and events and in support of organizational decision making.

Additionally, information systems typically serve in their organizational roles actively, not passively. Specifically, they initiate formal organizational transactions according to circumstances and schedule, and hence shape organizational events much as do the organization's human agents. Over time, their 'knowledge' further becomes institutionalized, a taken-for-granted feature of the organization.

Systems further embody organizational structure, establishing routines which employees follow and often controlling the contingencies and pace of work. They provide information linkages which co-ordinate both within the organization and between it and its customers and suppliers.

Nevertheless, information systems are by no means autonomous as organizational agents. Rather, they function in tandem both with their users and with the active support and intervention of IS staff. The development and distribution of organizational knowledge by means of information systems is thus the joint product of systems, users, and staff. It is fundamentally for this reason that attending to the relationships among and between systems, users, and staff is crucial to maintaining information systems in organizations.

The second important characteristic of information systems is that they tend to grow and elaborate as they are used (Belady and Lehman, 1976). Over time, their application software accumulates, their databases swell with added items, and their reports become more numerous. The rate of growth of the software itself is typically a substantial 10 per cent per year (Lientz and Swanson, 1980).

Why should systems grow as they do? Basically, one good use of an information system typically begets another. Therefore, for example, one report suggests another to a user, perhaps as a by-product of the first. This new report calls, in turn, for several additional items of data, which requires further that new software procedures be provided. Once provided, the added data and procedures serve not only the immediate need but become re-usable resources to be drawn upon for new purposes. Organizational learning is continuous, and so the cycle repeats itself.

Also, information systems grow over time because they must adapt to new situations and circumstances not originally foreseen (Lehman, 1980). Transaction-processing systems, in particular, confront a substantial stream of organizational transactions over time, some of which are inevitably exceptional in ways not anticipated by the software, which lacks the requisite processing variety and requires an infusion of additional procedures (Swanson, 1979).

The important consequence of this growth and elaboration is that systems tend to increase their appetites for scarce organizational resources. Over time, with increased functionality, they are likely to involve more rather than fewer users, and to be integrated into more of any one user's job rather than less. Also over time, systems are likely to need more IS staff support rather than less, and to need this more often rather than less.

The third important characteristic is that information systems tend to be long-lived (Zvegintzov, 1984). They are likely to serve the organization for a decade or more, and to remain in service long after those who originally brought them to life move on to other pursuits, within the organization or elsewhere. Maintaining such aging systems is, of course, expensive to the organization. However, replacing them is likely to be more expensive yet, at least in the short run. Systems thus persevere in organizations while users and staff come and go.

The important consequence is that the knowledge embodied by an information system is maintained with progressive difficulty as the system ages. Within an aging portfolio, relationships among and between systems, users, and staff become increasingly problematic.

Finally, the fourth important characteristic is that the information systems of an organization tend to congregate and develop as families. By original design or not, they come to rely upon each other for their data. Over time, newer systems originate in niches provided by older ones, and identifiable families of systems come to exist. Relationships among families are further established. Thus, over the long run, an organization is served more by its systems as a whole than it is by those taken individually. This aggregate whole is commonly referred to as the application systems portfolio.

As we shall see later, the application systems portfolio of an organization may be characterized in terms of important demographic features, in the same way as IS staff and users may also be described. The systems of a portfolio will vary in terms of age, origin, and technology, for example, while IS staff and users will similarly vary in terms of length of service, prior work experience, and education. Problems of fit, such as those described above, may therefore be diagnosed by demographic analyses of systems, IS staff, and users (Swanson and Beath, 1986). (Pfeffer, 1985, discusses the usefulness of organizational demographics in general.)

TOWARD A NEW VIEW OF IS MAINTENANCE

This book argues for a new view of maintaining information systems in organizations, and we outline here the elements of this view.

The first element is a focus on the application system portfolio of the organization, which is understood to include all major installed systems and new ones under development. Only by an understanding of the portfolio as a whole, and of individual systems as related parts of this whole, can IS and general management make intelligent sense of the maintenance and development tasks.

The second element of the view promotes maintenance to the foreground of the task as a whole. We will argue that there are good strategic reasons for inverting the current emphasis, and that top management will value and support the new vision. This new vision emphasizes quality of service to the host organization.

Finally, we will argue that successful maintenance of the application system portfolio requires that systems, staff, and users be related among and between each other in ways that we have illustrated above. We shall have much to say about this in the chapters which follow.

STRUCTURE OF THE BOOK

The balance of this book is decidated to the further exploration of the issues raised in this chapter. It is constructed around twelve cases, from which we have presented some short extracts above. The cases appear in full in Chapters 4 through 7.

Chapter 2 presents the background for our multiple-case study. It begins with a review of an earlier study which motivated the current work and continues with an articulation of the present research strategy and focus. It concludes with a description of the research methods employed.

Chapter 3 presents an overview of maintenance in the twelve organizations studied, on the basis of common data collected from each. It describes, in effect, the sample on which the study is based, and further compares this sample to known reference populations where possible. Thus the reader may compare the cases both among each other and among other organizational cases of interest.

Chapters 4 through 7 form the heart of the book. Each explores a major concern in the maintenance of information systems in organizations and further incorporates three full cases as an addendum. Any or all of the cases may be read in or out of the sequence in which they are presented. Introductory notes and concluding postscripts facilitate the navigation.

Chapter 4 discusses the maintenance of information systems in relation to the policies and strategy of the host organization. These are seen to establish an important context for maintenance, within which a strategy for maintenance itself may be formulated. Cases include: (4.1) Westcoast Refining and Marketing; (4.2) Western Aeronautics; and (4.3) United Food Stores.

Chapter 5 examines the organizational task of maintenance. Discussed first is the traditional view of maintenance within the context of the system development life cycle. A new view of the task, based in an application portfolio context, is then presented. Basic types of maintenance work are examined, along with requisite knowledge and skills and alternatives for specialization. A discussion of the differences between maintenance and new system development concludes the chapter. Cases include: (5.1) Advanced Technologies Manufacturing; (5.2) West Coast High Tech Manufacturing; and (5.3) Small City Manufacturing.

Chapter 6 is devoted to organizational designs for information systems maintenance. Managerial choices among alternative organizational structures, the selection of policies to govern maintenance, and other techniques of maintenance management are covered. Cases include: (6.1) Nationwide Soft Drink; (6.2) National Foods; and (6.3) Diablo National Laboratories.

Chapter 7 examines staff selection and development in information systems maintenance. Among staff selection issues discussed are those relating to educational preparation, prior work experience, and internal transfers. Among staff development issues considered are those relating to first assignments, in-class and on-the-job training, job expansion and rotation, and turnover and retention. Career path issues complete the chapter. Cases include: (7.1) Integrated Information Technologies; (7.2) Metropolitan Gas Company; and (7.3) Big City State University.

Chapter 8 presents a summing-up. Lessons for IS management are drawn and a reconstructed view of systems maintenance and development is proposed, with substantial implications for future practice. Directions for further research are also offered, completing the exposition.

REFERENCES

Belady, L. A., and Lehman, M. M. (1976) 'A model of large program development', *IBM Systems Journal*, **15**, 3, 225–52.

Boehm, B. (1986) 'Understanding and controlling software costs', in *Information Processing 86* (Ed. H.-J. Kugler), Proceedings of the IFIP 10th World Computer Congress, Dublin, Ireland, 1–5 September, North-Holland, Amsterdam, pp. 703–14.

Bohl, M. (1980) *Information Processing*, 3rd edition, Science Research Associates, Chicago.

Canning, R. G. (Ed.) (1972) 'That maintenance iceberg', *EDP Analyser*, October, 1–14.

Couger, J. D., and Colter, M. A. (1985) *Maintenance Programming: Improved Productivity Through Motivation*, Prentice-Hall, Englewood Cliffs, NJ.

Edwards, C. (1984) 'Information systems maintenance: an integrated perspective', *MIS Quarterly*, **8**, 4, 237–56.

Goguen, J. A. (1986) 'One, none, a hundred thousand specification languages', in *Information Processing 86* (Ed. H.-J. Kugler), Proceedings of the IFIP 10th World Computer Congress, Dublin, 1–5 September, North-Holland, Amsterdam, pp. 995–1003.

Harrison, R. (1987) 'Maintenance giant sleeps undisturbed in federal data centers', *Computerworld*, **21**, 10, 9 March, 81–6.

Lehman, M. H. (1980) 'Programs, life cycles, and laws of software evolution', *Proceedings of the IEEE*, Special Issue on Software Engineering **68**, 9, September, pp. 1060–76.

Lientz, B. P., and Swanson, E. B. (1980) *Software Maintenance Management*, Addison-Wesley, Reading, Mass.

Lientz, B. P., Swanson, E. B., and Tompkins, G. E. (1978) 'Characteristics of application software maintenance', *Communications of the ACM*, **21**, 6, 466–71.

Martin, J., and McClure, C. L. (1983) *Software Maintenance: The Problem and its Solutions*, Prentice-Hall, Englewood Cliffs, NJ.

Pfeffer, J. (1985) 'Organizational demography: implications for management', *California Management Review*, **28**, 1, Fall, 67–81.

Port, O. (1988) 'The software trap—automate or else', *Business Week*, Special Report, 9 May, 142–54.

Swanson, E. B. (1979) 'On the user-requisite variety of computer application software', *IEEE Transactions on Reliability*, **R-28**, 3, 221–6.

Swanson, E. B., and Beath, C. M. (1986) 'The demographics of software maintenance management', *Proceedings of the Seventh International Conference on Information Systems*, San Diego, 15–17 December, pp. 313–26.

Zvegintzov, N. (1984) 'Immortal software', *Datamation*, 15 June, 170–80.

Chapter 2

BACKGROUND FOR A MULTIPLE-CASE STUDY

INTRODUCTION

In this chapter we present the background for the study on which this book is based. We begin with a brief review of an earlier research project, the results of which directed the current study, and next describe the research strategy and focus of this one. Finally, we document the research method employed. This final section may be skipped without loss of continuity by those not interested in such matters.

AN EARLIER STUDY

The present study has its roots in earlier work, and it will be helpful to briefly review its history.

In an early paper on the subject of software maintenance, Swanson (1976) identified three basic types of maintenance work:

(1) Corrective maintenance, performed in response to processing, performance, and implementation failures;
(2) Adaptive maintenance, performed in response to anticipated changes in the data and processing environments; and
(3) Perfective maintenance, performed to eliminate processing inefficiencies, enhance performance, and improve maintainability.

This typology became the foundation for subsequent empirical studies, both by ourselves and by others, and has also become widely accepted among practitioners (Martin and Osborne, 1983).

Lientz *et al.* (1978) reported on a small exploratory survey (69 respondents) in which the substantial scale of maintenance work (comprising about half of the total application staff effort) was established, perfective maintenance was surprisingly found to be the largest of the three work components, and user demand for enhancements and extensions was identified as the most important management problem area. This preliminary study served as a pilot for a more ambitious effort which followed.

Five issues were the subject of the follow-on study, the overall results of which are reported in Lientz and Swanson (1980a):

(1) Conceptual issues, relative to the nature and composition of the maintenance task;

(2) Scale-of-effort issues, relative to resources allocated to maintenance;
(3) Organizational issues, relative to the division of labor in maintenance;
(4) Productivity technique issues, relative to the technology of maintenance; and
(5) Problem-area issues, as seen by managers of maintenance.

To address these issues, a two-part questionnaire was mailed to a randomly selected sample of 2000 Data Processing Management Association (DPMA) members employed as IS managers. The first part of the questionnaire focused upon the manager's IS unit as a whole, while the second asked questions about a significant system maintained by the IS unit. A total of 487 responses to the survey were received (a 24 per cent response rate).

Results of this survey confirmed and extended the findings of the preliminary study. Perfective maintenance was found to consume over half of the average maintenance effort, while providing user enhancements was seen to constitute most of the perfective task and more than 40 per cent of the total. Moreover, more than two-thirds of the enhancement effort went into providing users with new, additional reports or in adding new data to existing reports. Little effort was spent in filtering existing data or in consolidating current reports. Perhaps not surprisingly, therefore, the application software itself grew in size (as measured in modules or lines of code) at an average rate in excess of 10 per cent per year.

The amount of effort in maintaining a system, measured in hours per year, was found to depend upon four interrelated factors:

(1) The age of the system;
(2) Its size;
(3) The experience of the maintenance staff in the original development of the system; and
(4) The relative amount of corrective maintenance of the system required.

Thus because, as a system ages, it grows, it loses its architectural integrity, its staff becomes less familiar with it, and it requires relatively more repair, older systems tend, on average, to consume more maintenance resources.

Among the respondents, only 16.2 per cent organized maintenance separately from new system development. Significantly, these organizations, which also tended to be larger, with greater budgets supporting higher numbers of installed systems, spent smaller proportions of their efforts on maintenance, on average, than did those without separate maintenance units. This suggests, perhaps, that larger organizations may achieve efficiency in maintenance by means of specialization.

Six significant maintenance problems, as seen by IS managers, were identified:

(1) User knowledge, in terms of system understanding and training received;
(2) Programmer effectiveness, in terms of productivity, skills, and motivation;

(3) Product quality, in terms of design specifications, quality of original programming, and documentation;
(4) Programmer time availability, in terms of competing demands for programmers' time;
(5) Machine requirements, in terms of program storage and processing time; and
(6) System reliability, in terms of system hardware and software, and data integrity.

Of these, the problem of user knowledge accounted for most of the explainable difference in problems among organizations, underscoring again the importance of the user relationship in accounting for system success or failure (Lientz and Swanson, 1981).

Contrary to popular claims, the use of various development productivity techniques (e.g. test data generators, structured walk-throughs, and structured programming) was not associated with a reduced effort in maintenance. However, the use of such techniques was associated, on average, with fewer problems of product quality (Lientz and Swanson, 1980b).

In general, the study results confirm the importance of managerial and organizational aspects of application software maintenance. Inevitably, issues of the division of labor in maintenance among staff members arise. So, too, do those of the allocation of this effort among existing and future systems. Alternatives in the distribution of services to multiple clients raise further, related, issues. None of these lends itself to purely technical resolution (for example, by means of automated tools). Rather, resolution requires informed management choice among basic organizational alternatives.

Ultimately, research on the work of the individual IS staff member, e.g. the programmer, or on the task associated with a single application system is also too narrow to address such managerial issues. Such work fails to deal with the organization of these individuals around a shared task and a portfolio of systems. An organizational level of analysis is needed instead. For this reason, in the work which is the subject of this book we focus upon the IS unit and its application system portfolio as a whole.

RESEARCH STRATEGY AND FOCUS

The present study, designed to build upon the earlier work, involved the development of a set of twelve research cases. These focus on the comparative maintenance environments of IS organizations and on alternative management strategies for maintenance, including alternative approaches to organization design, task definition and assignment, work technique, and policies for co-ordination and control (Swanson and Beath, 1985).

Whereas the earlier work employed a large-scale mail survey, and focused on the maintenance of a single selected application system in each instance, the present study used on-site visits and data-collection procedures, and concentrated on the maintenance and development of the full application system portfolio within the organization. The intent was to conduct a more intensive and extensive examination of maintenance within the individual IS organization, though, of course, a much less extensive examination across organizations.

The study is conceptually motivated by a contingency theory perspective on application software development and maintenance. From this perspective, the IS organization is seen as linked to its host organization by means of its application system portfolio, which we define as the organized set of computer-based software and procedures which support automated data gathering, organizing, and processing, and thus information-providing and action-initiating applications in the host organization. Thus viewed, the application system portfolio is the vehicle for the information services provided to the host organization by the IS department.

Figure 2.1 summarizes pictorially the overall organizational task. Here the IS task is circumscribed by the smaller of the two bold circles, while the larger circle circumscribes in turn the task of the host organization. The task associated with the application system portfolio, which consists of system design, development, implementation, operation, maintenance, and use, is represented by the circular band which overlays the smaller circle, indicating that it is shared between IS and users within the host organization. The appropriate nature of this sharing and, in particular, the involvement or non-involvement of user organizations in system design, development, and implementation is a topic which has received

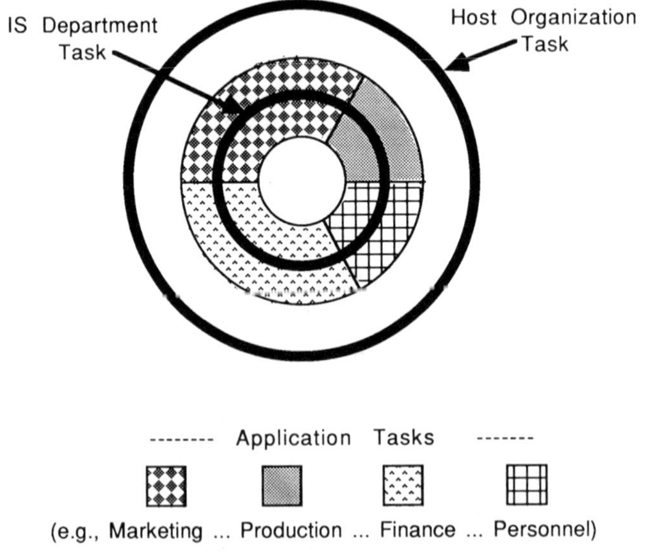

FIGURE 2.1 The system development and maintenance task

substantial attention in the IS literature. (See, e.g., Lucas, 1978; Zmud and Cox, 1979.)

In our view the application system portfolio establishes the fit of the IS organization to the host one, and provides the common ground on which both organizations meet. This suggests a guiding research hypothesis:

> *The Task Fit Hypothesis:* Problems in the maintenance and development of application systems occur in substantial part because of lack of fit among and between the systems and those who share in the task as a whole.

Strictly speaking, we postulate this hypothesis more than we advance it for a formal test here. That is, we employ it to frame our investigation on the whole.

More specifically, the task associated with an application system portfolio may be regarded as a set of subtasks associated with the systems of a portfolio and allocated between IS staff and system users, as also portrayed in Figure 2.1. In this context, it is the individual and collective characteristics of systems, staff, and users that provide the basis for subtask allocation. This suggests that problems in the management of the application system portfolio occur in significant part as a consequence of the effects and interaction among distributions of individual characteristics of (1) the application systems themselves; (2) the members of the IS staff; and (3) the users of the application systems.

Thus problems of maintenance may be viewed as shaped by certain fundamental 'IS demographics', i.e. distributions of individual characteristics associated with three populations: the application systems themselves, the members of the IS staff, and the users. Six categories of demographic effects and interactions are posited to be of relevance:

(1) Among systems;
(2) Among staff;
(3) Among users;
(4) Between systems and staff;
(5) Between systems and users; and
(6) Between staff and users.

In Chapter 1, the reader will recall, we introduced and summarized these in terms of a Relational Foundations Model, shown in Figure 1.1.

To illustrate, demographic effects among systems include those relating to compatibilities among underlying hardware and system software. Here, lack of compatibility may complicate maintenance where, for example, older systems are the prisoners of now-obsolete equipment. Effects among staff include those relating to career path implications of differences in educational backgrounds among IS personnel. Such differences may create problems for maintenance in that they might re-enforce a class structure within the organization—for example, where maintenance is a dead-end job. Effects among users include those relating to variation in computer literacy across major user groups. Here, maintenance may be made more difficult because of unrealistic expectations among, for example, the extremely naive.

Demographic effects between systems and IS staff include those relating to work-assignment substitutabilities based on programming language requirements and skills. Maintenance may be complicated by lack of substitutability among staff who, for example, are not skilled in more than one language. Effects between systems and users include those relating to requirements for continued training in the use of systems, and maintenance may be burdened by lack of user understanding of older systems due to turnover, for example. Effects between IS staff and users include those relating to their mutual understanding and effective communication with each other. Maintenance problems may arise where substantial gaps in business understanding prevail.

These and other demographic effects and interactions are best understood by data gathered and analyzed at the organizational level. Case study research, such as that employed here, offers one means toward this end. We describe our own use of this methodology next. Readers not interested in such matters are invited to skip this section, and move on to Chapter 3, where we summarize characteristics of the twelve organizational participants.

RESEARCH METHOD

The present research employs a case study methodology, an approach particularly suited to research on organizational, as opposed to individual, problem solving (Yin, 1984; Van Maanen, 1983). While case studies pose special challenges to the researcher because they focus on organizational issues in real world settings, they offer a special appeal to the practitioner, especially the manager, who can frequently identify with their situations. They thus also offer a common ground for communication and collaboration between researcher and practitioner.

Key characteristics of case study research are summarized in Table 2.1, adapted from Benbasat *et al.* (1987). Briefly, in a case study the phenomenon is examined in a natural, as opposed to a laboratory, setting, and experimental controls and manipulations are avoided. Only one or a few entities are studied, and each is examined intensively. The focus is on contemporary events. Data are collected by multiple means and changes in site selection and collection methods may take place while the research is underway. Results depend heavily on the integrative powers of the investigator. Research purposes involve exploration, classification, and hypothesis building. 'Why' and 'how' questions are particularly suited to examination.

Studies may further involve multiple cases, not just one, in which case a replication logic, as opposed to a sampling one, is suggested (Yin, 1984). Each case is considered equivalent to a single experiment, and analysis follows a cross-experiment rather than a within-experiment design and logic. Replication may be

TABLE 2.1 Key characteristics of case studies (adapted from Benbasat et al., *1987, by permission)*

(1) Phenomenon is examined in a natural setting
(2) Data are collected by multiple means
(3) One or few entities (person, group, or organization) are examined
(4) Complexity of the entity is studied intensively
(5) Exploration, classification, and hypothesis development are featured
(6) Experimental controls and manipulations are not involved
(7) Results depend heavily on the integrative powers of the investigator
(8) Changes in site selection and data-collection methods may take place during the research
(9) 'Why' and 'how' questions may be addressed through operational links traced over time
(10) Focus is on contemporary events

either literal or theoretical, and is dictated by the theoretical framework, which states the conditions under which case findings should be the same (literal replication—where equivalent case situations and actions prevail) and different (theoretical replication—where non-equivalent but closely related case situations and actions prevail).

In our own research we developed twelve cases using roughly a theoretical replication strategy. Each case was based on a study of moderate intensiveness over a limited time frame. Questionnaires were employed, as were on-site interviews, and reviews of organizational documents and publications, both internal and external. A common protocol was used throughout in assembling both quantitative and qualitative data, enabling triangulation as suggested by Jick (1983).

Together, the twelve participating organizations constituted a diverse group, and included four high-technology manufacturing companies, two food and beverage producers, an oil company, a retail grocery company, a defense firm, a public utility, a research and development laboratory, and a university. Their similarities and differences are further described in Chapter 3.

For those interested in particulars we document next our research design. We follow with a description of the data-collection process and conclude with a discussion of the data analysis and synthesis. (See also Swanson and Beath, 1988a, from which this material is adapted.) Those not interested in these details are invited to skip these sections and proceed directly to Chapter 3.

1. Research design

The overall research design was that of a multiple-case field study, involving the unobtrusive observation and examination of IS management in real organizational settings. This research strategy is recognized as strong with respect to realism of context but relatively weak on generalizeability and precision in control and measurement of variables (McGrath, 1982).

While no research strategy escapes its inherent weaknesses, various compensatory design features may provide added strength. The present design included a number of features intended to cope with weaknesses inherent in the simple field study.

As mentioned above, the present study involved multiple cases, not merely one, and used roughly a theoretical replication strategy. Thus a sample was involved, albeit a systematic one, not designed to be representative of any one population, despite its significant variety. Within the sample the case situations were closely related in that all involved the maintenance of an application system portfolio by an IS department within a host organization. However, important differences in organizational and management approaches also prevailed, enabling us to explore various aspects of the fit between portfolios, IS staffs, and users. Beyond this analysis, limited generalizeability from the sample was also possible in that its characteristics were comparable to those of a reference population, such as that surveyed earlier by Lientz and Swanson (1980a).

A common set of questionnaires was employed to gather data from the participating organizations. The first questionnaire focused on the IS organization and provided data on: the IS budget; levels of staffing; staff service length, prior job experience, education, training, and professional associations; allocation of effort to maintenance and development; amount of contact with users; and the use of various organizational techniques, work methods, and documentation tools. The second questionnaire focused on the application system portfolio and provided data on: the nature and number of the major installed systems and their integration; the size of the user population served; system age, size, development origin, and use of various technology; the hardware and system software base; and the nature and number of the new and replacement systems under development. Also included was a question in which the IS manager was asked to evaluate the problems of maintenance. Copies of both questionnaires appear in the Appendix to this book.

On the whole, the questionnaires solicited relatively objective, quantitative data, and, to the extent possible, used items validated in previous research (Lientz and Swanson, 1980a, 1981) on the same subject. Thus with common data to be obtained from multiple sites a small-scale sample survey was imbedded within the field study design.

On-site interviews and other sources were used to validate the questionnaire data and to gather further data in each case (Mitchell, 1985). This portion of the process was guided by a common protocol, along the lines suggested by Yin (1984), but was at times open-ended. Specific questions of interest were used to guide the interview process in all cases. However, each case was permitted to develop along its own story line; that is, questions of particular interest in the case context were pursued in depth and those of little interest were sometimes ignored.

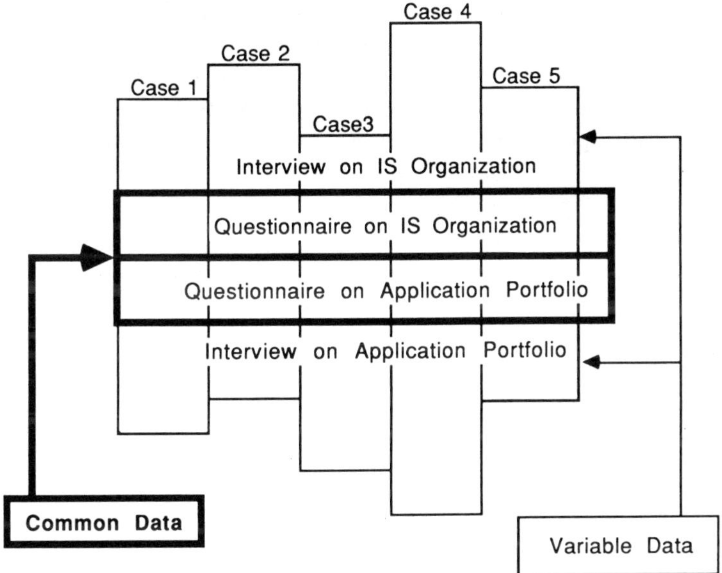

FIGURE 2.2 Combining common and variable data

As a consequence, in contrast to the questionnaires, the interviews and other sources generated variable data across cases. Some of these variable data were comparable but most were not.

Each case therefore includes both common and variable data, as depicted in Figure 2.2, which together provide the basic information for the individual case study. The aggregate of this case study data, across all cases, comprises the composite database for the study as a whole.

2. Data collection

A one-page project description was prepared for distribution to organizations which might be interested in participation. This document described the research purposes of the project, the general research procedure, and the research product from the practitioner's viewpoint. Potential participants were told that they would each receive a complimentary copy of the complete set of cases, that they would be debriefed on their own individual cases, and that identities of organizations and individuals would remain confidential.

Professional contacts were used to develop a short list of candidate organizational participants. Selection of a participant was made on the basis of mutual interest, determined on the basis of a brief introductory meeting with the IS manager, held in person where possible, by telephone where not. Development of the cases began with about half the participants determined. The balance was added incrementally as the work progressed.

The sample of cases was thus a systematic one. Convenience played a significant role in its determination. However, the criterion of diversity among organizational settings was also important in the selection process. This diversity was intended to ameliorate against the problem of generalizing from too few similar cases.

Development of the first case began in the fall of 1983 and ended in March 1984. The last of the twelve cases was completed in July 1985.

In addition to establishing the agreement to participate in the study, the introductory meeting was used to decide upon the scope of the study in the organization and to review the questionnaires to be used in data gathering. The latter often served to clarify a number of local issues in responding to specific questions. A staff liaison from the participating organization was also agreed upon to supervise the gathering of questionnaire data and to serve as the principal contact for the researchers. The task to complete the questionnaires was typically estimated as about one to two person-days over two weeks.

Completed questionnaires were returned to the researchers, who reviewed them as the basis for a series of follow-up interviews. These interviews were arranged and scheduled in consultation with the IS manager and staff liaison and involved at least one on-site visit by one or two of the researchers. Total interview time ranged from one to two days.

In preparation for the interviews the researchers also familiarized themselves with the host organization by reviewing various publicly available literature, typically business articles and annual reports. These provided a basis for understanding the environment of the IS organization, independent of the interpretations of the participants interviewed.

In the course of the interviews various internal organizational documents were typically identified, which provided additional important case data and enabled the interviews to focus on less-documented matters. These documents were added to the case dossier.

Researcher notes from the interviews, both mental and written, were formally documented as soon as possible after the conclusion of the interviews. Loose ends and inconsistencies were identified and resolved by means of follow-up phone calls.

The result of the data-collection process was a dossier of materials: completed questionnaires; background articles and reports; organizational documents; and interview notes. Inevitably, however, much of what the researchers learned remained in their heads; there was thus, in a sense, no well-defined closure to the database.

3. Data analysis and synthesis

The data collected have been subjected to both analysis and synthesis in addressing our research questions. A principal effort involved the development of twelve individually written cases in a self-contained narrative form, which provided a form of within-case analysis and synthesis. The nature of the synthesis, in each case, was a story that 'added up', i.e. made sense to the researchers.

Each case follows a standard format, reflecting the theoretical motivation for the research, and includes as much of the common data as possible to facilitate comparative analysis. Each begins with a description of the host organization environment. Major sections on the IS organization and the application system portfolio follow. A discussion of the management problem set concludes the case.

The resulting case narratives are intended to be essentially descriptive, without *ex-post* theoretical interpretation by the authors, even though, of course, such interpretation may be implicit in the nature of the data incorporated. On the whole, the cases constitute a second-order form of data, constructed primarily from the more basic information in the dossiers and supplemented by the recollections of the researchers.

Notably, the case-composition process also served to surface additional gaps and inconsistencies with the data. These were typically reconciled in follow-up discussions with case participants. A draft of the case was eventually submitted to the participating organization for review and comment, after which it was revised as necessary and considered completed.

Apart from the development of the individual cases, a small-scale sample survey was imbedded in the study, based on the responses to the questionnaires, as indicated above. These questionnaire data were coded and keyed into an SPSS (Statistical Package for the Social Sciences) file for analysis across cases.

Given the nature of the sample, its representative characteristics were not known. However, previous research based in random sampling had produced estimates of certain parameters of the population of organizations which maintain information systems (Lientz and Swanson, 1980a). Among these parameters were the problem factors in maintenance (Lientz and Swanson, 1981). Because the present study employed the same question used in the earlier research, scores on these factors could readily be computed and compared. Analysis showed the present sample to find maintenance more problematic on the whole. As might be expected, it is not representative of the population of all maintenance organizations. Rather, it apparently represents organizations for whom maintenance has a higher profile, as we discuss further in Chapter 3.

Given the absence of a clear basis for inferential reference, formal confirmatory analysis of the sample data would be of doubtful validity. Nevertheless, statistical analysis across cases is possible along several exploratory lines. In one such study we showed that demographic analysis of the IS organization and its application system portfolio is a likely means of understanding the problems of fit posed by the theory (Swanson and Beath, 1986).

The final research task, the results of which we present in the chapters to follow, again combines analysis with synthesis. Here the individual twelve cases are juxtaposed in comparative qualitative and quantitative analysis, and the earlier within-case synthesis is extended to the full set of cases to provide a comprehensive within-study interpretation. The design logic for this task is that of the multiple-case study with theoretical replication (Yin, 1984).

This book constitutes our cross-case report (Yin, 1984) and documents the overall effort. It is a progress report as much as it is a final one. The reader is invited to participate actively in the interpretation through the questions provided with each case.

REFERENCES

Benbasat, I., Goldstein, D., and Mead, M. (1987) 'The case research strategy in studies of information systems', *MIS Quarterly*, **11**, 3, 369–86.

Jick, T. D. (1983) 'Mixing qualitative and quantitative methods: triangulation in action', in *Qualitative Methodology* (Ed. J. Van Maanen), Sage Publications, Beverly Hills, Ca.

Lientz, B. P., and Swanson, E. B. (1980a) *Software Maintenance Management*, Addison-Wesley, Reading, Mass.

Lientz, B. P., and Swanson, E. B. (1980b) 'Impact of development productivity aids on application system maintenance', *Data Base*, **11**, 3, Winter/Spring, 114–20.

Lientz, B. P., and Swanson, E. B. (1981) 'Problems in application software maintenance', *Communications of the ACM*, **24**, 11, 763–9.

Lientz, B. P., Swanson, E. B., and Tompkins, G. E. (1978) 'Characteristics of application software maintenance', *Communications of the ACM*, **21**, 6, 466–71.

Lucas, H. C., Jr (1978) 'Empirical evidence for a descriptive model of implementation', *MIS Quarterly*, **2**, 2, 27–52.

Martin, R. G., and Osborne, W. M. (1983) *Guidance on Software Maintenance*, National Bureau of Standards, Special Publication No. 500-106, Washington, DC, December.

McGrath, J. E. (1982) 'Dilemmatics: the study of research choices and dilemmas', in *Judgment Calls in Research* (Eds J. E. McGrath, J. Martin and R. Kulka), Sage Publications, Beverly Hills, Ca.

Mitchell, T. R. (1985) 'An evaluation of the validity of correlational research conducted in organizations', *Academy of Management Review*, **10**, 2, 192–205.

Swanson, E. B. (1976) 'The dimensions of maintenance', *Proceedings of the Second International Conference on Software Engineering*, San Francisco, California, 13–15 October, pp. 492–7.

Swanson, E. B., and Beath, C. M. (1985) 'Field studies of software maintenance organizations: a target for software maintenance research', presented at the Conference on Software Maintenance, Washington, DC, 11–13 November.

Swanson, E. B., and Beath, C. M. (1986) 'The demographics of software maintenance management', *Proceedings of the Seventh International Conference on Information Systems*, San Diego, California, 15–17 December, pp. 313–26.

Swanson, E. B., and Beath, C. M. (1988a) 'The use of case study data in software management research', *The Journal of Systems and Software*, **8**, 63–71.

Swanson, E. B., and Beath, C. M. (1988b) 'Division of labor in software development and maintenance', unpublished working paper, Anderson Graduate School of Management, University of California, Los Angeles, revised 6 April.

Van Maanen, J. (Ed.), (1983) *Qualitative Methodology*, Sage Publications. Beverly Hills, Ca.

Yin, R. K. (1984) *Case Study Research: Design and Methods*, Sage Publications, Beverly Hills, Ca.

Zmud, R. W., and Cox, J. F. (1979) 'The implementation process: a change approach', *MIS Quarterly*, **3**, 3, 35–43.

Chapter 3

MAINTENANCE BY THE DOZEN

INTRODUCTION

In Chapters 1 and 2 we described maintenance problems as having their source in the interaction of characteristics within and among collections of users, IS staff members, and application systems, summarized in the Relational Foundations Model in Figure 1.1. In this chapter the focus of attention is on the variation of characteristics *within* each of the three large circles in Figure 1.1—within the user area, within the application staff, and within the portfolio—and, to some extent, the implications for these variations for maintenance. Chapters 4 through 7 attend to the relationships within application systems, IS staff, and users.

Chapter 2 describes the study of twelve organizations that we undertook to explore these relationships. As noted there, our sample size is too small to draw any definitive conclusions about the relative impact on maintenance of the characteristics we studied. Instead, the thrust of our discussion in this chapter about the data we gathered is to simply present the variation we found among the twelve organizations with respect to these characteristics and to put that diversity in a meangingful context. Thus in each of the following sections we describe why, based on prior research, we considered these particular characteristics relevant to the study of maintenance, followed by a summary of what we found at the twelve case-study sites.

Copies of the questionnaires on which the study is based are contained in the Appendix of this book. We suggest that you look at them now. If you are a practitioner, you might want to 'complete' the questionnaires, either literally or figuratively, to give yourself an idea of how your own IS organization would compare on the data we are using in this book.

Whether or not you complete the questionnaires, you may find while reading this chapter that one or another case seems to be quite like (or unlike) an organization with which you are familiar. Alternatively, you may be intrigued by some case situation. Jumping forward and reading a case that seems particularly relevant to your own experience may help you absorb the message in this book, so please feel free to do that, if you are so inclined. However, do read all of this chapter first. It sets the stage for the cases, so to speak, explaining much of why we asked the questions we did and how the responses might be interpreted. The chapter also concludes with a brief discussion of the maintenance problem section of the questionnaire, which is helpful in understanding the final section of each case on the Management Problem Set.

If you choose to read the cases in sequence, at the end of Chapters 4 through 7 you may discover later that you wish to know how a particular case compares with the others on some measure. You can make those comparisons (which are not made in the cases themselves) by referring back to this chapter, which summarizes data from all twelve cases. To help you find the relevant information to make such comparisons, we have included, in Table 3.7 at the end of the chapter, a list of figures and tables that summarize data on key characteristics of the organizations.

Before turning to the discussion of user, systems, and IS staff characteristics, a few general comments on the data and sample are in order. As you may have noticed in Chapters 1 and 2, we are concerned in this research with both the central tendency of certain characteristics as well as their variability or dispersion. To illustrate how both central tendency (or the average) and variance (dispersion or range) of a characteristic of systems, staff, or users can make a difference in maintenance, consider the following two examples.

First, with regard to central tendency, think of the difference in language and programming technology skills required to maintain 10 applications with an average age of 2 years compared with another 10 with an average of 12 years. In programs, 10 years can make a considerable difference in underlying technology, use of productivity techniques, or design architecture; maintenance of the older set of systems is likely to be more challenging.

Second, with respect to our interest in variance, consider how much more constrained maintenance assignments will be where many languages are used in a portfolio rather than just one. As a rule, we do not expect programmers to be skilled in more than a few languages, and so where many languages must be supported there will naturally be some reduction in flexibility regarding maintenance assignments.

Composition, the proportion of a distribution that is above or below some criterion, and cohort effects, characterized by lumpiness in the distribution, can also affect maintenance. A single Assembler language program, for example, lurking in a portfolio that is otherwise written in high-level languages, is likely to be more problematic for maintainers than two dozen Assembler programs. Infrequently used skills, such as the single Assembler program might require, tend to deteriorate over time, and quality work using obsolete skills can be difficult to motivate.

In our questionnaire, therefore, we often asked about distributions of characteristics, such as staff tenure or system age, from which we calculated distribution means and variances or with which we looked at composition and cohort effects.

Our sample, as we noted in Chapter 2, was not randomly selected. Rather, pursuing a theoretical replication we specifically sought variety in our twelve sites. The sample includes large host organizations as well as medium-sized ones;

information systems departments with an emphasis on new systems development as well as ones devoting all their resources to maintenance; companies located on the east coast as well as ones on the west coast, in small towns as well as large cities; and public organizations as well as private ones. As a result, the organizations studied represent a broad variety of types of host organizations and information systems departments. The variation across maintenance organizations is marked, and this is an important theme of this chapter.

In general, how does this sample compare to that of 487 information systems managers randomly selected from DPMA membership roles for the Lientz and Swanson (1980) survey? The IS departments studied here are larger: median annual budget is nearly $12 million in the current study versus $250 000 in the 1980 one, median application staff size is 102 in this study versus five in the earlier study. As will be discussed in more detail below, the IS managers studied here report maintenance issues to be somewhat more problematic than did the information systems managers surveyed in the previous study. This is undoubtedly a consequence of our solicitation process and the fact that participation in this study required a much greater commitment of time than did the previous one. This greater time commitment may have tended to eliminate organizations that did not find maintenance to be an interesting topic.

We have included in this chapter, where possible, comparative data from other software maintenance studies. In this way, a more detailed understanding of the representative nature of the twelve organizations can be developed by the reader. However, all too few such statistics are available.

We turn now to consideration of variation among users, or within the user circle, in terms of the Relational Foundations Model.

THE HOST ORGANIZATIONS

In our study we sought to describe the host organizations of the twelve cases in terms of industry, geographic location, competitive strategy, and size of the user population served by the IS department. These are key features of the context within which application maintenance takes place and are important aspects of the relationships among users that can affect the organization and management of maintenance. Chapter 4 considers in more detail the relationship between the host organization and the IS department and between the host organization and the application portfolio.

Table 3.1 lists the industry of each host organization and shows the pseudonyms and abbreviated names of the twelve cases. We call the reader's attention to the abbreviated names, as they are used in the figures and tables to refer to the cases where the longer names would not fit.

Four of the host organizations are strategic business units of high-technology manufacturing firms; another is a division of an aeronautical manufacturer. Four firms are concerned primarily with marketing: two of these market consumer

TABLE 3.1 The cases: names, abbreviations and industry

Case	Case name (and abbreviation)	Industry
4.1	Westcoast Refining & Marketing (Ref&Mkt)	Petroleum
4.2	Western Aeronautics (WestAero)	Aerospace
4.3	United Food Stores (FoodStor)	Retail marketing
5.1	Advanced Technologies Manufacturing (AdvTech)	Manufacturing
5.2	West Coast High Tech Manufacturing (HighTech)	Manufacturing
5.3	Small City Manufacturing (SmallMan)	Manufacturing
6.1	Nationwide Soft Drink (SofDrink)	Consumer goods
6.2	National Foods (NatFoods)	Consumer goods
6.3	Diablo National Laboratories (Diablo)	Research
7.1	Integrated Information Technologies (InfoTech)	Manufacturing
7.2	Metropolitan Gas Company (MetroGas)	Utility
7.3	Big City State University (BCSU)	Education

goods (foods and soft drinks); one refines and markets petroleum products; one is a retail marketer of foods. The remaining three organizations are in service or distribution businesses: one is a research contractor, one a university and one a gas utility. The sample does not include any financial organizations such as banks or insurance companies. While it is possible that application maintenance work might differ across industries, particularly across those of greater or lesser maturity with respect to the use of information systems, our sample is much too small to show such differences. Our interest, therefore, was simply to have a variety of industries represented in our study.

The host organizations are geographically distributed across the United States. Six are in Southern California and the other six are scattered across the country in the Southwest, the Southeast, New England, the Upper Midwest, and Northern California. The eight host organizations located in California and the Southeast are in major metropolitan areas, but the other four are in relatively small towns. No particular differences in maintenance contexts were expected due to geographic location and none were observed in our sample. In rural areas large organizations may face some unique employment problems and opportunities, as is discussed further in Chapter 7.

The competitive strategies (Porter, 1980) pursued by the twelve host organizations vary considerably. One firm, Western Aeronautics, is currently in a holding pattern, waiting out a down cycle in its industry. Metropolitan Gas Company, a regulated utility, is just beginning to think of itself as having a competitive environment made up of alternative energy sources. The four high-technology manufacturing units and the food processor all pursue differentiation on the basis of producing a quality product. Diablo National Laboratories and Big City State University both strive to maintain high-quality standards and, in some senses, compete on the basis of that quality, but primarily they both pursue political strategies to ensure a steady flow of financial resources. Nationwide Soft Drink, like most soft-drink producers, differentiates on the basis of image. Two of the marketing firms, United Food Stores and Westcoast Refining and Marketing, actively pursue a low-price strategy.

While many IS researchers (e.g. McFarlan, 1984; Ives and Learmonth, 1984) have pointed out the importance of linking the host organization's competitive strategy and application development strategy, very few associations are drawn between host organization strategies and maintenance work. We believe this is an oversight, as we will discuss in Chapter 4.

We investigated the size of the user populations served by the IS departments. Size of the user population testifies to the scope of the audience for service, administrative complexity (Kimberly, 1976), complexity of the maintenance task itself (larger user populations are probably more heterogeneous), and penetration of the portfolio within the host organization. Figure 3.1 shows the size of the user populations in the host organizations served by the cases' IS departments. In most of the host organizations, with the exception of West Coast High Tech Manufacturing and Small City Manufacturing, services are provided to users throughout the host organizations. At West Coast High Tech Manufacturing and Small City Manufacturing the IS department serves a highly automated manufacturing function, staffed by a relatively small number of people. In most of the other organizations the size of user population is strongly influenced by the size of the host organization.

In some cases the size of the user population reflects the spread of computing in the organization. Western Aeronautics, for example, was an early leader in the use of information systems, and these systems now pervade the management environment there. As might be expected, those cases with larger user populations

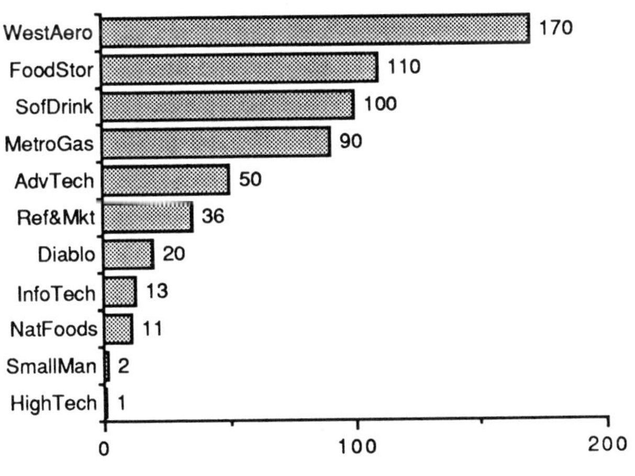

FIGURE 3.1 Size of user population

also tend to have older portfolios (Pearson correlation coefficient = 0.66, significant with $p = 0.01$). Sometimes a larger user population is linked to the presence of a pervasive strategic application. At United Food Stores, for example, the IS department is responsible for distributing information to a large system of retailers. Hence its user population comprises a larger proportion of the host organization than in most of the other cases.

It is perhaps important to note that the notion of what constitutes a 'user' of the IS department is somewhat equivocal, both among our respondents and in the IS literature. That is, some IS organizations probably recounted to us the number of 'serious users', or perhaps dependent users, or the users they deal with directly. Others included all information recipients. Differences in the definition of 'user' are undoubtedly related to differences among the IS department missions. (Who is being served? What service is being offered?)

THE INFORMATION SYSTEMS DEPARTMENTS

The study also sought to describe the people and organizational devices assembled in information systems departments to carry out application maintenance and development, the 'staff' circle in the Relational Foundations Model. Chapters 5, 6, and 7 discuss various aspects of the relationship between IS staff and the application system portfolio, and Chapter 4 considers aspects of the relationship between IS staff and users. With respect to the maintenance staff, we believe the size of the staff, its organizational location, and certain tool and technique choices, as well as some characteristics of the application staff members themselves, as described below, to be relevant to maintenance.

1. Size of the application staff

The number of application systems and programmers (or full-time equivalents) working in the IS departments in our cases ranges between seven and 266, as shown in Figure 3.2 and Table 3.2. During the two years for which we have data (the data-collection year and the prior one) the staff sizes were essentially unchanged. Five staffs contracted slightly, three are a little larger, and four remain the same. In general, these dozen sites could be classified as 'larger' IS departments. With one exception (West Coast High Tech Manufacturing), they are considerably larger than the average of the IS organizations surveyed in Lientz and Swanson (1980), as noted earlier.

Figure 3.3 shows the average budget breakdown for the eight IS departments that provided us with budget figures. The allocation of funds in these organizations, with equipment and facilities consuming about half the budget and wages the other half, are in line with our expectations (see, for example, Verity, 1986). The median total IS budget for our sample is just under $12 million (1984 or 1985 data); this is another indication that these are not small IS departments.

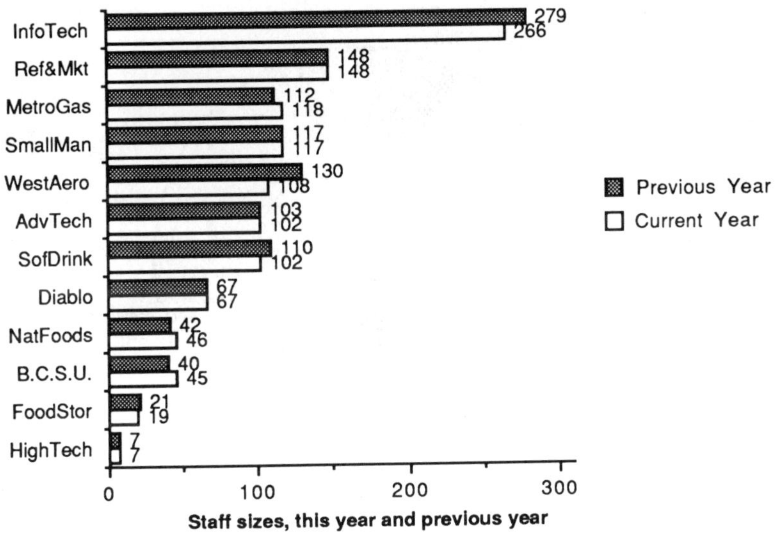

FIGURE 3.2 Size of application staff

By way of comparison, the median IS budget in the Lientz and Swanson (1980) study was about \$250 000 (1977 data). In the *Datamation* survey of 1985 budgets (Verity, 1986), a small group of *Fortune 1000* companies reported average total IS budgets of about \$3 150 000, still considerably smaller than the average here.

On a per person basis, the budgets for annual systems and programming wages range widely, from about \$36 000 per application staff member per year to more than double that (about \$74 000 per year). In comparison, in *Datamation's* 1985 salary survey (Datamation, 1986) firms with DP budgets over one million dollars report average salaries for programmer/analysts to be about \$28 500. It is likely

TABLE 3.2 Distribution statistics for application staff size. Number of application systems analysts and programmers (FTE) (excludes contractors and managers) (N = 12)

	Mean	Standard deviation	Range
Current year	95	69	7–266
Previous year	88	79	7–279

T-test for differences in means between current and previous years: $t = 0.72$ ($p = 0.49$). Not significant.

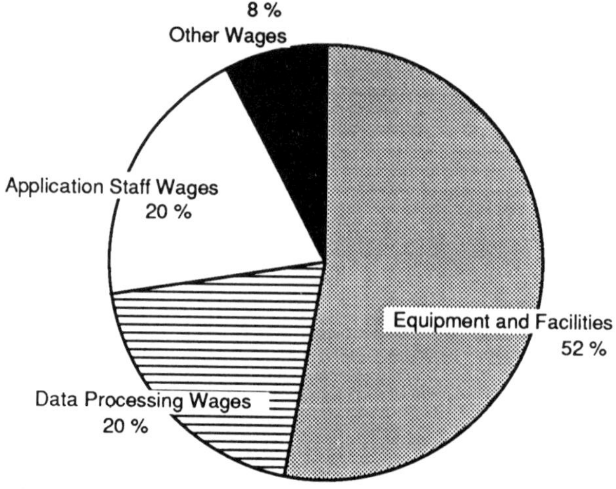

FIGURE 3.3 Average budget breakdown (N = 8)

that part of the difference among the twelve companies and between the twelve companies and the *Datamation* survey is due to differences in policies on the allocation of overhead costs and fringe benefits. We do note, however, that wage budgets per person in our data are systematically higher where the application staffs are larger (Pearson correlation coefficient = 0.67, significant with $p = 0.02$). The association of higher wages with larger staffs might occur because larger firms have more slack resources in their IS departments.

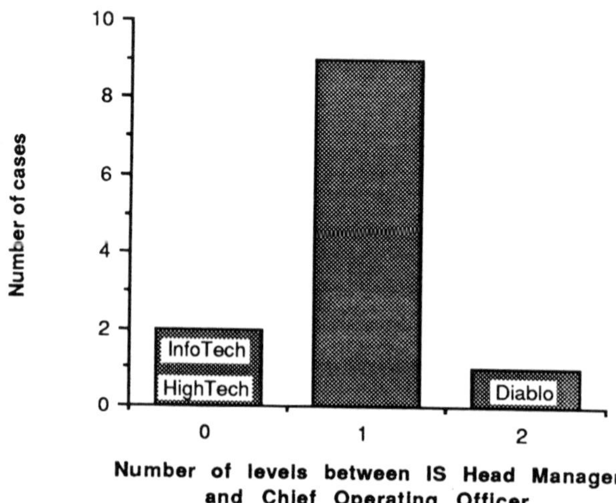

FIGURE 3.4 Reporting relationship of IS head manager

2. Organizational location of the application staff

In our interviews we asked about the location of the IS department within the host organization. Most of the IS department heads report to a manager who, in turn, reports to the head of the firm or strategic business unit. That is, as shown in Figure 3.4, in nine out of twelve cases there is one level of management between the head of IS and the Chief Operating Officer of the host organization. The exceptions are at Diablo National Laboratories, which has a relatively steep hierarchy and an extra layer of management between IS and the top executive, and at Integrated Information Technologies and West Coast High Tech Manufacturing. These two firms are both manufacturing business units, and the head of IS reports directly to the plant manager, who is the Chief Operating Officer of the business unit.

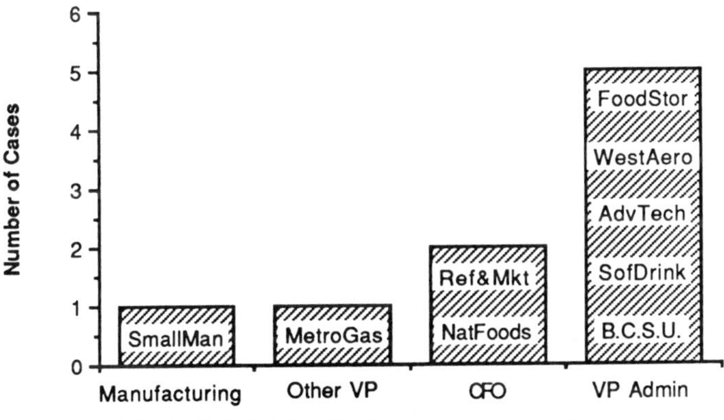

FIGURE 3.5 The IS head manager's boss

Five of the IS heads in our sample report to Administrative Vice-Presidents (see Figure 3.5), who are generally responsible for other service functions such as purchasing or human resources. Only two of the IS heads report to a Chief Financial Officer. One IS department reports to the head of manufacturing, who also happens to be that IS department's primary user.

Because we view application maintenance and development as work requiring interaction with the customer we asked about the frequency with which application programmers and analysts interact with users. As shown in Figure 3.6, most of the application staffs in our cases have face-to-face contact with users at least weekly, but nearly a quarter of them see users no more often than monthly, if at all.

3. Staff characteristics

Prior research suggests that several characteristics of the application staff have a bearing on the ability to maintain systems. One of these characteristics is

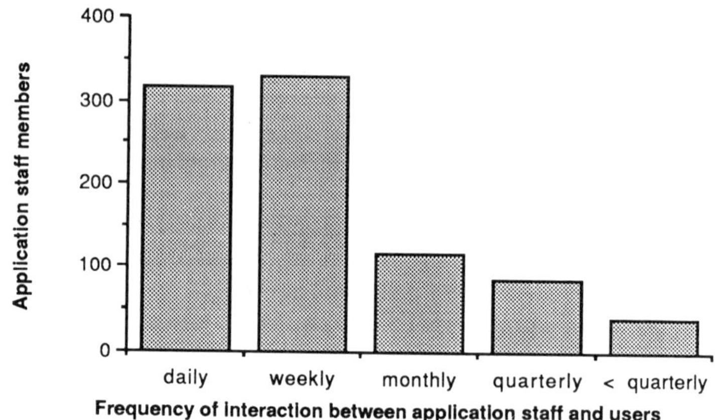

FIGURE 3.6 Interaction between IS and users (twelve case total)

application staff tenure, or years on the job. Since experience in development of systems contributes to productivity in maintenance (Lientz and Swanson, 1980), it seemed likely that longer staff tenures would be associated with greater knowledge of the portfolio and thus higher maintenance productivity.

The distributions of application staff service lengths among the twelve cases are quite varied. Figure 3.7 presents a scatter plot of service length means and variances for the cases. The cross bars show the locations of the twelve-case averages (about 5.5 years for service length mean and 22 for service length variance). At two extremes in Figure 3.7 are Big City State University and Small City Manufacturing, which illustrate differences in the distribution of service lengths. The IS department at Big City State University is a 'young' (that is,

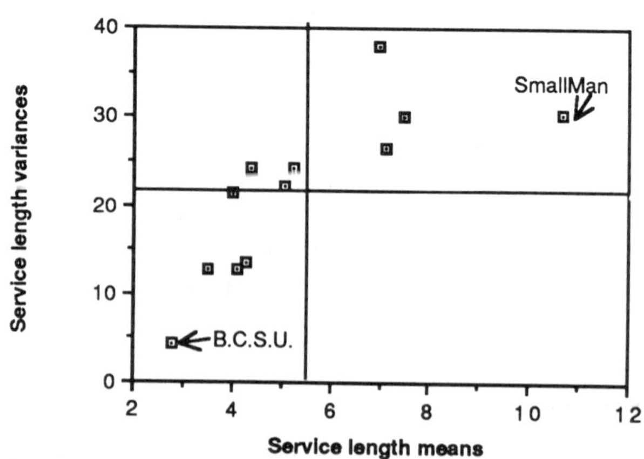

FIGURE 3.7 Service length of the IS staff

characterized by short tenures) and homogeneous department. It was spun off from another organization only six years ago, and a quarter of its staff has less than a year of tenure. Big City State University experiences consistently high but expected turnover, as its employees, many of whom are students, graduate from the university and take other jobs. The IS department at Small City Manufacturing, on the other hand, is an 'old' organization and has an extremely heterogeneous staff in terms of service length. More than half the staff has been in the IS department for over 10 years, reflecting perhaps Small City Manufacturing's culture of lifetime employment, while another quarter has been in IS three years or less.

Closely related to tenure is the question of prior job experience. Figure 3.8 shows how the application programmers and analysts in the twelve cases were occupied immediately prior to joining the IS departments where we encountered them in our study. In about equal numbers, they came to the IS departments from four main places: they left IS professional positions in other firms, they left school, they transferred from a non-IS position in the same firm, or they transferred from IS professional positions in the same firm. They did not, as a rule, transfer from non-IS positions in other firms. However, as will be seen in the individual cases, this fairly even distribution is not typical of any of the twelve cases. Rather, the IS departments we studied tend to concentrate on one or two of these sources when seeking candidates for their application staffs. Chapter 7 discusses the relationship between staff selection and maintenance in much more detail.

Programmer quality is another characteristic that is hypothesized to be related to maintenance effectiveness (e.g. Vessey and Weber, 1983), but reliable evaluations of programmer quality are difficult to obtain. As a substitute for programmer quality, we investigated staff professionalism, which we measured in

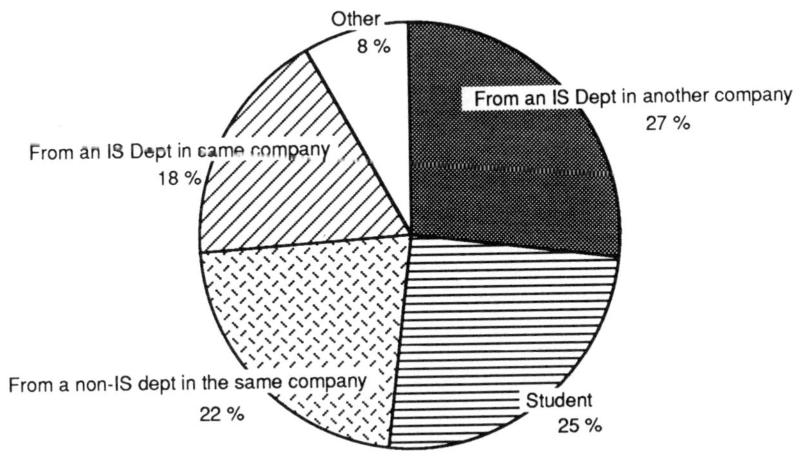

FIGURE 3.8 Immediate prior job experience (average across twelve cases)

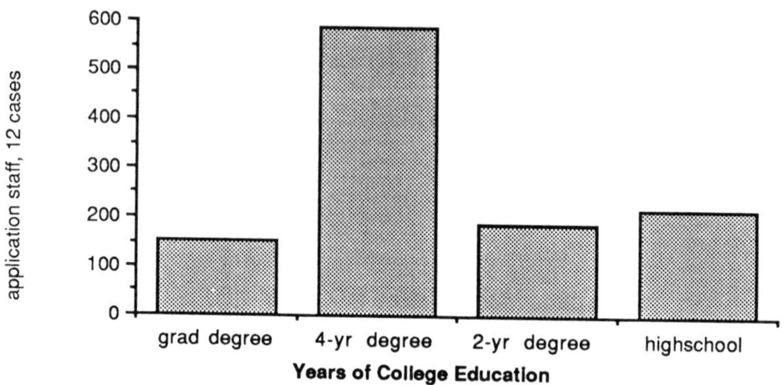

FIGURE 3.9 Years of college education(twelve case total)

a variety of ways, including years of college education, professional association, and job-related training.

The level of professionalism of the application staffs in the twelve cases is reflected in Figures 3.9 and 3.10. Figure 3.9 shows the distribution of college education for all the application staffs of the twelve cases. Among the twelve cases the mean number of years of college education is 3.5, or equivalent to just under a four-year degree. Figure 3.10 shows the distribution of days of on-the-job classroom education and training received by the application staffs across the twelve cases. It will surprise few IS managers to learn that the application staff members received, on average, about two weeks (10.5 days) of job time formal education and training during the year we gathered data.

Among the application staff members we studied, formal professional ties are few. The number of memberships in professional societies, specifically the

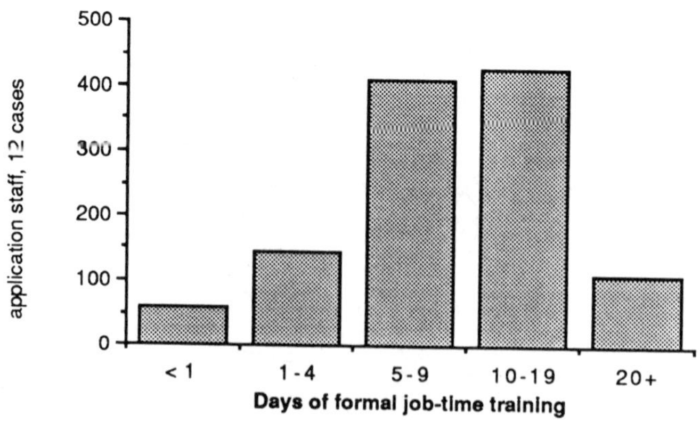

FIGURE 3.10 Job-time training (twelve case total)

Association for Computing Machinery, Data Processing Management Association, or Association of Systems Management, and certification awards, specifically in the Certificate in Data Processing, are low for a 'profession'. On average, the application staffs have about 13 memberships or certifications per 100 staff members; the range across the twelve cases is 0 to 43 memberships or certifications per 100 staff members. In some cases, of course, memberships in more than one society may be held by a single externally oriented or gate-keeping individual. The highest proportion, equivalent to 43 per 100, is found at West Coast High Tech Manufacturing, in the smallest IS department, where a few individuals are active professionally.

4. Organizing for maintenance

Following Lientz and Swanson's (1980) finding that separate maintenance organizations seemed to be more productive, we were interested in whether or not maintenance staffs were separated from development ones. There is little consensus on how to manage the division of labor among maintenance and development in the twelve cases. Five departments told us that they organize their maintenance and development as separate departments, seven said they do not.

Even where maintenance is not organized as a separate department some people work primarily on maintenance. We asked each IS department how its staff allocated their time: do they spend more than two-thirds of their time on development, more than two-thirds on maintenance, or no more than two-thirds on either development or maintenance (splitting their time more evenly between the two)? As shown in Figure 3.11, about a third of the combined application staffs of the twelve cases fall into each category. Within the individual cases, however,

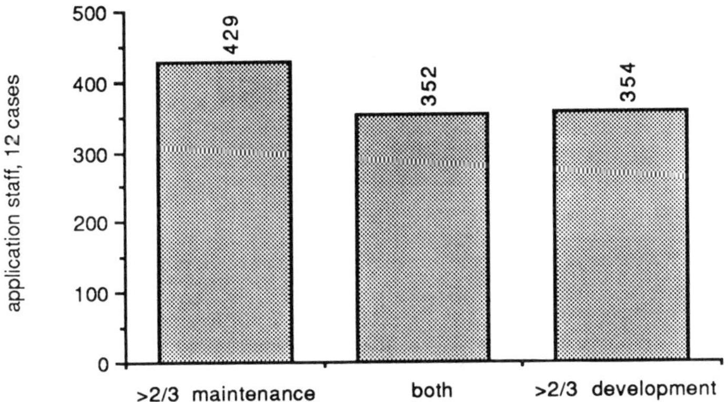

FIGURE 3.11 Allocation of effort (twelve case total)

the allocation is never so uniform. At Western Aeronautics, for example, the entire application staff devotes more than two-thirds of their time to maintenance. In no firm, however, does the entire application staff fall into the 'more than two-thirds on development' category. At Advanced Technologies Manufacturing everyone divides their time between maintenance and development.

Since certain tools and techniques, such as structured programming, are alleged to reduce the maintenance burden (Guimaraes, 1983; Vessey and Weber, 1983), we were also interested in the degree of institutionalization of some maintenance-enhancing or maintenance-supporting mechanisms. Therefore we asked each IS department to tell us what organizational techniques had been established for managing application system maintenance. Specifically, we asked about techniques related to controlling the allocation of maintenance budgets or verifying quality in maintenance work. As shown in Figure 3.12, a user change request procedure is the only technique all twelve departments have implemented. All the techniques listed in Figure 3.12 are supportive of maintenance work, and it is interesting that only one has been universally adopted by IS management.

We also asked each IS department what work methods had been established for application maintenance and development. Specifically, the question asked about the adoption of methods that make maintenance work easier or of higher quality by either improving the development product or the maintenance process. As seen in Figure 3.13, the structured work methods are the only ones that have been adopted by more than two-thirds of the twelve cases. In general, it appears that those work methods having some immediate impact on development are more well institutionalized than those with their payoff in maintenance. For example, 'structured retrofit' packages are expensive (costing between $50 000 and $75 000)

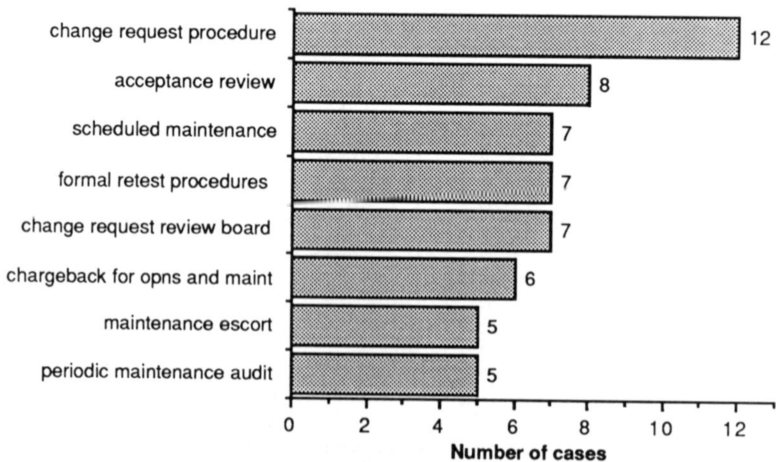

FIGURE 3.12 Use of organizational techniques

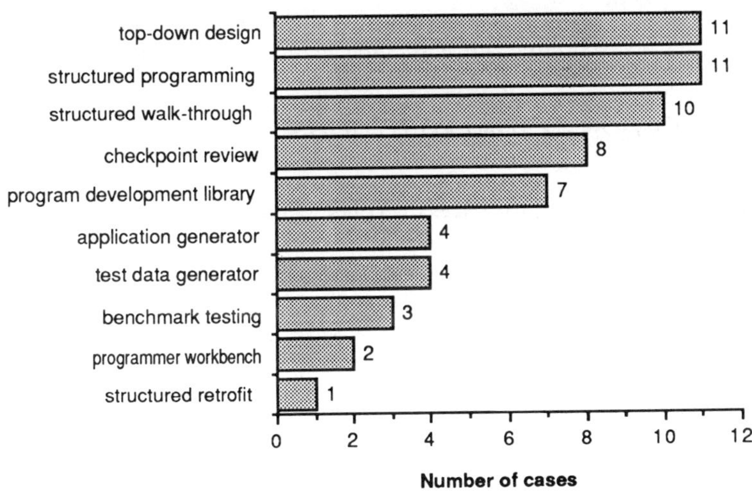

FIGURE 3.13 Use of work methods

and are useful only after development. It does not seem coincidental that only one organization has seen fit to invest in this approach.

Finally, we also asked the IS department to tell us what documentation tools they use. Very little uniformity exists among the twelve cases, as can be seen in Figure 3.14. We believe this reflects a lack of consensus as to what constitutes the right documentation.

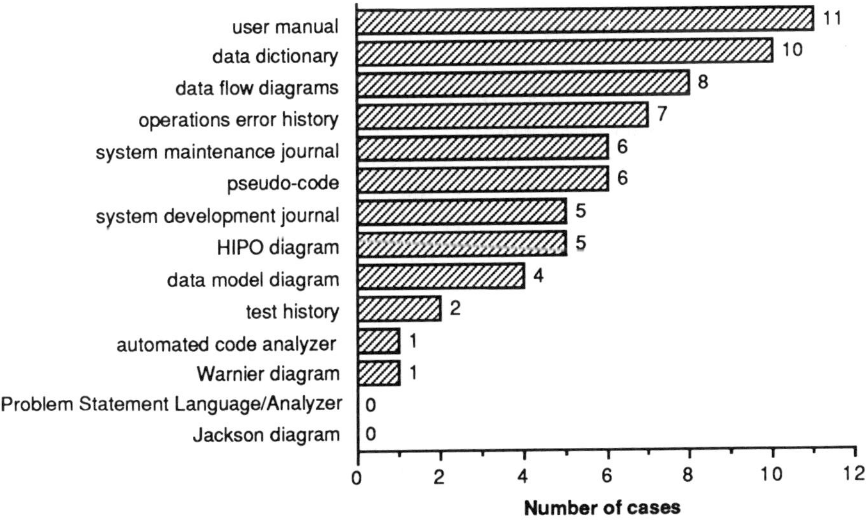

FIGURE 3.14 Use of documentation tools

Chapter 6 further explores issues related to the separation of maintenance from development and techniques for managing maintenance work.

THE APPLICATION SYSTEM PORTFOLIOS

The third basic element of interest in our research, as shown in the Relational Foundations Model in Figure 1.1, is the collection of major systems in the current installed application systems portfolio. We are particularly interested in certain characteristics of the portfolio and in certain policies governing the development of the portfolio that are thought to make maintenance more or less problematic. Given that the relationship between many characteristics of the portfolio and the maintenance burden is fairly well established, as we will describe below, it was interesting to us to discover that many IS departments found it difficult to compile data on these characteristics for us.

In part, this predicament comes about because most of these IS departments do not think of their systems as a portfolio. For example, five of the twelve departments could not, without considerable effort, tell us anything about the distribution of system size in their portfolios. We speculate that many IS managers avoid quantification of the maintenance task in order to avoid the appearance of overbearingly close supervision. They steer clear of measuring lines of code simply to avoid any hint of measuring individual programmer productivity. One consequence of this circumvention is that it becomes difficult to demonstrate the effectiveness of any productivity-enhancing tools or techniques.

1. Size and domain of the portfolio

We asked the firms to tell us about the major systems in their portfolios. We offered no particular definition of 'major' systems, but each firm seemed to have no trouble in distinguishing between those systems they considered 'major' and the rest of the systems in their portfolios. We concentrated on major systems to simplify the data-collection effort for the participants and to permit us to ignore the large number of small, isolated systems in the portfolio, which, we believe, pose relatively less of a problem for maintainers. The reader should keep in mind, however, that the data we collected describe only a part, albeit the most important one, of the application portfolio.

We were interested in the size of the application portfolio because this is considered to be related to the size of the maintenance task, in particular to the amount of corrective maintenance (Gremillion, 1984). The size of the application portfolio is a function of the number of systems and the size of those systems. The numbers of major systems in the application systems portfolios during the year of data collection, the previous year, and the following year are shown in Figure 3.15. In contrast to the stability we observed in application staff size (see Table 3.2 and Figure 3.2, above), the portfolios in these dozen IS departments are definitely

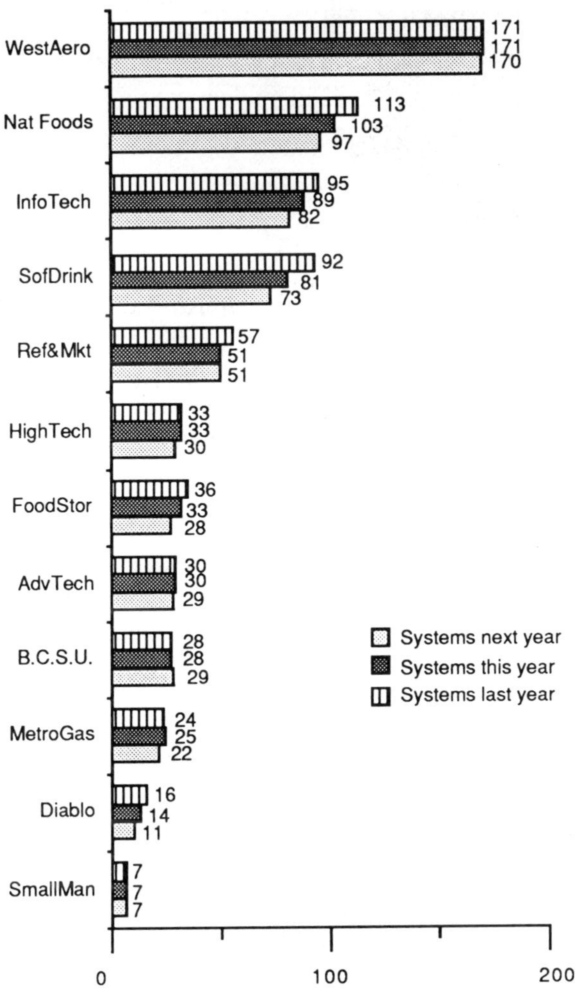

FIGURE 3.15 Portfolio growth

growing (last year compared to this year: Student's $t=3.52$, significant with $p=0.005$). Only Metropolitan Gas Company will have a smaller portfolio next year, and that is because a number of small systems are being combined in the process of replacement.

Replacement is a significant portion of much of the development activity in these firms, as can be seen in Figure 3.16. The firms developing replacement systems are replacing about 10 per cent of their portfolios (see Figure 3.17). The

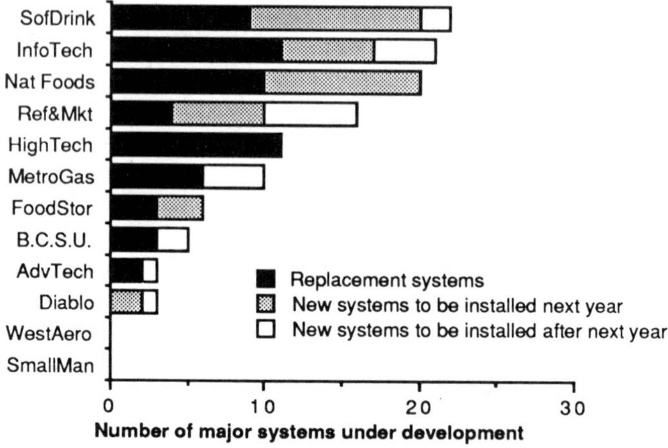

FIGURE 3.16 Focus of development activity

systems being replaced are, in general, older ones, averaging nearly 12 years in age. Most replacements are undertaken because the old systems are hard to maintain and use (see Figure 3.18), which seems likely with systems that are more than 10 years old. Many of the replacements involve upgrades from batch to on-line systems.

To determine the size of the systems within the portfolios we asked each firm to describe the size distribution of the application systems in the current portfolio by telling us, roughly, the median, lower quartile, and upper quartiles of the sizes of the systems in its portfolio. Only seven of the IS organizations were able to supply

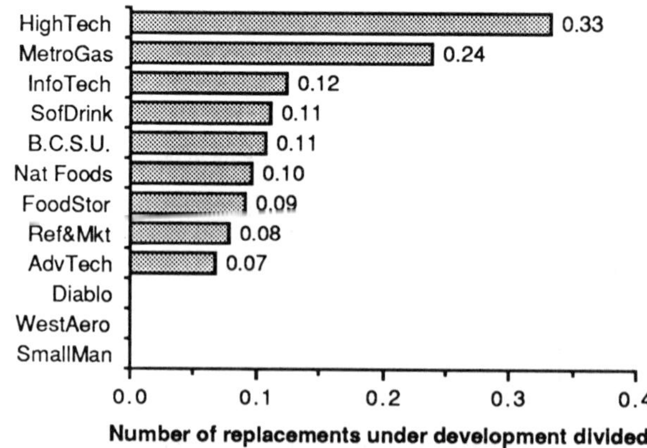

FIGURE 3.17 Replacement rates

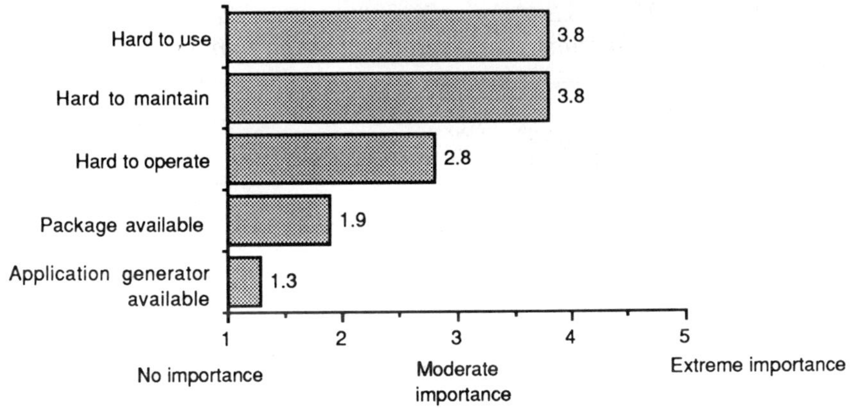

FIGURE 3.18 Reasons for replacement

us with this (or any other) information on size of the major systems in their portfolios. As Figure 3.19 shows, most of what are called 'major' systems in these seven portfolios are small, although a few are very large. This distribution of sizes is very similar to one reported in Walston and Felix (1976) for 60 projects at the IBM Federal Systems Division.

We asked each IS department to describe the domain of its portfolio, or the functional areas supported by the major systems. Later, we categorized the groups of major systems according to their value chain role (Porter, 1985), yielding the distribution of systems shown in Table 3.3. As we asked the IS departments only about the *major* systems in their current installed application systems portfolios,

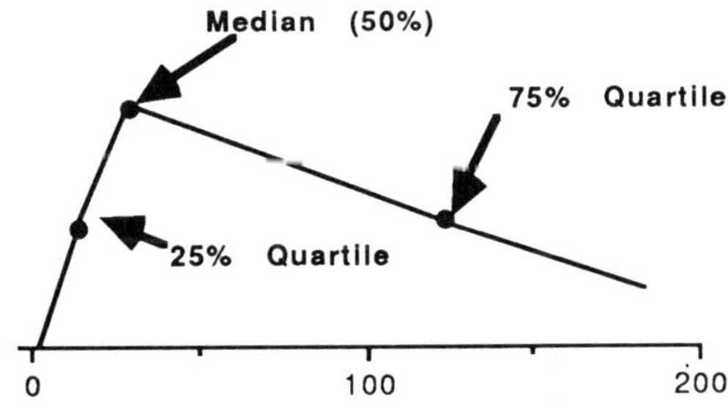

FIGURE 3.19 Size distribution of systems in the portfolios

TABLE 3.3 Application domain in value chain terms (285 systems at seven firms)

	%
Primary activities	
Inbound logistics	9
Operations	25
Outbound logistics	11
Marketing and sales	15
Service	0
Support activities	
Firm infrastructure	37
Human resource management	2
Technology development	0
Procurement	1

this distribution should be treated with caution. The high proportion of operations systems reflects, perhaps, a manufacturing bias in our sample.

We were interested in the degree to which the portfolio of a firm offered competitive advantage, either by supplying functionality beyond that typically available to its competitors or by providing direct service to customers or suppliers (McFarlan, 1984). King (1986) reported that 70 per cent of respondents to his survey had customer-oriented strategic systems, but, as can be seen in Table 3.4, only a relatively small proportion of the portfolios in the twelve cases are devoted to applications of these types. Variance among the cases, however, is high. Most firms have very few systems supporting customers; a few claim to have many. We did not discuss strategic systems at length with our participants, for security reasons. It was our observation, however, that most of the systems linking these firms with their customers exist where there is a large administrative burden in doing business with the customers, not because the firm is consciously, or with forethought, attempting to create a competitive advantage.

TABLE 3.4 Competitive advantage in the portfolios (N = 12)

	Mean	Standard deviation	Range
Percentage of current portfolio that provides users with functions beyond those typically available in competing firms	0.16	0.13	0.0–0.43
Percentage of current portfolio that provides direct services to customers or suppliers of the host organization	0.08	0.13	0.0–0.36

2. Other portfolio characteristics

Besides size, other characteristics of the portfolio, such as the distribution of system ages, integration among systems, the source of the system, and the use of modern tools and techniques, are known to influence maintenance tasks. We used characteristics such as these to describe the application portfolios in the twelve cases.

System age is important to maintenance in several ways. As noted earlier, older systems are sometimes hard to maintain because their underlying technologies, business objectives, and data and process models become increasingly less familiar to the maintenance staff as time passes. Moreover, systems increase in size with age (Lientz and Swanson, 1980), thus increasing the amount of code to be maintained. Corrective maintenance has been hypothesized to decrease with age (Gremillion, 1984), but this is probably outstripped by increases in requests for adaptive maintenance as the business environment for the system gradually changes.

The distribution of ages of the installed systems in the twelve cases is shown in Figure 3.20, and reflects a gradual accumulation of newly developed systems followed by the replacement or elimination of very old ones. Within the individual cases, however, the distribution of system ages can be quite wide, as can be seen in Figure 3.21, which shows a scatter plot of means and variances of portfolio ages for the twelve cases. (The cross lines mark the averages of age mean, 6.6 years, and age variance, 19 units.) As can be seen in the figure, Diablo National Laboratories' systems are mostly new; at Western Aeronatucs, where new development and replacement have been on hold recently, the systems are mostly much older;

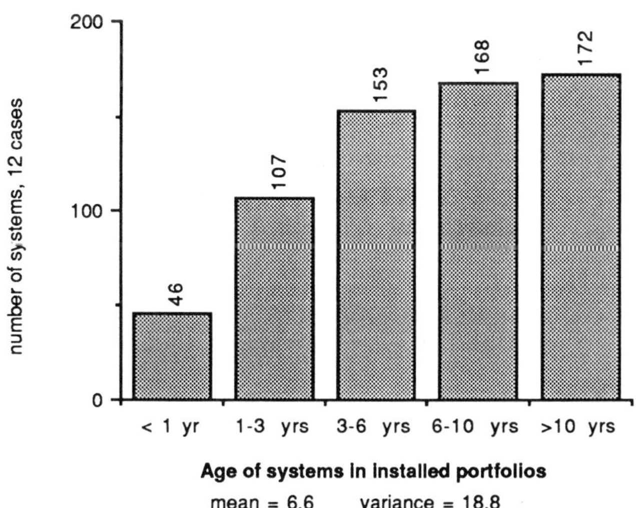

FIGURE 3.20 Age distribution of portfolios (twelve case total)

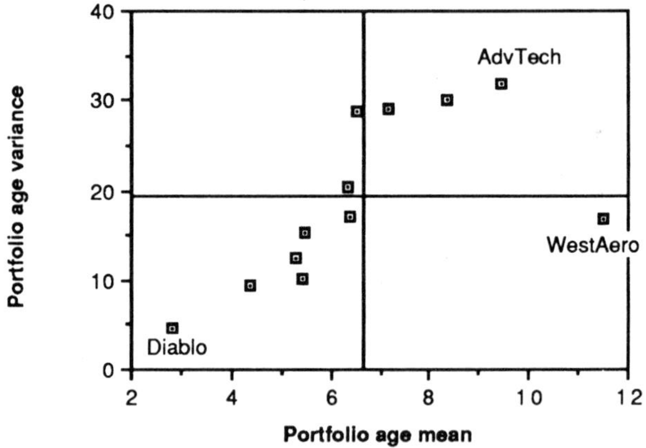

FIGURE 3.21 Portfolio age

Advanced Technologies Manufacturing's portfolio, by contrast, is made up of a variety of both new and old systems.

We asked about integration of the portfolio, or the degree to which systems depend on one another for data or provide data to one another, since integration can increase the testing and re-installation portion of a maintenance task. In order to understand the degree to which a portfolio was integrated or linked we asked the IS departments to tell us how many of their major systems received or gave data to other major systems. From this we calculated a simple index of integration for the portfolio, indicating the proportion of the systems in the portfolio that relied on or were relied on by other systems in the portfolio. The mean index of integration in the twelve portfolios is 0.56, and the range of this index is from 0.19 to 1.00. A mean index of 0.56 indicates that about half the major systems are connected to other major systems, and that the other half are stand-alone systems. As reflected in the wide range of integration indices, and as will be seen in the individual cases, some of the twelve portfolios are much more integrated than others.

Given the Lientz and Swanson (1980) finding that development experience enhances maintenance productivity, we asked whether or not the systems in the portfolio were developed in the IS group or elsewhere. Almost all (81 per cent) of the systems in the twelve application portfolios were custom built by the IS departments in which they are installed (see Figure 3.22). A sizable proportion (12 per cent) of the entire set of systems was inherited by IS departments from a parent IS department—usually corporate headquarters or a predecessor department—but these are almost all found in three cases—West Coast High Tech Manufacturing, Big City State University, and Integrated Information Technologies.

We asked about language and operating environments for the portfolio not because we think that one language or another is easier or harder to maintain but

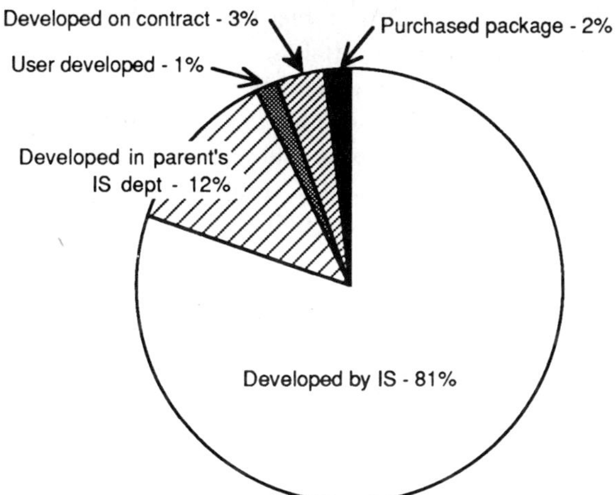

FIGURE 3.22 Development backgrounds of portfolios (average across twelve cases)

because we were interested in the impact of diversity in language or operating environment on maintenance. The operating environment of ten of the twelve cases is IBM or IBM-compatible mainframes. IBM's share of the overall market is lower than this (more like 60 per cent, estimates Guimaraes, 1983). COBOL is the most frequently used third-generation language in the combined portfolios, as seen in Figure 3.23, with PL/1 and Assembler accounting for most of the balance of the portfolios. Individual cases, however, have less variation in their portfolios. Most organizations use a single language, COBOL or PL/1, supplemented with a fourth-generation or a retrieval language. Integrated Information Technologies' portfolio

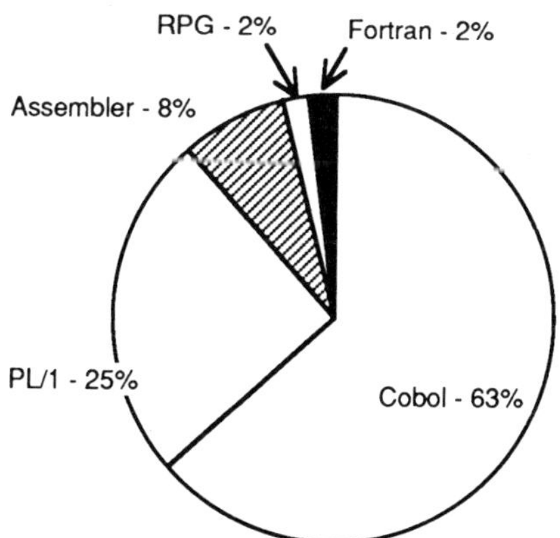

FIGURE 3.23 Languages in the portfolios (average across twelve cases)

includes a significant number of Assembler systems, accounting for most of the Assembler use among the twelve portfolios.

Finally, we asked about the penetration of maintenance productivity-enhancing techniques, such as the use of structured techniques, in the application portfolio. It can take several years for a policy to use a new technique to achieve any significant penetration in a mature application portfolio; we wanted to distinguish between firms with productivity-enhancing *policies* and those with productivity-enhancing *portfolios*.

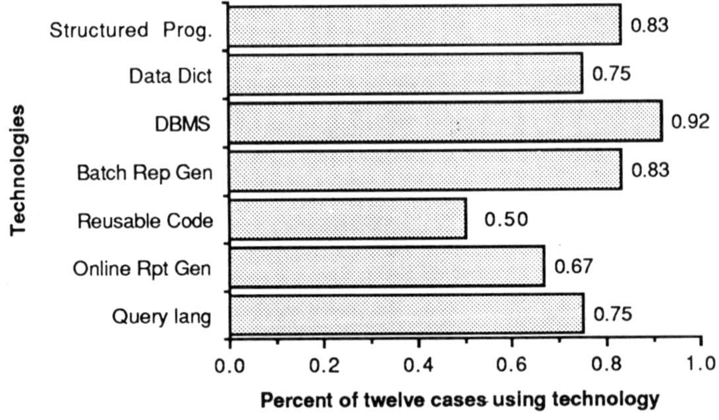

FIGURE 3.24 Technology policies

Specifically, we asked the IS departments about the extent of penetration within the current installed application system portfolio of the technologies shown in Figure 3.24. While all twelve firms have apparently adopted policies favoring the use of many of these techniques, the results of the policies have been slow to penetrate the portfolio (see Figure 3.25). Particularly worth noting is the limited penetration of the data dictionary, considering that most experts suggest that all major systems, or at least the principal data elements in them, should be cataloged in a data dictionary (Ross, 1981). It is easier to understand that old code might not be structured and that some systems simply do not require a DBMS system, but surely more than 30 per cent of the major systems should have at least a few entries in the enterprise data-tracking system, particularly when we consider that, on average, half of the major systems share data with another. We suspect that organizations lack commitment to data administration because the payoff to *developers* from data dictionary efforts is frequently less than that to *maintainers*.

Chapter 5 considers in more detail the relationship between characteristics of the portfolio and the maintenance task of the IS staff.

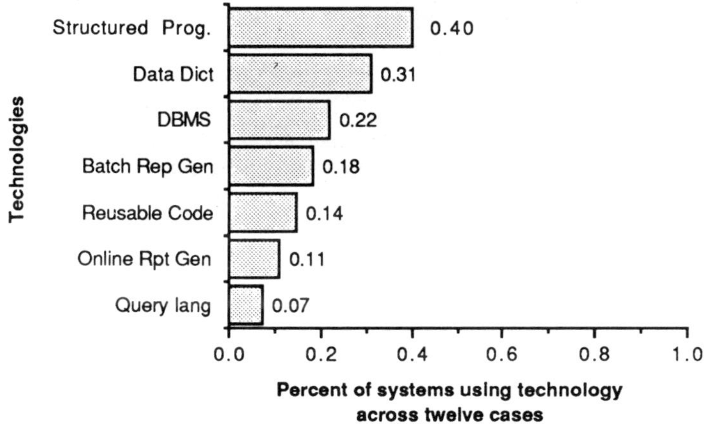

FIGURE 3.25 Technology penetration

THE MANAGEMENT PROBLEM SET

As described in Chapter 2, the managers of the IS departments were asked to evaluate the severity of 26 possible problems in maintaining the current installed application system portfolio. Most problematic in relationship to maintaining systems were 'User demands for enhancements and extensions to application systems', 'Competing demands for maintenance programming personnel time', and 'Quality of application system documentation'. Items seen as least problematic were 'Management support of application system', 'Storage requirement of application system programs', and 'Application system run failures'. The predominance of non-technical problems over technical ones is quite apparent in all twelve cases. (The ratings for the entire problem set are presented in Table 8.2, in Chapter 8, along with a more detailed discussion of the problem factor scores.)

In each of the cases that follow we report a series of six problem factor indices, which were computed from standardized scores of 13 of the 26-item scores. The index calculation (that is, the factor score coefficients and the standardizing) are based on the sample of 487 respondents who completed the problem factor scale reported in Lientz and Swanson (1980, 1981). Table 3.5 shows the six factor indices and their problem item components.

Table 3.6 shows the distribution of the problem factor index scores for the twelve cases. An index score of zero is equivalent to the mean in the reference sample of 487 IS managers. Scores below zero indicates that the IS manager views the factor as less problematic than did the reference sample; scores above zero indicate that the IS manager views the factor as more problematic. Using the Lientz and Swanson (1980) distributions, we designate an index score in the cases as 'Normal' if it falls within one standard deviation of zero (the mean), 'above (or below)

TABLE 3.5 Problem factor indices and their item components

(1) User knowledge	Lack of user understanding Inadequate user training
(2) Programmer effectiveness	Maintenance programming productivity Maintenance programming motivation Skills of maintenance programmers
(3) Product quality	Adequacy of system design specifications Quality of original programming Documentation quality
(4) Programmer time availability	Competing demands for programmer time
(5) Machine requirements	Program storage requirements Program-processing time requirements
(6) System reliability	System hardware and software reliability Data integrity

normal' if it is between one and two standard deviations away from zero, and 'substantially above (or below) normal' if it is more than two standard deviations away from zero.

The IS managers who completed the problem factor survey in the twelve cases found the problem factors to be normal more often than not (that is, within one standard deviation of the reference population mean of approximately zero), even though the mean scores are consistently above zero. The factors related to user knowledge, programmer time availability, and system reliability were each found to be more problematic than normal at four IS departments. One IS department found programmer effectiveness to be more problematic than normal, and two found product quality to be so. Only one IS department reported any problem factor (programmer time availability, in this case) to be less problematic than normal. We found that IS managers were frequently undertaking programs

TABLE 3.6 Distribution of problem factor index scores (N = 12)

	Mean	Standard deviation	Range
User knowledge	0.24	0.44	−0.32–1.11
Programmer effectiveness	0.38	0.61	−0.54–1.70
Product quality	0.55	0.37	−0.04–1.18
Programmer time availability	0.52	0.68	−1.19–1.15
Machine requirements	−0.08	0.47	−0.59–0.57
System reliability	0.31	0.52	−0.31–1.15

addressing the factors they saw as underlying their maintenance problems. We discuss this further in Chapter 8.

CONCLUSIONS

In this chapter we have described the host organizations, the application staffs, and the portfolios of the twelve sites we studied. By referring back to this chapter as you read an individual case you can see how that case compares to the others. Table 3.7 can be used to locate distribution characteristics of any particular sample parameter to assist you in making this comparison.

Two different kinds of diversity or variation can be seen in this chapter. First, across the cases there can be quite large differences in host organization, IS staffs, and application systems. That is, some firms have staffs with outside professional

TABLE 3.7 List of figures and tables in Chapter 3

Table 3.1	The cases: names, abbreviations and industry
Figure 3.1	Size of user population
Figure 3.2	Size of application staff
Table 3.2	Distribution statistics for application staff size
Figure 3.3	Average budget breakdown
Figure 3.4	Reporting relationship of IS head manager
Figure 3.5	The IS head manager's boss
Figure 3.6	Interaction between IS and users
Figure 3.7	Service length of the IS staff
Figure 3.8	Immediate prior job experience
Figure 3.9	Years of college education
Figure 3.10	Job-time training
Figure 3.11	Allocation of effort
Figure 3.12	Use of organizational techniques
Figure 3.13	Use of work methods
Figure 3.14	Use of documentation tools
Figure 3.15	Portfolio growth
Figure 3.16	Focus of development activity
Figure 3.17	Replacement rates
Figure 3.18	Reasons for replacement
Figure 3.19	Size distribution of systems in the portfolio
Table 3.3	Application domain in value chain terms
Table 3.4	Competitive advantage in the portfolios
Figure 3.20	Age distribution of portfolios
Figure 3.21	Portfolio ages
Figure 3.22	Development backgrounds of portfolios
Figure 3.23	Languages in the portfolios
Figure 3.24	Technology policies
Figure 3.25	Technology penetration
Table 3.5	Problem factor indices and their item components
Table 3.6	Distribution of problem factor index scores

experience, others do not; some IS departments build all their own systems, others do not; some host organizations see information systems as central to their operations, others do not. This diversity across cases was important to our study, as we believe there is more than one way to manage maintenance.

Second, within the cases, it is clear that variation within the areas of users, portfolio, or applications staff is inevitable. Staying on top of the naturally occurring diversity in staff tenure, application ages, and application technologies, for example, can be a challenge for a maintenance manager. Recognizing that diversity is part of the problem is an important theme of our research.

This chapter has also described why we think diversity within users, IS staffs, and portfolios—the elements of the Relational Foundations Model—are related to maintenance issues. Subsequent chapters focus more on the relationships between these elements—the lines between circles in Figure 1.1. Chapter 4 focuses on the relationship between users and IS staff and users and the portfolio. Chapters 5, 6 and 7 concentrate on different aspects of the relationship between the IS staff and the portfolio. Chapter 5 shows how the portfolio influences the maintenance task for the IS staff; Chapter 6 discusses the organization of the staff for maintenance of the portfolio; and Chapter 7 considers IS staff career management.

REFERENCES

Datamation (1986) 'Salary survey: small change for DP pros', *Datamation,* **32**, 18, 15 September, 72–87.

Gremillion, L. (1984) 'Determinants of program repair maintenance requirements'. *Communications of the ACM*, **27**, 8, August, 826–32.

Guimaraes, T. (1983) 'Managing application program maintenance expenditures', *Communications of the ACM,* **26**, 10, October, 739–46.

Ives, B., and Learmonth, G. (1984) 'The information system as a competitive weapon', *Communications of the ACM*, **27**, 12, December, 1193–1201.

Kimberly, J. (1976) 'Organizational size and the structuralist perspective: a review, critique and proposal', *Administrative Science Quarterly*, **21**, December, 571–97.

King, W. (1986) 'Seeking competitive advantage using information-intensive strategies', *Proceedings of the New York University Symposium on Strategic Uses of Information Technology*, May, pp. 1–27.

Lientz, B. P., and Swanson, E. B. (1980) *Software Maintenance Management,* Addison-Wesley, Reading, Mass.

Lientz, B. P., and Swanson, E. B. (1981) 'Problems in application software maintenance', *Communications of the ACM,* **24**, 763–9.

McFarlan, F. W. (1984) 'Information technology changes the way you compete', *Harvard Business Review*, **62**, 3, May–June, 98–103.

McFarlan, F. W., McKenney, J. L., and Pyburn, P. (1983) 'The information archipelago—plotting a course' *Harvard Business Review*, **61**, 1, January–February, 145–56.

Porter, M. E. (1980) *Competitive Strategy: Techniques for Analyzing Industries and Competitors*, Free Press, New York.

Porter, M. E. (1985) *Competitive Advantage: Creating and Sustaining Superior Performance*, Free Press, New York.

Ross, R. G. (1981) *Data Dictionaries and Standard Data Definitions: Concepts and Practices for Data Resource Management*, Amacom, New York.

Verity, J. W. (1986) '1986 DP budget survey', *Datamation*, **32**, 7, 1 April, 74–8.

Vessey, I., and Weber, R. (1983) 'Some factors affecting program repair maintenance: an empirical study', *Communications of the ACM*, **26**, 2, February, 128–34.

Walston, C. E., and Felix, C. P. (1976) 'A method of programming measurement and estimation', *IBM Systems Journal*, **15**, 3, 182–211.

Chapter 4

THE POLICY AND STRATEGY CONTEXT FOR MAINTENANCE

INTRODUCTION

Chapters 1 and 2 described our view of how the host organization, the application portfolio, and the IS department are interrelated with respect to software maintenance, as summarized in the Relational Foundations Model (Figure 1.1). In this chapter we turn to the relationships between the host organization and the IS department and between the host organization and the application portfolio. In particular, the chapter considers how the IS department is affected by a host organization's policies and how the host organization's business strategy is related to maintenance of the application portfolio.

The application portfolio, we said in Chapter 1, can be thought of as an artifact of joint efforts by the host organization and the IS department in pursuit of certain business strategies. These strategies rest on a foundation of policies, both explicit and implicit, embraced by the host organization. The policies provide a relatively enduring context in which more opportunistic strategies are pursued. The IS department is subject to these same policies, naturally, while it develops and maintains the application portfolio. In this chapter we consider three policy areas that seem particularly pertinent to the management of the application portfolio: the organization's approach to control, the approach to change, and policies related to the management of human resources. These three policy areas are important features of the context within which software maintenance takes place.

Another part of the context for maintenance is the host organization's business strategy. That the IS department and the host organization should have congruent strategies has become a commonplace in the IS literature (Boynton and Zmud, 1987; King, 1978; Cash *et al.*, 1988). Lately, the concept of the supportive IS strategy has been extended to include arguments that strategic information systems can shape or influence the host organization's business strategy (Cash and Konsynski, 1985; Ives and Learmonth, 1984; McFarlan, 1984; Porter and Millar, 1985; Wiseman, 1985) or the structure of the host organization (Malone *et al.*, 1987). The bulk of this literature, however, pays little or no attention to the role of *maintenance* in either shaping or supporting the host organization's strategy, even though the existing application portfolio provides the foundation for the strategic systems that generate such keen interest. The emphasis in the IS literature is, by far, on the development strategy, on identifying new applications, and on planning new campaigns. We consider the strategic role of maintenance in the second part of this chapter.

Finally, we describe how the host organization and IS department policies and strategy can be captured in what we call a 'maintenance philosophy'. The IS department's maintenance philosophy is expressed in managerial choices related to several of the topics that are the focus of later chapters, such as maintenance task definition (Chapter 5), IS department management (Chapter 6), and application staff career path development (Chapter 7). The chapter concludes with three cases illustrating three very different maintenance philosophies.

THE HOST ORGANIZATION POLICY ENVIRONMENT

As mentioned above, three policy areas seem to be particularly important for the management of the application portfolio. These are: the host organization's approach to controlling its operations, its attitudes and policies regarding change or innovation, and its human resource management approach. We consider each of these below.

1. How is control effected?

Anthony *et al.* (1984) describe several different ways in which an organization can control its operations. They note that control has both informal and formal aspects, but in their discussion they focus on the formal design of organizational units as revenue, expense, profit, or investment centers. Each of these 'centers' uses the same basic control mechanisms, including organization responsibility and reporting relationships; budgeting or other resource-allocation schemes; information systems to report the use of resources; and control or adjustment mechanisms used to bring the organization closer to the desired strategy. The differences among the centers are basically a matter of focus; thus in expense centers the budgets, information systems, and adjustment mechanisms focus on expenses, whereas in profit centers these same control mechanisms concentrate on profits.

It is not uncommon for an IS researcher or management consultant to argue that IS should be treated as a profit center, or an investment center, to improve control of IS resources (e.g. Allen, 1987). It seems more likely, however, that a firm with a strong functional organization, in which central services are managed as unallocated cost centers, should manage IS as an unallocated cost center, and, similarly, a firm that is heavily decentralized into profit or investment centers, with a tradition of charging out central services, would do better to organize IS in a like manner. That is, rather than controlling information services in the same way in every firm, the control approach taken with IS should be similar to that used by other service or support organizations in that firm. More generally, IS managers who are subject to the same controls as their major users probably find that communications with their users are eased.

Cash *et al.* (1988) make a related but more general point in discussing what they call top management's 'leadership style'. As they note, an upper management vision emphasizing the autonomy of operating units sets a different context for organization design and planning choices than one emphasizing tight central control. This observation also holds for IS organizations. An overall formality in the host organization with respect to planning and decision making creates pressure for IS to be formal, too. In more informal settings IS can be successful without formal planning or decision referral and approval processes.

In the functionally organized companies in our sample we frequently observed that the IS department's organization charts mirrored those of the host organization. The IS managers in these organizations noted that such a structure simplifies budgeting and other resource-allocation processes, particularly for maintenance.

Many factors influence the control environment in which IS operates. Larger organizations need more formality—evident in their increased reliance on information processing—both to communicate to their more numerous employees and to control the complexity inherent in size. Geographical distance can also impose a need for additional formality in an otherwise informal organization. In contrast, informal management can be much more responsive than formal management; a highly volatile business environment may dictate a need for reactive, informal control. The level of trust between the head of IS and his or her superior probably also has an immediate effect on the type of control structures imposed on the IS department. If the head of IS is an IS professional, as opposed to a general manager, we might expect to find that the IS department might be subject to somewhat more formal controls.

2. What is the climate for innovation?

Considerable research in organizational innovation has shown that firms differ with respect to their climates for innovation and change (Hage and Dewar, 1973; Zaltman *et al.*, 1973; Pierce and Delbecq, 1977; Maidique, 1980; Kanter, 1983). For example, norms and policies that directly facilitate change processes or reduce the risk of failure encourage innovation. Organization structures or work assignments that promote interdependence among work units provide access to resources for initiating innovations as well as avenues by which innovations diffuse within an organization. Similarly, network-forming devices, such as employment security (but not job-assignment security) and team work, ease the sharing of information which is so important to the innovation process. Firms without features such as these make innovation much more difficult.

Since the IS department is an organizational change agent its work can be made easier by the presence of innovation-promoting policies in the host organization. IS's change agent role is made easier by policies that reward innovative behavior (regardless of its outcome) or provide access to information and resources needed to experiment and make transitions. On the other hand, policies that impose penalties on failed experiments, favor the *status quo*, or impose tight control over all resources make IS's job harder. The climate for innovation affects the maintenance agenda as well as the development slate, particularly if maintenance work is tied to operational or administrative innovations.

If the attitude toward innovation cannot be read directly from the policies of the host organization it can usually be observed in the users. If the climate for innovation is supportive, users who have occasion to directly experience information systems implementation or operation, and who are thus knowledgeable about information systems, are usually willing to take more of a partnership role with respect to direction setting and control of IS investments. On the other hand, users who tend to be too short term, too problem oriented, or too willing to forego investments in information systems staff professionalism or infrastructure may be operating in a climate that does not reward their innovation.

The host organization's attitude about innovation can sometimes also be observed in the IS department itself. Does the IS department have programs of experimentation or not? Are project failures treated as the natural inevitable consequences of empiricism or as personal failures? Do users share responsibility for tasks with IS, making the evaluation of personal success or failure difficult to determine, or are user tasks carefully distinguished so that individual performance can be protected? The allocation of resources to experimentation, giving 'room to fail', and promoting interdependence between IS and the users are all policies that encourage innovation in the use of information resources.

3. What is the nature of the employment relationship?

The third host organization policy area that is very important to application maintenance is that of human resource management, including policies that affect human resource planning, selection, hiring, training, rewarding, and dismissal. Chapter 7 discusses the implications of different human resource policies. Here we simply wish to point out that the applications staff in the IS department is governed by the employee-management policies of the host organization, with relatively minor exceptions attributable to the labor market for IS professionals. The host organization's employee-management policies are a product of the history of the host organization, and they frequently provide a set of constraints on the employee relationship within IS and between IS and its user community.

If, for example, the host organization is a major employer in its geographical area, potential employees may be more likely to be seeking long-term employment as fewer alternative positions are available. Alternatively, if the host organization is in a small town the IS department may find that its application staff has fewer opportunities to participate in professional society activities, and thus tends to be less professional. Also, host organizations with job-rotation policies tend to have more application staff members who have had some experience in business operations and more users with IS experience. Host organizations in industries with lower salary structures—the nonprofit firms, for example—also offer lower salaries to their IS staff members. Rewards that may be uniquely valued by systems analysts and programmers, such as flex-time and other signals of autonomy, may be difficult to arrange if most other employees in the host organization traditionally punch a clock.

Unfortunately, an IS manager might also find that a very stable host organization, where employees have a strong emotional attachment to the company, performance evaluations are infrequent, and lifetime employment is assured, can be problematic in different ways. Chapter 7 discusses in more detail the consequences of different human resource policies. For now, the point we wish to make is that the host organization's human resource policies create a relatively enduring context within which maintenance work is managed, as does its approach to control and its attitude toward innovation.

HOST AND IS STRATEGIES

In contrast to the host organization's policies, which are relatively long lived, business strategies are usually more short term and goal oriented. The host organization's business strategies thus provide another part of the context within which maintenance work is managed.

Information is one of the key resources of every business, along with people and capital, and so it follows that information technology has a potential role in every business strategy (Benjamin *et al.*, 1984; Porter and Millar, 1985). For firms pursuing a strategy based on being a low-cost producer, information technology can be used to drive down labor costs, improve utilization of assets, reduce inventory costs, improve collection of receivables, and reduce waste. For those following strategies based on product differentiation, information technology-intensive products or services may be attractive. Alternatively, information technology might be used to reduce lead time in product development (using CAD/CAM, perhaps), permit service differentiation, customize products, or allow market segmentation of products. Firms in a survival mode can use information systems to reduce production costs, improve cost accounting, or support contribution analysis. Those following a growth strategy can use information technology to manage increased volume, clone administrative processes, and consolidate financial information. Industry differences in strategic uses of technology may also be relevant; industries that are more information intense (Porter and Millar, 1985) are probably, by necessity, more innovative and more aggressive users of information technology.

1. The strategic role of IS

The strategic role of IS has received increasing attention in recent years, as noted earlier, but most of the attention as been on the identification of new opportunities

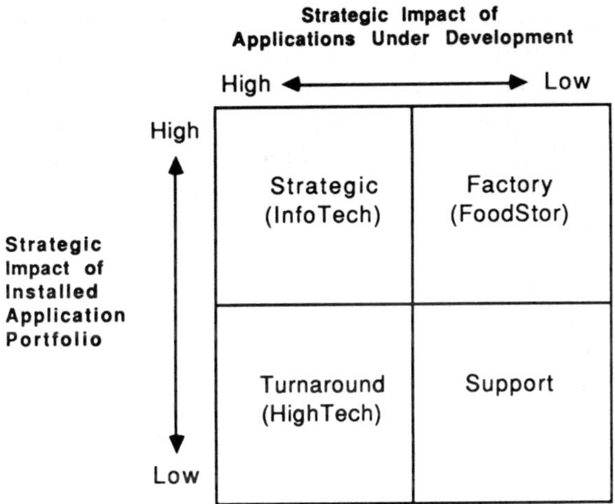

FIGURE 4.1 The Strategic Grid (adapted from Cash et al., *1988, p. 23, by permission)*

for the use of information technology. One exception to this is found in the Cash *et al.* (1988) 'Strategic Grid' concept. As shown in Figure 4.1, the grid defines four types of IS situations depending on the strategic impact of the applications under development and of the installed application portfolio. The cells describe four different strategic roles for IS.

Integrated Information Technologies is a good example of an organization in which the IS department plays a 'strategic' role. A relatively high proportion (28 per cent) of their existing application portfolio offers leading-edge manufacturing capability. These systems are highly interdependent with each other and with the manufacturing process. In addition, several new systems that will accompany additional innovative manufacturing procedures are currently under development.

West Coast High Tech Manufacturing's IS department could be said to be in a 'turnaround' role. While none of the current applications are considered to be 'leading edge', a set of new manufacturing control systems is under development. When installed, these systems will be vital to the achievement of the firm's strategic mission.

The VP-MIS at United Food Stores told us that his IS department is a 'factory'. United Food Stores is heavily dependent on the cost-effective, reliable functioning of its inventory-control applications. Even a short disruption in service can have severe operating consequences for the retail operations. Beyond these installed systems, however, no additional applications of such high importance are under development.

The Cash *et al.* (1988) notion of an IS department having a 'support' role is one in which business operations are not dependent on smooth functioning of the current application portfolio nor are any new applications critical to the current business strategy under development. While their research claims to have uncovered 'a surprisingly large number of companies in this category' (p. 24), we take issue with this finding. A burgeoning interest in disaster planning for information services speaks to the dependence of most large firms on their information technology infrastructures. Moreover, many strategic development opportunities have their foundations in fairly mundane transaction processing or administrative support systems. The three most famous 'strategic systems', American Hospital Supply's order entry system, American Airlines' reservations system, and Merrill Lynch's cash management system, all have their roots in seemingly mundane transaction-processing systems. Thus we believe that the high incidence of IS departments in a 'support' role is a thing of the past.

In a similar vein, Porter (1985) describes the important strategic advantages that can be gained by establishing links across the value chain of the firm, using information technology, among other ways. Galbraith (1977) makes a related point about managing uncertainty in organizations through the use of lateral processes, such as teams or liaison roles, to link across the organizational hierarchy. Information systems applications are another way of providing lateral linkage within the firm; computer-aided design linked to computer-aided manufacturing is an example of this. Order-processing systems, linking sales, manufacturing, distribution, and accounts receivable, are another example. Hayes (1985) discusses the need to look for strategic opportunities to leverage existing assets, including the information assets of the organization. The potential for making strategic linkages exists in many application system portfolios.

It is important to be very clear about the strategic potential of the existing application portfolio. Where information technology is seen as strategic, Cash *et al.* (1988) predict that IS managers will have higher reporting relationships in the organizational hierarchy, the IS departments will be able to tolerate higher-risk projects, the technology infrastructures will be state of the art, and more user involvement (and higher levels of user competence) will be evident throughout the systems life cycle. All these would seem to ease maintenance of the application portfolio.

2. The IS strategy

Whether or not information technology has the potential to offer strategic advantage for a particular firm is sometimes less important than whether or not the firm's senior management has an explicit strategy for the use of information. Even when information technology applications are central to the day-to-day operations of a firm, the IS department is not necessarily subjected to close scrutiny by senior management. In fact, the importance of an information technology application may mean that responsibility for the application is moved from IS to the users in the functional area supported. Information systems, that is, can be too important to leave to the IS department. As a rule, however, where there are more strategic applications, ones which offer leading-edge functionality or direct information services to customers, we find that the IS department receives relatively more attention from senior management.

Strategic attention to IS by senior management can be manifest in several ways. One, of course, is in budget growth. Among our twelve cases the budgets and portfolios were increasing in size but the application staff sizes were not. The staffing policy seems to be 'keep the IS staff size stable'. This policy gives a sense of stability and permanence to the IS department—that is, systems maintenance and development are not seen as something that one can finish, once and for all.

The existence of an IS plan signals a senior management agenda for IS. Quinn (1980) argues that firms develop overall strategies by developing a set of incremental, locally opportunistic plans, thus taking into account the cognitive and process limitations on planning. In Quinn's terms an application development plan and a replacement strategy are two elements of an overall strategy for using information technology. It is through partial plans such as these that the firm's managers probe the future, experiment, test the acceptability of approaches, and learn from a series of partial commitments rather than through global formulations of total strategies. The presence of a formal IS plan is evidence of an awareness of the role of information technology in the host organization's strategy.

We observe, however, that, among the organizations with which we are familiar, conscious strategies for maintenance, even partial ones, are rare compared to the nearly universal systems development plan, or 'development slate', as it is frequently called. For example, policies for determining when replacements are warranted are virtually nonexistent among our twelve cases. Even where the level of maintenance is significant, there is little active pursuit of an understanding of the factors giving rise to maintenance requests. Of course, absence of a plan does not necessarily indicate absence of a strategy. As Hax and Majluf (1984) point out, the degree of formal planning needed by an organization is a function of the complexity of its economic, competitive, social, political, technological, demographic, and legal environments. However, it seem unlikely that where development plans are needed, maintenance plans are not.

THE IS MAINTENANCE PHILOSOPHY

As shown in Figure 2.1, the IS department exists within the host organization, and, as we have discussed in this chapter, it is subject to the policies and strategy of the host organization. Consciously or not, the management of the IS department can be said to develop an 'IS maintenance philosophy', integrating elements of the host organization's policies and strategies with professional standards for maintenance and their own understanding of the task of maintaining the organization's application portfolio. As we talked to the IS managers at our case sites we began to distinguish between two philosophies, which we call a 'short-term view' and a 'long-term view'. None of the twelve IS departments subscribes wholly to either, and neither view is superior to the other in and of itself. Rather, a sometimes paradoxical balance of short- and long-term views seems the preferred arrangement, as we will discuss later.

1. The short-term view

The short-term view emphasizes the near-term, product-oriented, ephemeral nature of IS work. Typically, proponents of this view see the primary task of the IS department as development. Development is clearly a temporary activity—a project has a beginning and an ending date. Symptomatic of the short-term view is the perceived need to reduce the formally recognized maintenance task. One way of doing this is to classify enhancements as 'development' work. Replacements, similarly, may be viewed as 'new development'. In this way, the bulk of the work done by IS is seen as temporary, transient, and short term.

One consequence of the emphasis on development as the primary task or mission of the IS department is the view that maintenance is somehow 'not OK'. Maintenance is caused by design or implementation errors and user ignorance. It is an onerous task, which must be shared among the unlucky or out of favor. Maintenance work is viewed as a training ground for developers, where one 'pays one's dues', so to speak. People who cannot be trained, who do not make the grade, stay in maintenance, where, one might conclude, they are likely to do less harm.

Holders of the short-term view concentrate their investments in tools and techniques that have short-term payoffs, which almost, by definition, means they will show a return in the development cycle. Methods and documentation packages are chosen for their usefulness in development and then subsequently adapted to maintenance work. The short-term view also emphasizes short-term deliverables. Maintainers are sometimes isolated to protect developers from user demands for modifications and enhancements to operational systems. A cap may be put on the maintenance staff and the users told, 'You have these three people to maintain your systems. Now, what do you want them to do first?' The backlog becomes a graveyard for low-priority requests.

Holders of short-term views spend the bulk of the planning period negotiating priorities and budgets for development projects. Maintenance, on the other hand, is budgeted as a slush fund, to be used for 'whatever comes up' or to pull overrunning development projects out of the fire. Control reports for short-term view holders review, in great detail, monthly milestones and accomplishments for development projects. Maintenance milestones, on the other hand, do not exist, and maintenance accomplishments are summarized in a few lines or may not be reported at all.

If it is not balanced by some elements of the long-term view, described below, the short-term view can lead host management to perceive IS as performing only a temporary systems development activity, ultimately to be absorbed into user functions or replaced by more cost-effective outside data-processing services.

2. The long-term view

The long-term view sees IS as an ongoing service operation, with permanent responsibility for obtaining maximum value from information assets like the application portfolio. Proponents of this view see the primary activity of the IS department as providing professional information services to the host organization. The application portfolio is understood to be an integral part of business operations, contributing directly to the means of producing profits for the host organization. The information technology expertise embodied in the application staff may also be seen as an information asset. Maintenance combats deterioration of information assets in the application portfolio, and the maintenance staff accumulates and conserves knowledge and expertise regarding the use of information in the organization.

The long-term view thus emphasizes the permanent links between IS and the host organization's day-to-day operations. The idea of IS and its clients sharing responsibility for information, just as sales and manufacturing do for production planning, is seen as both necessary and problematic. In order to minimize disruption to operations investments are made to speed up and improve the reliability of maintenance activities. Code analyzers, which can be costly, and test support systems are justified because they help bring critical operational support systems back on-line quickly and unerringly.

Holders of the long-term view, like their short-term view associates, separate maintenance from development but with an eye toward improving the effectiveness of the maintenance activity rather than the development activity. A separate organization can more easily institute acceptance tests for newly developed software and for re-installation of modified software. Complexity measurement can be undertaken, maintenance techniques standardized and professionalized, and planning for maintenance can be rationalized. (See Chapter 6 for more on measurement.)

Maintenance career paths, peaking out in responsibility for ongoing operations, can also be defined. Compared to the relatively protected activity of systems development, isolated from the vagaries of business operations, responsibility for an operating application system can be seen to be the appropriate stepping stone to either a managerial position in a user area or in IS. (See Chapter 7 for more on career paths.)

However, if not balanced by elements of the short-term view, the long-term view may admittedly lose touch with the innovative world of information systems: new technologies, new challenges, and new opportunities to use information technology. Our argument in this book is that a strong dose of the long-term view in the IS department is critical to effective management of application systems as a whole.

3. The paradox of a balanced view

As we have described them here, a short-term view is associated with an emphasis on development or the delivery of products to the host organization, and a long-term view with an emphasis on maintenance or ongoing service to the host organization. The IS maintenance philosophy, however, should be a combination of short- and long-term views. Maintenance work has critical short-term deadlines. Responsiveness and an intelligent sensitivity to the client's immediate needs are an important ingredient in a well-managed maintenance group. Paradoxically, the most effective foundation for this highly desirable responsiveness is found in a long-term view that values investments in technical skills, knowledge of the portfolio, and tools and techniques that support the ability to react to the needs of the moment. A similar observation could be made about an IS development philosophy: the ability to quickly deliver quality development products rests on a foundation that includes a high-quality application portfolio, a keen understanding of the host organization's policies and strategy, and, most important, a long-term vision of the role of information in the organization.

The majority of the twelve organizations we studied subscribed to combined short- and long-term views in their maintenance philosophies. Even where a strong emphasis on development work was evident, for example, the IS managers did not seem to think IS was working itself out of a job, the logical conclusion of the extreme short-term view. Also, we sometimes found a short-term view of IS hand in hand with policies of lifetime employment in IS, an element of the long-term view. Frequently a short-term view of IS would disappear when we stopped talking to developers and started interviewing maintainers, who were managing to create pockets of long-term vision and quietly co-exist with their development counterparts. In the few organizations holding strong long-term views attention to development schedules, innovations, and experiments—elements of a short-term view—could also be found. We leave to the reader the exercise of describing the maintenance philosophy of each case and of relating it to his or her own organizational experience.

In this chapter we have described how the host organization's policies and strategies provide a set of opportunities and constraints within which the IS department operates. We have also argued that the IS department is guided by a maintenance philosophy that is influenced by these opportunities and constraints, IS professional concepts of maintenance, and the particular maintenance tasks that the IS department confronts. In the next chapter we look at the ways in which the maintenance task can vary across IS departments, depending in part on the characteristics of the application portfolio. Later, in Chapter 6 and 7, we discuss in more detail how a long-term view of maintenance can affect how maintenance is managed.

REFERENCES

Allen, B. (1987) 'Make information services pay its way'. *Harvard Business Review*, **65**, 1, January–February, 57–63.

Anthony, R. N., Dearden, J., and Bedford, N. M. (1984) *Management Control Systems*, 5th edition, Irwin, Homewood, Ill.

Benjamin, R. I., Rockart, J. F., Scott Morton, M. S., and Wyman, J. (1984) 'Information technology: a strategic opportunity', *Sloan Management Review*, **25**, 3, Spring, 3–10.

Boynton, A. C., and Zmud, R. W. (1987) 'Information technology planning in the 1990's: directions for practice and research', *MIS Quarterly*, **11**, 1, March, 59–71.

Cash, J. I., and Konsynski, B. (1985) 'IS redraws competitive boundaries', *Harvard Business Review*, **63**, 2, March–April, 134–42.

Cash, J. I., McFarlan, F. W., and McKenney, J. L. (1988) *Corporate Information Systems Management: The Issues Facing Senior Executives*, Dow Jones–Irwin, Homewood, Ill.

Galbraith, J. (1977) *Organization Design*, Addison-Wesley, Reading, Mass.

Hage, J., and Dewar, R. (1973) 'Elite values vs. organization structure in predicting innovation', *Administrative Science Quarterly*, September, 279–90.

Hayes, R. H. (1985) 'Strategic planning—Forward in reverse?' *Harvard Business Review*, **63**, 6, November–December, 111–19.

Hax, A. C., and Majluf, N. S. (1984) *Strategic Management: An Integrative Perspective*, Prentice-Hall, Englewood Cliffs, NJ.

Ives, B., and Learmonth, G. (1984) 'The information system as a competitive weapon'. *Communications of the ACM*, **27**, 12, December, 1193–1201.

Kanter, R. M. (1983) *The Change Masters*, Simon and Schuster, New York.

King, W. R. (1978) 'Strategic planning for MIS', *MIS Quarterly*, **2**, 1, March, 27–37.

Maidique, M. A. (1980) 'Entrepreneurs, Champions, and technological innovation', *Sloan Management Review*, **21**, 2, Winter, 59–73.

Malone, T. W., Yates, J., and Benjamin, R. I. (1987) 'Electronic markets and electronic hierarchies: effects of information technology on market structures and corporate strategies', *Communications of the ACM*, **30**, 6, June, 484–97.

McFarlan, F. W. (1984) 'Information technology changes the way you compete', *Harvard Business Review*, **62**, 3, May–June, 98–103.

Pierce, J. S., and Delbecq, A. (1977) 'Organization structure, individual attitude and innovation', *Academy of Management Review*, January, 27–37.

Porter, M. E. (1985) *Competitive Advantage: Creating and Sustaining Superior Performance*, Free Press, New York.

Porter, M. E., and Millar, V. E. (1985) 'How information gives you competitive advantage', *Harvard Business Review*, **63**, 4, July–August, 149–60.

Quinn, J. B. (1980) *Strategies for Change: Logical Incrementalism*, Irwin, Homewood, Ill.

Wiseman, C. (1985) *Strategy and Computers: Information Systems as Competitive Weapons*, Dow Jones–Irwin, Homewood, Ill.

Zaltman, G., Duncan, R., and Holbeck, J. (1973) *Innovations and Organizations*, John Wiley, New York.

CASES

Introduction

With this and the following three chapters we present three cases each, a total of twelve. Each case, as was described in Chapter 2, follows a standard format reflecting the theoretical motivation of the research. The host organization is described first, including a brief statement of the host organization's business strategy. Host organization policies toward control, innovation, and human resources are touched on in both this beginning section and throughout the case. Following the brief discussion of host organization environment, other sections describe first the IS department, with emphasis on the application staff, and then the application portfolio. The cases end with a discussion of IS management's view of maintenance problems.

Because the cases follow a standard format each could have been associated with any of the four chapters containing cases. However, as we were developing the cases we found that unique themes arose with each, and we attended more closely to these themes as we wrote the case. Where possible, therefore, we have associated cases with chapters that are particularly relevant to understanding those themes. Nevertheless, because of the common format, if the reader is interested in a particular aspect of maintenance, such as the maintenance philosophy, he or she might read all twelve cases to see how the maintenance philosophies differ among the cases.

In the cases that follow in this chapter there are marked differences in host contexts and concomitant differences in maintenance philosophy that permeate the discussions of application staffs and portfolios. In Case 4.1, Westcoast Refining and Marketing, the host organization is pursuing a low-cost producer strategy. The IS Department is part of the company's financial operation, and the application portfolio is dominated by financial applications. IS is functionally organized, mirroring its user population, and maintenance is the responsibility of a small pocket of maintainers located in each functional area. Recently, a task force was assigned the task of identifying ways to improve maintenance, and it identified 22 problem areas. The list of problems will seem very familiar to many experienced maintenance managers.

Case 4.2, Western Aeronautics, describes maintenance in an aeronautics firm that is conserving resources while competing for its next big contract. Upon the signing of a new contract, IS activity is likely to increase sharply. The rapid changes in resource management policies in the host organization—conserve today, spend tomorrow, then conserve again—may account for the many unusual characteristics of this case. The current focus on maintenance, for example, may mask an organization that is basically tuned for development.

In Case 4.3, United Food Stores, we encounter an IS department that is tightly integrated with its host organization. The CIO describes his operation as a 'factory', in terms of the Cash *et al.* (1988) Strategic Grid (see Figure 4.1), because the application portfolio includes applications on which the day-to-day operations of this food retailer are heavily dependent. However, the relatively small IS department finds it a challenge to find and retain good IS professionals. Their maintenance philosophy helps them overcome this potential problem on several fronts.

Case 4.1 Westcoast Refining & Marketing

The organizational environment

Westcoast Refining & Marketing (Ref&Mkt) is one of seven divisions of Westcoast Corporation, a diversified natural-resource company producing a variety of petroleum, mineral, and chemical products. Westcoast Corporation's net income for the year 1981 was in excess of $1.5 billion, providing a return on total assets of nearly 10 per cent. Pretax earnings of Ref&Mkt were $600 million.

The mission of Ref&Mkt is to refine, distribute, and market petroleum products and foodstocks. The division maintains four refineries and one crude oil-topping plant. Retail outlets include about 3000 service stations, all of which are concentrated in high-volume markets. A central Ref&Mkt strategy is to be the low-price seller in its markets.

The basic organization structure of Ref&Mkt is shown in Figure 4.2, and it is seen to consist of five major departments. The structure of the Planning and Control department is broken down to indicate the position of the Information Services department within Ref&Mkt.

The Information Services organization

The current (1984) annual budget of IS is approximately $56 million for all categories of expense. The current personnel budget is approximately $28.5 million (51 per cent of the total). The annual budget for 1983 was approximately $48.5 million. Of this, about $25 million (52 per cent) went to personnel.

Reporting to the Vice-President for Planning and Control (Figure 4.2), IS consists of four departments organized as shown in Figure 4.3. The development and maintenance of the application system portfolio is the responsibility of the Systems and Programming department. Operations are conducted by the Data Processing department. The other three departments, substantially smaller in scale, provide special services and support.

The manager of IS is new to his position and has no prior experience in IS, having come from another department within Marketing.

Each of the four IS departments is itself departmentalized, and the composition of Systems and Programming is shown in Figure 4.3. Four departments within Systems and Programming are responsible for development and maintenance of application systems serving major Ref&Mkt functional areas: Manufacturing, Supply, Marketing, and Planning and Control. (See Figure 4.2.) A fifth department is responsible for the development of a significant new system, Product Marketing Logistics (PML). The sixth provides planning and technical support, including database and data dictionary administration.

H.B., manager of Systems and Programming, while relatively new to his position, has several years of experience in IS, where he began his Ref&Mkt career.

Total applications staff (those working directly on application systems) is 148

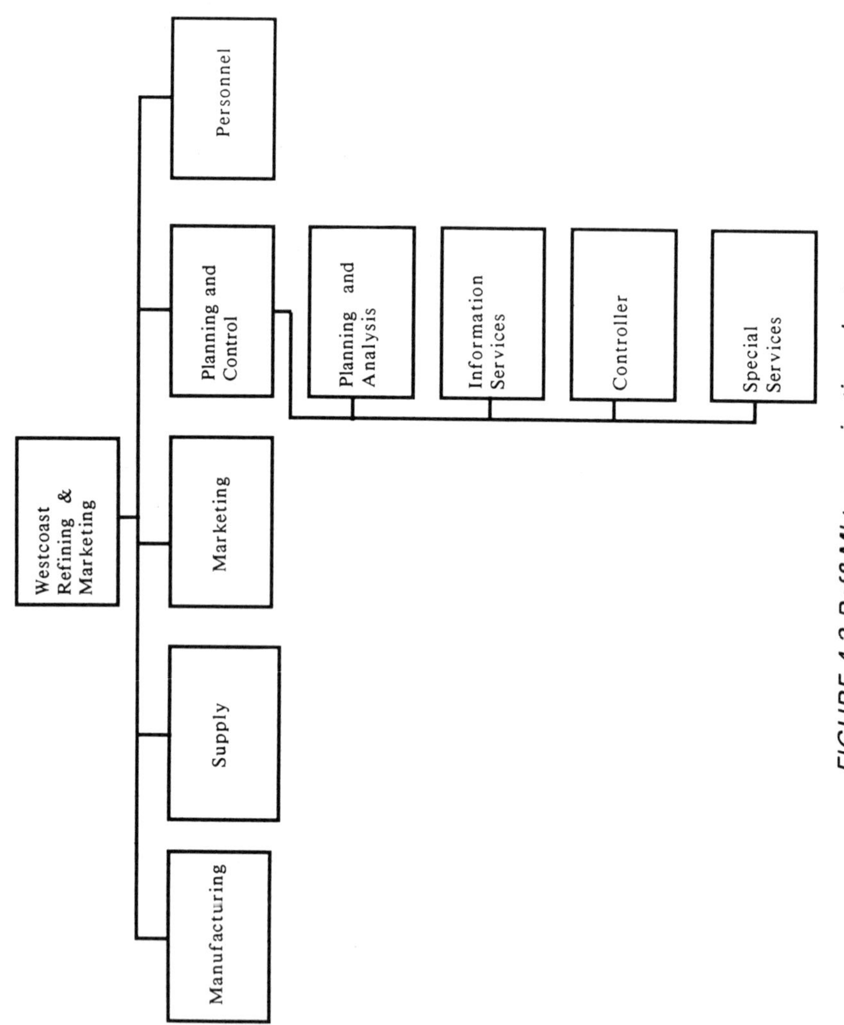

FIGURE 4.2 Ref&Mkt organization chart

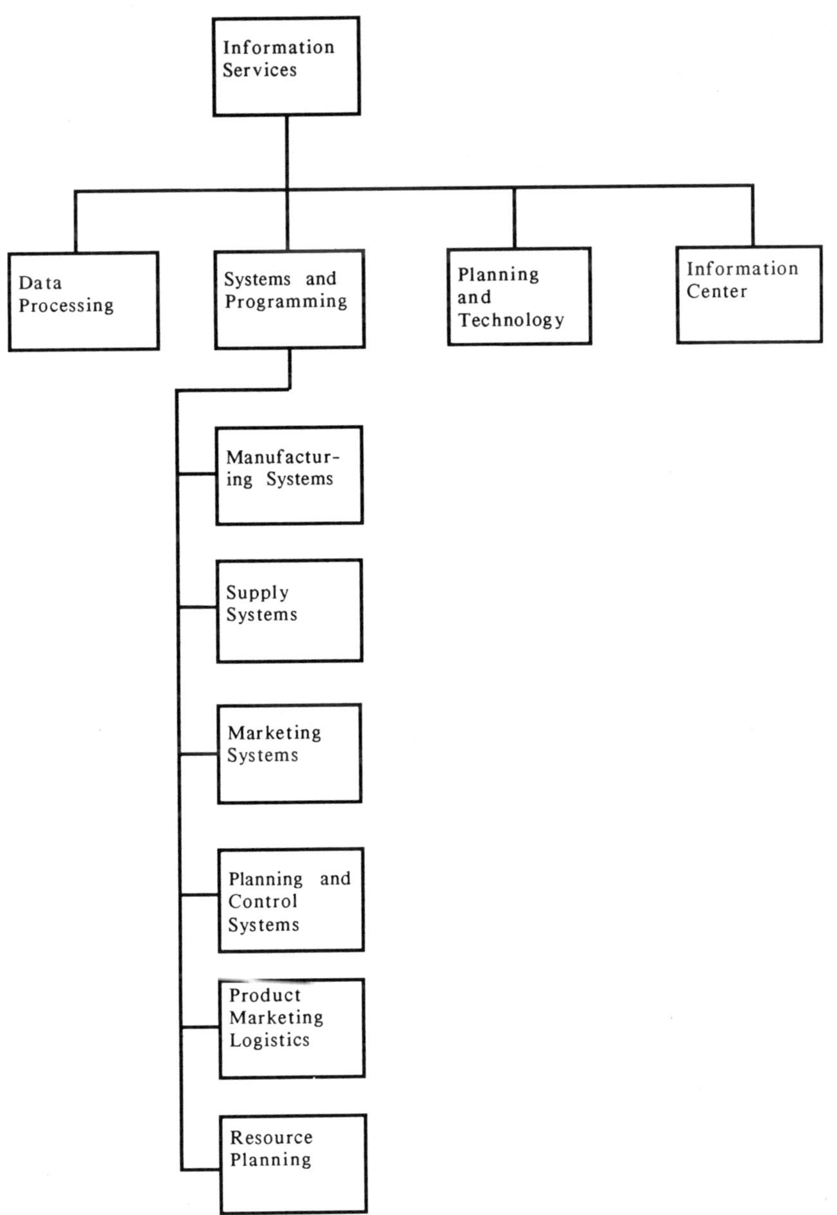

FIGURE 4.3 Information Services organization chart

full-time employees, of which 20 are first-level managers (supervisors). This staffing level is the same this year as last. Median length of service of the applications staff is approximately two years. Fifty-three staff members (36 per cent of the total) have been with the organization for less than one year.

The great majority (85 per cent) of the applications staff has no job experience in Ref&Mkt, apart from their current positions in IS. Sixty-four individuals (43 per cent) were formerly students and 62 (42 per cent) held positions in information systems units in other parent organizations. Of those with prior Ref&Mkt experience (15 per cent), ten persons (7 per cent) held positions in other IS units within Ref&Mkt and 12 (8 per cent) came from other Ref&Mkt units.

The applications staff is also substantially college educated. A total of 120 individuals (81 per cent) possess a four-year college degree and 45 of these (30 per cent of the 148 total) have an advanced one. Professional association memberships are, however, not extensive. Only ten individuals (7 per cent) are members of ACM, DPMA, or ASM, and only three (2 per cent) hold the Certificate of Data Processing (CDP).

The average applications staff member received between one and two weeks of working-hour classroom education and training during the past year.

Although the applications staff is organized primarily according to area of service, as indicated in Figure 4.3, at any particular time the individual staff member tends to work primarily on either new system development or on maintenance. A total of 57 applications staff members (38 per cent) currently allocate more than two-thirds of their effort to maintaining and enhancing the installed application system portfolio. Eighty-seven individuals (59 per cent) currently allocate more than two-thirds of their effort to new system development. Four (3 per cent) currently balance their effort between maintenance and new system development.

There exists no IS policy for the assignment of applications staff to maintenance or to new system development. A trainee may conceivably be assigned to either. The judgement of the responsible department manager is relied upon. Maintenance can be a good development ground for new hires, in the opinion of some. On the other hand, the corrective maintenance of certain vulnerable systems may require a sensitive, experienced touch. A similar set of considerations applies to new system development. Here, political knowhow and the ability to work well 'from a blank sheet' may be relatively more important skill factors, in the view of M.U., manager of Resource Planning.

Among the work methods used by IS are: structured programming, structured walk-throughs, top-down design, and checkpoint reviews. Among the documentation tools are: data dictionary, user manual, HIPO diagram, pseudo-code, data-flow diagram, system development journal, and operations error history. SDM/70 is the principal development methodology employed.

Organizational techniques supporting application system maintenance include: user change request procedure, change request review board, operation and maintenance cost charge-back system, acceptance review in transferring software from development to maintenance, and scheduled (batched change) maintenance. In the case of maintenance cost charge-back, all costs, regardless of maintenance type, are charged back to user departments, except for enhancements estimated to require six man-months or more of effort. These are classified as development work, subject to authorization and prioritization by a User Steering Committee. Operational costs of installed systems are also charged back to the using departments. Interestingly, development costs are not charged back but are borne by a development cost center.

The personnel budget for all development work is currently frozen at 90 individuals and that for maintenance work is targeted to the size of the installed application system portfolio. However, the maintenance budget is expected to show a productivity gain of 8–12 per cent per year in terms of programs maintained per person.

All application staff personnel work directly (face to face) with users.

The application system portfolio

The current application system portfolio consists of 51 major installed systems, serving a user population of 3600. The average age of these systems is 4 years 6 months. Sixteen major new systems are currently under development, with ten of these scheduled to be installed within the next year. Four of the new systems under development are replacement ones, and these will replace twelve existing systems of average age 4 years 6 months. No major new systems were installed during the past year.

The current portfolio has its origins in Ref&Mkt's consolidation of its administrative offices in the early 1970s. At that time, choices between alternative systems in the various offices were made, establishing the initial set of application systems in the portfolio. These systems and their replacements now constitute about one-third of the current portfolio while new applications make up the balance.

A more recent factor in the shaping of the current portfolio was a Business Systems Planning (BSP) study undertaken in 1982. A principal product of this study was a set of information priorities, which have set the agenda for subsequent IS work. A User Steering Committee was also established as a result of the BSP. This committee guides current development work according to the agreed-upon information priorities.

The application domain of the current major installed systems is as follows (numbers of systems in each category are indicated in parentheses):

Crude Oil Accounting (7)
Basic Manufacturing (12)
Distribution (4)
Sales Processing (6)
Sales Reporting (9)
Payments and Receivables (7)
Financial Accounting (6)

Seven of the installed systems are considered by IS management to be leading-edge applications in terms of user functions provided. One system provides direct services to customers or suppliers.

COBOL is the predominant application system language. The median size of an application system is estimated at 100 000 executable source statements (lines of code). The quartiles of the size distribution are estimated as 50 000 and 300 000 source statements (lines of code).

The operating environment of the application systems is IBM and IBM-compatible. Thirty-five of the major systems operate in IBM 3033 OS/MVS environments. (Seven of these operate under IMS DB/DC.) Twelve major systems operate in IBM 4331 DOS/VSE environments (two of these under CICS) and four systems run in other IBM environments.

A data dictionary supports all 51 application systems. However, only nine systems employ a database management system, of which five utilize a user-query language. Two systems make use of an off-line report generator and five are written in structured program code. Ten of the systems (20 per cent) are relatively independent, in that they rely on no other major systems. Twenty-six of the systems (51 per cent) constitute the core of the portfolio in that they are relied upon for input data by other major systems. Fifty of the systems were developed by IS and one was purchased off-the-shelf.

The management problem set

How does IS management view the problems of application software maintenance? To provide an overall perspective, H.B., manager of Systems and Programming, completed the Problem Assessment Questionnaire. Among 26 candidate problem items, eight were considered by H.B. to be 'somewhat major': quality of application system documentation; user demand for enhancements and extensions; skills of maintenance programming personnel; quality of original programming of application system; competing demands for maintenance programming personnel time; unrealistic user expectations; budgetary pressures; and meeting scheduled commitments.

Statistical analysis of the problem item responses, and comparison of the results with a reference survey population, produced the following problem factor profile:

User knowledge	0.16	Normal
Programmer effectiveness	0.71	Normal
Product quality	0.73	Normal
Programmer time availability	0.57	Normal
Machine requirements	0.18	Normal
System reliability	0.10	Normal

The problems of maintenance in Information Services, as assessed by H.B., are thus interpreted as normal on the whole when compared to those of other IS organizations.

M.U., manager of Resource Planning, offers another perspective. In his view, maintenance in IS is not a serious problem, on the whole. However, two matters need to be addressed. The first is the prevalent view that maintenance is not desirable work to which to be assigned. That 'maintenance is the pits' is not necessarily so, and should not be, he argues. The second is the skepticism and lack of understanding about the costs of maintenance which exists within some areas of the Ref&Mkt organization. 'What is this maintenance bullshit?' is a question occasionally heard.

A third perspective is that of B.W., manager of Manufacturing Applications. In an earlier organizational structure, maintenance of manufacturing and marketing applications was centralized under B.W.'s leadership. The subsequent decentralization of maintenance, which accompanied a general organizational rearrangement, 'was probably a mistake', B. W. offers. Economies in maintenance might be gained by re-establishment of the specialized function, he suggests.

Maintenance has, in any case, been identified by IS to be a problem worth special management attention. Upon assuming his current management position as manager of Systems and Programming, H. B. initiated a series of employee-discussions on ways to effect organizational improvement. Five problem areas were identified in this process as important enough to warrant task force efforts, and maintenance was one of these.

The Maintenance Task Force has since identified the following set of problems to be addressed:

(1) Absence of a maintenance philosophy, a fundamental set of concepts and principles that govern the maintenance function;
(2) Inadequate planning for maintenance;
(3) Failure to define maintenance training requirements;
(4) Lack of systematic and periodic check-up of systems being maintained;
(5) Organization of maintenance within area of application;
(6) Tracking of maintenance activities;
(7) Lack of formal change control process;
(8) Lack of systems and programming knowledge of data-processing environment;
(9) Lack of recognition of maintenance function and its accomplishments;
(10) Lack of systems and programming knowledge of business functions;
(11) Absence of system maintenance policy with regard to individual roles and responsibilities;
(12) Absence of development philosophy with respect to maintenance;
(13) Unreasonable work hours for maintenance personnel;
(14) Lack of application knowledge by Data Processing;

(15) Improper attention to maintenance documentation requirements;
(16) Failure to handle user expectations by means of formal maintenance commitments;
(17) Absence of comprehensive testing;
(18) Indiscriminate charge-out of all maintenance costs;
(19) Lack of adherence to operational standards established by Data Processing;
(20) Work environment constraints on maintenance productivity;
(21) Lack of knowledge with respect to the use of maintenance tools; and
(22) Weak maintenance staffing philosophy.

H.B. does not find this list surprising. 'About 90 per cent of what has bubbled up was predictable,' he offers. Currently, the Maintenance Task Force is generating, organizing, and prioritizing a set of proposed solutions to the above identified problems.

Apart from maintenance, what other problems concern IS management? H.B. identifies project management as the major overall problem. There exists a consistent failure to deliver what is promised on time and within budget. 'We do it to ourselves,' H.B. believes. Poor estimating is judged to be the difficulty, and this is attributed to an inexperienced base of project managers.

A second problem is a burdensome administrative process within IS. A lack of uniformity and consistency in data collection and use is seen to be a particular difficulty in this regard.

A lack of understanding of individual roles and responsibilities, both within IS and in relationships with user departments, is a third problem of concern. In this case not knowing whom to talk to when an issue arises is the too-frequent symptom.

Finally, productivity is an area of company concern generally and also a focus of IS management attention. With regard to software productivity tools, 'We're looking,' remarks H.B. A pilot project employing re-usable code is targeted for the coming year as one effort in this drection. Also planned is a prototyping experiment.

Questions

(1) What is Westcoast Refining & Marketing's maintenance philosophy? How can you tell?
(2) Can any of the maintenance task force's list of issues be traced to Westcoast Refining & Marketing's maintenance philosophy?
(3) What impact on maintenance would you expect from IS's choice of work technologies? What impact would you expect if they implemented some of the work technologies they do not have? (See Figures 3.12–3.14 and 3.24 for lists of work technologies.)

Case 4.2. Western Aeronautics

The organizational environment

Western Aeronautics (WestAero) is one of twelve operating companies comprising a large US corporation with annual sales totaling more than $8 billion. Primary businesses involve research, development, and production in the areas of aerospace and defense. Sales are primarily to governments, both US and foreign.

The twelve operating companies are organized into four groups. The Aeronautics Group, to which WestAero belongs, builds special-mission and high-performance aircraft for both military and civilian uses. Group sales total more than $3.5 billion.

Characteristic of its industry, profitability at WestAero is closely tied to its success in obtaining major government contracts and to its ability to deliver on its obtained contracts on schedule and with minimal cost overruns. Contractual competition is thus fierce.

Currently, the company is engaged in a 'survival war' around a major contract viewed as the last opportunity of its kind within the foreseeable future. Success in winning this contract has the highest management priority. For this reason, in positioning itself for the contract WestAero is committed to the demonstration of its expertise and leadership in the relevant areas of high-technology engineering and manufacturing. In this context it is recognized that older manufacturing ways must yield to new factory automation technology.

Because 'computing is a microcosm of the world of which it is a part', in the words of S.R., a senior staff member of the Information Services organization at WestAero, the current IS agenda reflects the facts of competitive life just described. This involves keeping current costs low (new systems development work is currently frozen) while at the same time building forward-looking IS skills in anticipation of the major project opportunity (the manager of IS currently serves full time on the company committee charged with development of the project proposal).

The Information Services organization

Information Services at WestAero is organized as shown in Figure 4.4. Its manager, G. J., reports to the Vice-President of Administration, who reports in turn to the President of the company.

The current annual Information Services budget is approximately $48 million, of which $34.5 million (72 per cent) is allocated to equipment and facilities. The current equipment budget represents a 5.2 per cent increase over that of the previous year.

As seen in Figure 4.4, IS is composed of four divisions and two departments. The divisions include Business Computing and Scientific Computing, which develop and maintain the computer applications for the company; Computing

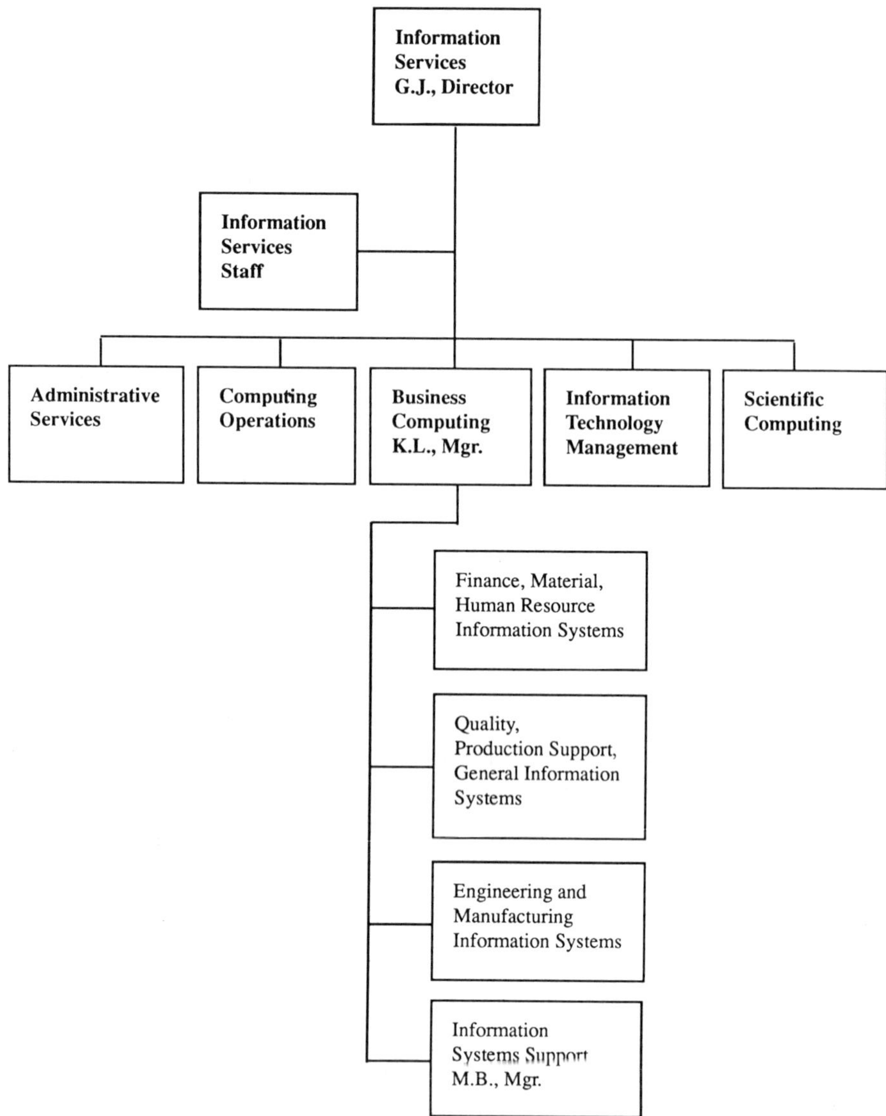

FIGURE 4.4 The IS organization at WestAero

Operations, which processes these same applications; and Administrative Services, which is responsible for publications, graphic arts, and photographic, reproductive, and other office services.

The two departments include Information Services staff, which provides budgets and forecasts, personnel and equipment reports, and other administrative support; and Information Technology Management, an organizational unit that has grown out of an earlier information center effort, described further below.

Business Computing, managed by K.L., is responsible for the application portfolio that supports the manufacturing plant while Scientific Computing is largely concerned with the support of product development engineering. The current annual budget for the Business Computing Division is approximately $13.3 million. Applications staff number 108, down 16.9 per cent from the 130 of the previous year. These are managed by 24 supervisors organized into four departments as shown in Figure 4.4.

Included among the four Business Computing departments are Finance, Material, and Human Resource Informations Systems; Quality, Production Support, and General Information Systems; Engineering and Manufacturing Information Systems; and Information Systems Support. The latter supports and integrates the efforts of the first three departments, which have primary responsibility for the application portfolio.

Average length of service of a staff member is approximately 5 years. Thirty-four employees have been with Information Services more than 10 years. However, turnover of personnel in recent years has been significant, reaching a rate of 45 per cent in one year, according to K. L. Most of those leaving have been employees with 2 to 5 years of experience. With new system development currently frozen, 'people perceive we're not going anywhere', K. L. remarks.

Most staff members have come to Information Services with significant prior work experience. Forty (37 per cent) held positions in other IS organizations, not in WestAero. Forty-five (42 per cent) held positions elsewhere in the company, 15 of these in other IS units. Only 18 (17 per cent) were previously students. Five came from non-IS positions outside the company.

Of those staff who came from elsewhere in WestAero, a significant number were formerly systems analysts in user areas. These were originally hired by users to fill a void left by an earlier cutback and resulting layoff of analysts from Information Services. Subsequently, these replacements were eventually transferred into Information Services. This pattern could conceivably repeat itself, according to K.L.; the problem is that in a forced cutback, analysts are seen to be more expendable than programmers.

About 50 of the staff (46 per cent) possess a four-year college degree as their highest educational degree obtained. Another 30 (28 per cent) hold a two-year one. About 20 (19 per cent) have a high-school diploma or less. Eight have earned a graduate degree. Professional associations are few. Two staff members hold the Certificate of Data Processing (CDP). Two belong to the Data Processing Management Association (DPMA) and one to the Association for Computing Machinery (ACM).

Working-hour classroom education and training is significant. Thirty-five staff members (32 per cent) are estimated to have received between two and four weeks of training during the past year and an identical number received between one and two weeks. Thirty-eight (35 per cent) received less than one week.

As indicated above, with a general freeze on new system development Information Services staff presently work primarily in a 'maintenance mode'. Almost all (100, 93 per cent) spend more than two-thirds of their individual efforts on tending to existing systems.

Contact of staff with users is scattered. Twenty (19 per cent) are estimated to work daily with users. Another twenty meet with users at least weekly and ten more meet with users monthly. However, 58 (54 per cent) are estimated to meet with users no more frequently than quarterly, if at all.

Computer-service requests are the principal organizational means of work justification and allocation of effort. A charge-back system was previously used but proved ineffective. 'The real problem [was that the users] were being tracked to a number they had no control over,' K.L. recalls.

Among the work methods in use are: structured programming; structured walk-throughs; top-down design; and checkpoint reviews. Documentation tools in use include: data dictionary; HIPO diagrams; data-flow diagrams; and an operations error history. A development methodology based on SDM-70 has been established but is not consistently used. However, it is planned to feature this methodology in the development of selected 'major projects' in the future.

The application system portfolio

The current installed application system portfolio consists of 171 major systems, an increase of one system over last year. Areas of application are mirrored by the three departments responsible for development and maintenance.

The Finance, Material, and Human Resource Systems Department includes the major financial systems (e.g. payroll, accounts payable and receivable, cost accounting, and project management), personnel and wage systems, and systems for marketing, legal, and administrative services. The Quality, Product Support, and General Information Systems Department includes systems for quality assurance, commercial and government product support (e.g. maintenance and spare parts), and various engineering and manufacturing systems support. The Engineering and Manufacturing Information Systems Department includes systems for engineering drawings support, job tracking, parts requirements, manufacturing orders and location, engineering change notices, and schedules and forecasts, among others. The portfolio serves a user population of approximately 17 000 employees at three principal locations.

Fifteen of the application systems are considered leading edge. Examples are: a system for planning and generating manufacturing operations routings; a database with CAD/CAM interface in support of the engineering drawing process; and a quality assurance system that includes a cost-assessment component. An older 'integrated wiring system' is also notable; it supports automatic wiring of aircraft from design through manufacturing, installation, and test.

Four of the application systems provide direct services to customers or suppliers and one of these has a 'drive-in theatre' maintenance facility for customer-purchased aircraft. Another supports the installation of engineering changes. Two systems provide information to suppliers as a by-product of their principal functions: one enables the tracking of subcontractors; the other supports buyers in the field.

The majority of systems in the portfolio are of significant age. A total of 95 (56 per cent) are more than 10 years old. Another 60 (35 per cent) are 6–10 years old, and 12 (7 per cent) are 3–6 years old. Only four systems are 3 or fewer years of age.

The median size of an installed system is approximately 11 000 executable source statements. The quartiles of the size distribution are estimated at 15 000 and 6000 statements, respectively.

The application systems possess a moderate degree of integration. Forty-five of the systems rely on other major systems for their inputs. Fifty are, in turn, relied upon for the same purpose. With two exceptions, all systems in the portfolio were developed by the Information Systems Division. The operating environment for the portfolio is IBM 3081 MVS XA (Extended Architecture) and two machines are employed.

The principal programming language used is COBOL (in approximately 150 of the installed systems). However, other languages are selectively employed and included are Mark IV, D 280, Assembler, FORTRAN, Artemis, BQL, and RAMIS.

About 50 of the installed systems possess structured program code. Twenty use a database management system (IMS). Only two major systems make use of a user-query language, or an interactive report generator. No major new systems are under development, given the current freeze described above. The excessive burden to maintain and use current systems in the portfolio is considered of substantial importance in considering their replacement should the present development freeze be lifted.

The management problem set

The Problem Assessment Questionnaire was completed by S.R., senior staff member of the Information Systems Support Department. Two problem items were evaluated by S.R. as 'major': user demand for enhancements and extensions; and competing demands for maintenance programmer personnel time. Five others were considered 'somewhat major': turnover of maintenance personnel; quality of application system documentation; changes made to system hardware and software; skills of maintenance programming personnel; and lack of user interest in application systems.

Statistical analysis of the problem item responses, and comparison of the results with a reference survey population, produced the following problem factor profile:

User knowledge	−0.32	Normal
Programmer effectiveness	0.73	Normal
Product quality	0.17	Normal
Programmer time availability	1.15	Above normal
Machine requirements	0.58	Normal
System reliability	0.73	Above normal

Apart from the problems of maintenance, K.L. characterizes the major problem of Information Services as '[our] inability to convince upper management that we're doing enough'. The essence of this difficulty may be 'terminology and communications' in the view of one Vice-President, K.L. continues. However, whatever the reason, top management is seen as essentially skeptical of the IS contribution.

The image problem carries over to user organizations as well. Faced with a service organization unable to develop new application systems, users blame Information Services for its inability to sell itself to top management.

End-user computing is also seen as a growing problem. This movement began in the 1970s with the acquisition by Engineering of a distributed VAX network. Direct user access to the 3081 followed, in the form of VSPC (Virtual Storage Personal Computing). The period 1980–81 saw the introduction of the first Information Center, and in late 1982 a VM network was created, with 'user self-sufficiency' an established goal. Currently, 1200 users are actively supported by the network, and regular office communications between selected managers take place routinely, by means of PROFS. PCs have also begun to be acquired in quantity, though these remain under Information Services control (within its budget).

The looming difficulty is data availability, M.B., manager of Information Systems Support, believes. Users increasingly expect ready access to the databases maintained by Information Services, but substantial technical challenges are posed in responding to these expectations. There is some doubt that the necessary tools are there to make user self-sufficiency a reality, M.B. adds.

Responsibility for the development of user self-sufficiency now rests with the Information Technology Management Department, which has evolved from the earlier Information Center. Among its other related responsibilities are: quick-response programming; VM and PC software and hardware evaluation; office automation; user decision support systems; and information resource management (the development of strategies, plans, policies, standards, and procedures for the management of information as a company-wide resource).

With respect to maintenance of the existing application system portfolio, a new organizational approach is currently being implemented. Responsibility for programming maintenance support of the full range of applications will be assumed by the Information Systems Support Department. A staff of up to 20 individuals will accept all systems put into production, maintain and control the libraries of production software, and provide the first line of operational support (corrective maintenance in the event of ABENDS and related difficulties). In management's view, this staff should eventually be an elite group, possessing the best talent within Information Services. In launching the group, however, it has been necessary to recruit individuals primarily on the basis of their interest in doing this type of work.

With the maintenance task thus re-allocated, the other three departments within Business Computing will begin to orient themselves to major development projects, supported by the new development methodology as described above. This is expected to necessitate a long-term strengthening of systems analysis and supervisory skills within the organization.

Questions

(1) What is Western Aeronatics' maintenance philosophy? How can you tell?
(2) Why do you think the management of Western Aeronautics' Information Services department is concerned about programmer time availability?
(3) According to a senior staff member, the strategy at Western Aeronautics' Information Services department is to keep current costs low while at the same time building forward-looking information systems skills. Which of these goals is easiest to accomplish?

Case 4.3. United Food Stores

The organizational environment

United Food Stores (FoodStor), one of the West Coast's most successful supermarket chains, is one of 18 operating divisions of Consolidated Stores, Inc. (CSI). According to a recent annual report, CSI is a 'diversified retail firm serving customers across the nation through their department and specialty stores'. FoodStor is CSI's only supermarket operation; the other 17 divisions are upscale department store chains in major cities across the nation. All CSI's divisions operate on a decentralized basis; this is particularly true of FoodStor, because of its uniqueness among the CSI divisions and its financial success.

In 1983 FoodStor's sales approximated $1.5 billion, accounting for 17 per cent of CSI's total sales. FoodStor's profit margin in the same year was 3.4 per cent, whereas the overall CSI profit margin was about 1.5 per cent. In addition to being more profitable than the department and specialty store divisions, FoodStore plays an important stabilizing role in CSI's earning picture, since its earnings are relatively insensitive to seasonal fluctuations and are predominantly cash, rather than credit.

FoodStor was founded in 1873, and its first branch store was opened in 1911. The chain expanded to 74 stores by 1968, when it was acquired by CSI for about $60 million of stock. The chain currently operates 127 supermarkets in two highly competitive metropolitan areas. In 1982 and 1983 it added about 40 stores and increased store footage by 50 per cent, to 4.5 million square feet of space. This recent rapid growth has presumably been funded by CSI, in part because it is pleased with FoodStor's internal return on investment.

FoodStor's marketing strategy has shifted recently to a low-price theme in an attempt to recapture the reputation of a chain that seeks to be competitive on prices. Cost-cutting measures have been combined with a low-price advertising campaign to communicate this realignment to the buying public. Previously, FoodStor emphasized what an annual report called 'the art of meaningful differentiation'. The company is recognized as a national leader in the merchandising of generic products and the installation of automated check-stands.

The overall organizational structure of FoodStor is along functional lines (see Figure 4.5). Heading the organization, in the office of the Principles, are the Division Chairman and the President. The Chairman is responsible for all administrative functions, such as personnel, legal, administration (including MIS), and the controller's office. Two Senior Vice-Presidents report to him, the SVP of Administration and the SVP of Planning and Development. The President is responsible for the main line of business; the SVP of Stores and the SVP of Marketing report to him. Also reporting to the Office of the Principles is the Executive Vice-President who is responsible for support functions such as warehousing, distribution, trucking, and manufacturing (meatcutting, bakery, dairy and deli).

The Vice-President of MIS reports to the SVP of Administration, as do the heads of real estate, internal audit, risk management, and office services.

The Management Information Systems organization

The mission of the Management Information Systems (MIS) organization at FoodStor is twofold: (1) to provide high reliability for the processing of the critical applications in the current portfolio and (2) to adapt to changes in a dynamic business environment. The MIS staff views itself as 'an operations department, not just a service department' according to L.C., Director of MIS Planning. This requires the MIS staff's in-depth knowledge of FoodStor's day-to-day activities and operations.

According to G.E., Vice-President of MIS, the MIS department can be viewed as a 'factory' in the McFarlan *et al.* framework (see above or Cash *et al.*, 1988). That is, the strategic impact of existing applications is relatively high while that of

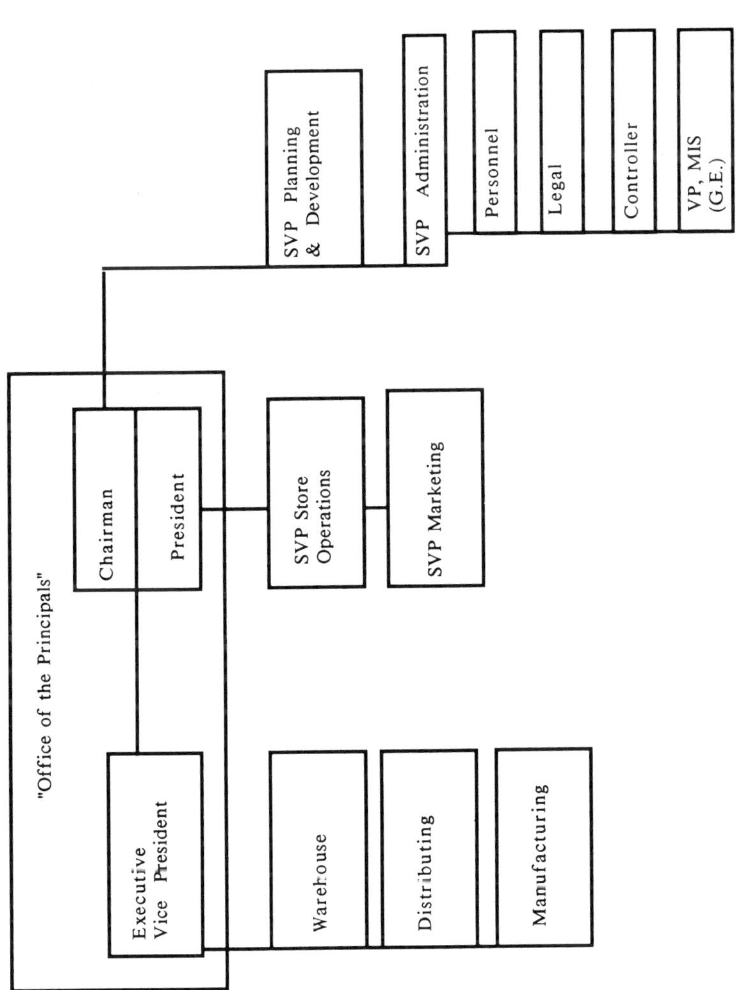

FIGURE 4.5 FoodStor's organization

applications under development is relatively low. An example of the strategic nature of an existing application are the systems that run FoodStor's warehouse. The need for these systems to be operational at all times partly accounts for the great emphasis on maintenance of existing systems in this organization.

G.E. summarizes the mission:

> We don't just handle data. We look for systems that are big cost savers. In order to compete successfully we must keep our prices close to the lowest-price supermarket in our trade area. What allows us to do that is cutting costs. Since we have a large application portfolio and can't be down for any length of time, we are in a position where software maintenance is a big issue for us and where we spend a great amount of time.

The 1984 budget for MIS is approximately $8 million, a 3.8 per cent increase over 1983. Forty-nine per cent of the budget is allocated to equipment and facilities and 48 per cent to personnel. Of the total budget, comprising hardware, software, and people, 86 per cent is spent on support and maintenance, according to G.E. This is a much higher percentage than most other food chains spend on support and maintenance, in his assessment, and may be partially accounted for by FoodStor's relatively large applications portfolio.

The MIS department is divided into four groups: Data Processing, the operations group; Information Systems, the software maintenance and development group; Supermarket Systems, the operations group which handles the decentralized computers; and MIS Planning, the planning group for the department (see Figure 4.6). The Supermarket systems group has recently reorganized as a single group within MIS after a period of being scattered among Information Systems, production control, and computer operations. Apart from this change, the structure of the MIS organization has been relatively stable. Information Systems, which develops and maintains the software, is further broken down into three sections: Systems and Programming (S&P), Data Administration, and Information Services. Information Services analyzes universal product code data in support of market research projects and for sale to marketing organizations and distributors. Data Administration handles systems security. The S&P section actually develops and maintains the software.

The S&P section is in turn broken down into three groups: Warehousing and Distribution Systems, Financial and Administrative Systems, and Store Systems. These three groups have full responsibility for development and maintenance of the software in their areas of jurisdiction. The division of duties in the S&P section mirrors that found at the top level of FoodStor between the Chairman, the President, and the Executive Vice-President.

The applications systems staff (those working directly on application systems) currently number 19. Three of these personnel are first-line managers. Last year the applications systems staff numbered 21.

All applicants for FoodStor-exempt positions, which includes all MIS

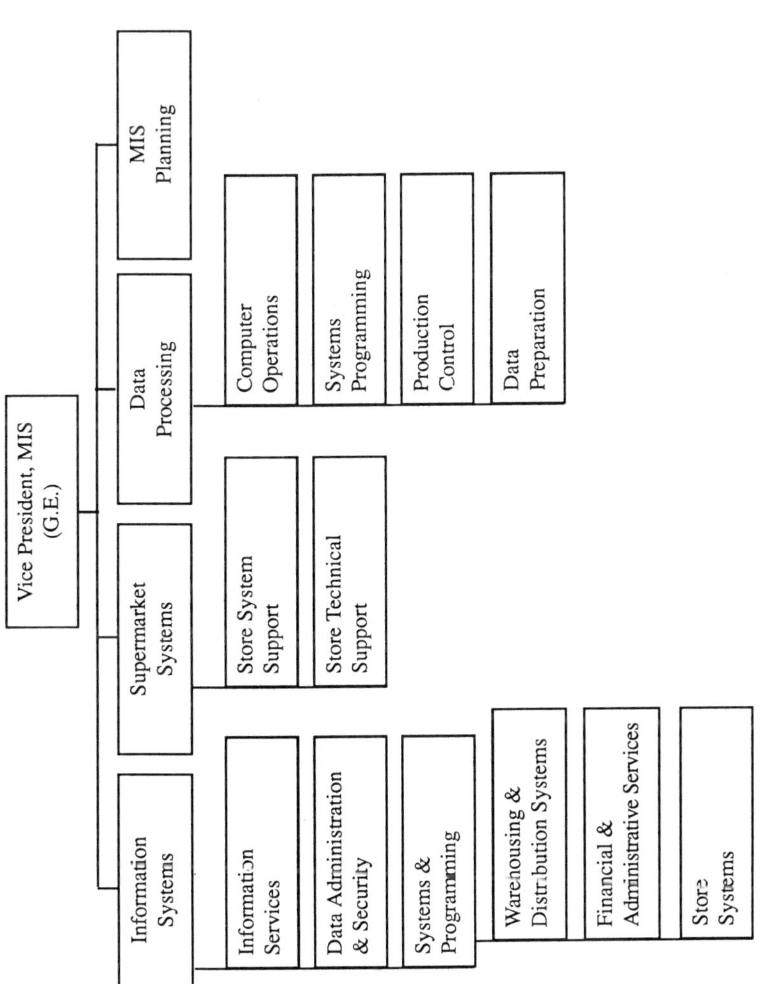

FIGURE 4.6 The MIS organization

applicants, undergo 7 to 8 hours of testing with a psychologist. According to G.E., the profile of a successful systems candidate includes the following characteristics:

(1) A technical problem-solving orientation;
(2) Ability to work independently;
(3) Being at least in the 90th percentile on intelligence tests; and
(4) Strong identification with, and career involvement in, data processing.

In addition, applicants for management positions should score in at least the 95th percentile on intelligence tests.

In general, FoodStor prefers to hire applicants with previous experience in data processing and, if possible, in food service or related industries. Of the 19 applications systems staff members, 16 (84 per cent) came to FoodStor from IS departments in other companies. Two came to MIS from FoodStor's operating departments. Only one person was hired immediately out of school with no prior work experience. Among the managing staff, the Director of Information Systems was recruited from another food industry firm.

All the 19 application systems staff members have at least a two-year college degree. Of these, 13 (68 per cent) have bachelor's degrees, four (21 percent) have two-year college degrees and two (10 per cent) have graduate college ones. Two of the four Directors reporting to G.E. have MBAs, one has an MS and one has no degree. None of the current application systems staff members hold the Certificate of Data Processing (CDP) or membership of ACM, DPMA, or ASM.

In general, FoodStor has found it more economical to hire staff members with natural intelligence and prior education and/or training rather than provide formal training. Most of the current application systems staff (16, 84 per cent) received less than one week of formal training last year. One person (6 per cent) received between one and two weeks of training and two people (10 per cent) received two to four weeks.

With respect to career paths, the preference at FoodStor is to promote internally, although it has been necessary to hire several of the Directors from the outside. For example, the supervisors of the S&P section (the three first-level managers) were hired in at the staff level and worked their way up to their present positions. G.E. was previously Director of Information Systems. His predecessor in the VP, MIS, position is now a Vice-President in Retail Store operations. The majority of the Directors, on the other hand, were hired for their current positions.

The 19 application systems staff members have a median length of service of 1–3 years. Almost all (16, 84 per cent) have been in MIS 6 years or less. In G.E.'s view, turnover among the staff members (which he estimates at 10 per cent per year overall) is high. The median tenure among the S&P first-level managers is 4 years. The median management tenure overall is 5 years. G.E. regards the turnover among his management staff as low.

There exists a large application systems portfolio to support and more time is spent on maintenance than development. G.E. considers this to be one of the problems contributing to the high turnover among the younger staff members, who prefer development work. As a result, an attempt is made to spread the development assignments among the staff members equitably. Currently, 11 (58 per cent) split their time equally between development and maintenance. Only three people (16 per cent) work principally on development and five (26 per cent) on maintenance.

Several systems in the application portfolio are considered to be critical; if they go down, the operation which they support comes to a halt. Because the systems are so important to FoodStor, responsibility for their maintenance is reserved for senior people.

Contact between the applications system staff and users is relatively infrequent. Fourteen (74 per cent) of the Staff work face to face with members of the using departments at least monthly; however, only five (26 per cent) work directly with users at least weekly. Contact between the MIS management team and the users, on the other hand, is much more frequent. For example, G.E.'s office is located in the same area as FoodStor's Senior Management, with whom he is in daily contact.

Organization techniques supporting application systems maintenance include user-change request procedures, acceptance reviews, and formal retest procedures. Any changes to a major system are simulated for one week before being put into operation and special test data sets are reserved specifically for this purpose. Any new data needed for incorporation into a system are provided by the user who requested the change. Dual processors are maintained, one specifically for back-up and testing.

The user participates in the testing and verification of any major change involving functions or processes. EDP auditing performs audits either along with or subsequent to the user-verification procedure. In the past, any major change to a critical system could only be made on weekends, but because of increasingly efficient methods of handling changes, and extensive test procedures, this rule is currently being loosened.

Among the work methods established by the S&P organization for application systems development and maintenance are: structured programming, structured walk-through, and checkpoint review. Documentation tools used are user manuals, HIPO diagrams, and data-flow diagrams.

The application systems portfolio

The current applications portfolio includes 33 major installed systems, an increase of 18 per cent over 1983, serving a user population of 11 000 in over 120 stores. One-third of the systems are less than 6 years old; another third are 6–10 years old and the last third are more than 10 years old. There are six major new systems currently under development, all to be installed next year, with three of these being replacements. Of the three systems being replaced, one has been installed for 1–3 years, one for 6–10 years, and one for more than 10 years.

The most important reason given for replacing systems is to support the growth and changing objectives of business operations. For example, the focus of FoodStor advertising has moved in recent months to emphasize lower prices. As a result, the S&P organization has sought ways to lower costs throughout the company, and this has triggered major system changes. Other reasons for replacing systems include changes in store districts (due to organizational restructuring) and changes in merchandising philosophy.

The major functions supported by the applications portfolio are: merchandsing (six systems), manufacturing (three systems), inventory control (three systems) store operations support (four systems), labor control (three systems) fleet control (two systems), and financial control (12 systems). According to L.C., 60 per cent of the systems in the portfolio are considered to be critical. That is, the function that the system supports does not operate without the computer, and, in addition, system support is required on a 24-hour basis. In inventory control, for example, the critical systems are the billing, electronic order entry, and warehouse management systems. Critical systems in store operations support are the host-to-store, store-to-host, store support, and item movement systems. Centralized returned check processing and product information are two other critical systems.

Two-thirds of the systems in the application system portfolio were developed in-house. The rest were developed by outside firms on custom-build contracts. According to L.C., there are several advantages for FoodStor in using an outside firm for systems development. Purchased systems are considered to have a more consistent structure and superior documentation. If purchased software can provide 60 per cent of desired functionality for a proposed system, then purchase is considered to be warranted. The application systems staff will then tailor the system to FoodStor's particular needs. Maintenance is subsequently performed internally rather than by the selling firm.

The warehouse system is an example of a critical system that was originally purchased from an outside firm. It is 6 to 7 years old, and now little resembles the originally purchased system.

There are several systems considered to be leading edge from a technological standpoint. The scanning system is one example (it was at the leading edge when first installed). Currently at the leading edge is a dynamic shelf-allocation system, which allocates shelf space in each store based upon customers' buying patterns. One of the systems now being developed, a robotic warehouse, will be another leading edge application.

Integration among FoodStor's application systems is relatively high. Twenty-one (64 per cent) of the systems rely on other major systems for input data and eight (25 per cent) are relied upon for data by other major systems.

All systems are written exclusively in COBOL and operate in an IBM 3033/MVS environment on dual processors (one processor for production and one for backup and testing), with all channels redundant. The processors are supported by an uninterruptable power supply, which is used about twice a month. CICS is used by seven systems.

Only two systems use a database management system (IMS). It is felt that, in general, systems with DBMSs make MIS too dependent on individuals with special database knowledge and skills. In addition, according to L.C., the majority of FoodStor's data is best thought of as being organized horizontally rather than vertically, which makes using hierarchical systems impractical.

Other technologies employed within the current installed application system portfolio are an off-line report generator for the general ledger program and a data dictionary maintained by the data administrator.

The management problem set

The Problem Assessment Questionnaire was filled out by G.E., Vice-President of MIS, to provide an overall perspective on the extent of various problems experienced at FoodStor in maintaining the application portfolio. Among 26 possible problem items, one was considered to be major: competing demands for maintenance programming personnel time. Three were considered a somewhat major problem: user demand for enhancement and extensions to application systems, lack of user understanding of application systems, and processing time requirements of application systems programs.

Statistical analysis of the problem item responses and comparison of the results with a reference survey population produces the following problem profile.

User knowledge	−0.13	Normal
Programmer effectiveness	−0.20	Normal
Product quality	0.28	Normal
Programmer time availability	−0.02	Normal
Machine requirements	0.16	Normal
System reliability	−0.32	Normal

It is seen that maintenance problems at FoodStor, as assessed by G.E., are normal in comparison with the reference survey population.

G.E. feels that maintenance activies are well managed overall. 'People here do a good job of taking care of things,' he says. He expects to hear from users if things go awry and interprets absence of complaints as indication of user satisfaction. G.E.'s involvement in maintenance, as a result, is minimal, centering principally on planning (choosing systems to be replaced, setting maintenance budget targets, and prioritizing tasks) and staffing (insuring that the MIS staff is talented and works well together).

Quality maintenance of the strategic applications in FoodStor's portfolio is extremely important. However, in a computing environment changes are always being made to hardware, system software, and application software. G.E.

attempts to balance a motivation for excellence with some circumspection. 'We have a policy here that we don't have the same problem twice,' he says, 'but my feeling is that some problems are inevitable. If we can, we get the system up and running and then diagnose the problem.' The emphasis is thus on providing continuous service, not on systems analysis.

In G.E.'s estimation, two major strengths of MIS are its extremely reliable data-processing operation and the quality of the MIS staff. The operation group has very favourable rerun and downtime rates, in his opinion. 'That lets us focus our attention on more productive issues. The MIS staff is fairly young, but has, "pound for pound", as much raw talent and intelligence as any MIS department', says G.E. A major issue for FoodStor is providing operating and supervisory experience to its people so that the potential of their abilities can be fulfilled. Experience is also an issue at the MIS management level. G.E. and his immediate staff are all relatively new to their current positions (13 months or less) and so they are also still learning.

Questions

(1) What is United Food Stores' maintenance philosophy? How can you tell?
(2) Why might United Food Stores have trouble keeping application staff?
(3) Does the Information Systems department take quality seriously? Why do you think so?

Postscript

Other cases in the three chapters to follow offer additional examples that emphasize the significance of the policy and strategy context for maintenance. Small City Manufacturing (Case 5.3) illustrates the reorganization of maintenance in the context of a new corporate emphasis on decentralized profit responsibility. Diablo National Laboratories (Case 6.3) describes maintenance in a context shaped by the ebbs and flows of Federal priorities and budgets. Integrated Information Technologies (Case 7.1) portrays maintenance in a high-technology manufacturing environment where innnovation, high quality, and the control of costs are all at a premium.

Chapter 5

THE MAINTENANCE TASK

INTRODUCTION

In Chapter 4 we established a linkage between information system maintenance and the business policies and strategies of the host organization. We argued that a maintenance philosophy based on a long-term view of the IS task can strengthen this linkage.

In this chapter we examine the maintenance task itself. Earlier, in Chapter 1, we argued that maintenance is substantially an organizational problem. Here we revisit this theme. We begin by considering the traditional view of maintenance, which, we argue, derives from the popular notion of the system development life cycle. This view is deficient, we find, inasmuch as it ignores the relational foundations of maintenance in general and the systems–staff relationship in particular.

We present a new, alternative view of the maintenance task and first describe and emphasize the portfolio context within which maintenance must be understood. We then consider the basic types of maintenance work, following which we discuss requisite knowledge and skills and the issue of specialization as well as the tools of maintenance.

Finally, we consider the ways in which maintenance differs from new system development. From this discussion a new view of the maintenance task emerges, one which differs significantly from the established view of maintenance as an unfortunate-but-necessary backwater operation. This new view shifts the focus of IS away from the development of new software products toward its ongoing business services, with clear implications for IS organization and management, the subject of Chapter 6.

MAINTENANCE AS TRADITIONALLY VIEWED

The traditional view of maintenance is largely attributable to the concept of the system development life cycle. As most widely understood, this cycle describes the task of system development in terms of a sequence of phases such as those portrayed in the 'waterfall model' shown in Figure 5.1. It will be helpful to briefly review this model, which also distinguishes between the systems analysis and programming portions of the overall task.

The early phases of the development life cycle—the establishment of system

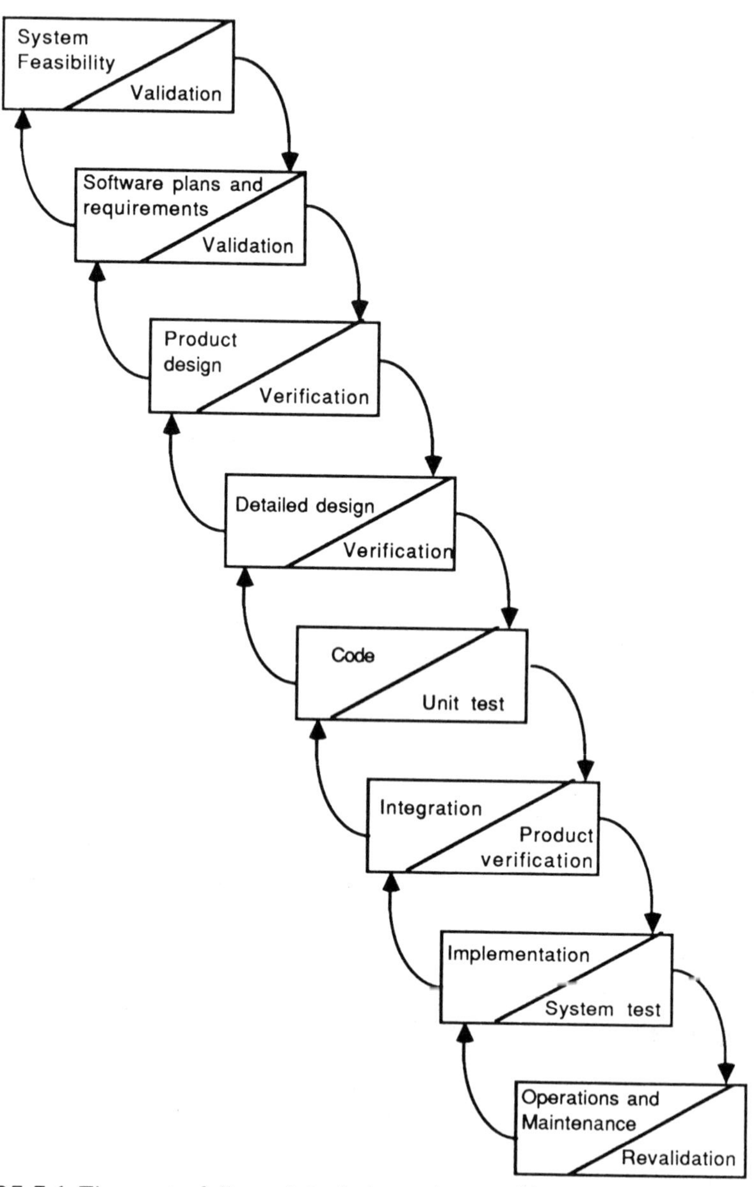

FIGURE 5.1 The waterfall model of the software life cycle (adapted from Boehm, 1981, by permission)

feasibility, plans and requirements, and design specifications—are commonly recognized to constitute the task of systems analysis. The next phases—those of detailed software design, coding, and unit testing—make up the task of programming. The remaining phases—those of integration, implementation, operations, and maintenance—are tasks shared among a number of parties, including operations and user personnel.

In the case of any new system under development the overall task is accordingly differentiated across its phases. Depending upon progress, the current task may be dominated by systems analysis, by programming, or by other, subsequent, activities. Notably, the task of maintenance is subordinated to the overall development concept. It is also last among the phases, almost as if it were an afterthought.

Hand in glove with the waterfall model of system development, the traditional job distinction in the overall task is between systems analysis and programming. Significantly, the work of the system analyst is understood to precede that of the programmer. The analyst studies system feasibility, develops plans and requirements, and produces a set of system specifications. The programmer works from the established specifications to design, code, and test the software.

The programmer is thus the software technician. The systems analyst, in contrast, works in a mediating role between the system user and the programmer. The programmer, buffered from the user by the system analyst, is not presumed to understand the application system in the user's terms. The system analyst, on the other hand, must understand the application both from the user's point of view and from that of the programmer. Table 5.1 summarizes the difference in skills needed for the two positions, as viewed by IS managers surveyed by Cheney and Lyons (1980). Interestingly, the difference is not as pronounced as might be expected, probably because application-specific skills were not included among those listed in the survey. (See also Cheney, 1988, for an update.)

Job specialization in terms of systems analysis and programming facilitates the development of two professional elites within IS, those who are intimately familiar with and knowledgeable about computers and those who know enough about computers and their applications to act in the critical boundary spanning role in which contractual understandings are negotiated with users.

However, these traditional roles are perhaps most easily associated with the development of new systems rather than the maintenance of installed ones. Historically, the maintenance task has been left to the programmer, although continued development of the system after installation is characteristic. The term 'maintenance programmer' is commonplace; 'maintenance analyst' has not been used to our knowledge.

Why should this be the case? A closer look at the waterfall model is revealing in answer to this question. Note that while the overall process is sequential, it is nonetheless iterative in that problems with any one phase feed back to the preceding phases. Viewed narrowly, maintenance consists simply of keeping the

TABLE 5.1 Skill needs ranked in order of importance (adapted from Cheney and Lyons, 1980, by permission)

Systems analyst	Programmer
(1) Introductory computer and information systems concepts	(1) Introductory computer and information systems concepts
(2) System design topics	(2) File design
(3) Information-gathering techniques	(3) Applications programming languages
(4) File design	(4) Operating systems
(5) Human relations in systems development	(5) Database management systems
(6) Applications programming languages	(6) System design topics
(7) Database management systems	(7) Telecommunications
(8) Human factors in equipment design and work layout	(8) Computer hardware
(9) Telecommunications	(9) Human relations in system development
(10) Project planning and control	(10) Sorting

system 'up and running'. However, what is meant by this goes largely undefined in the waterfall model. Substantive changes to the system, especially those which imply a revised specification, require additional development iterations within the model, and the role of 'maintenance' in this context is largely reduced to serving as the trigger for yet another round of development activity.

No wonder that, for some, 'maintenance is the pits', as we heard the expression. Ed Yourdon, among the most widely known authorities on system development, has therefore commented:

> Maintaining a computer program is one of life's dreariest jobs. For most American programmers, it is a fate worse than death. They dread it . . . no, that's not quite right. It is not that programmers are afraid of maintenance, but rather that they look upon it as demeaning work. To be called a maintenance programmer is to be called a second-class citizen. A junior programmer must put up with this because that is all he is offered; but as soon as he has enough experience and/or seniority, he looks for ways to remove himself from this form of indentured servitude. If his employer won't help him, he quits (Zvegintzov, 1988).

However, as we know from Chapter 2, at least half of the effort in system development and maintenance is typically devoted to maintenance, when the task is viewed more broadly (Lientz and Swanson, 1980). Many more systems are maintained at any one moment than are under new development. If maintenance is 'the pits', many people nonetheness toil there. We suggest that a more enlightened view of the task is needed.

MAINTENANCE VIEWED ANEW

It will be helpful to recall that the overall task of systems development and maintenance is the establishment and deployment of the application system portfolio for the IS department (Nolan, 1979). It is primarily by means of this portfolio that IS services are provided to the host organization.

The term 'portfolio' emphasizes the significance of both diversity and complementarity among an organization's application systems. Within the portfolio, systems may be functionally differentiated in terms of, for example, user groups supported. They may also vary in their strategic significance to the host organization, as we have seen earlier. Whatever the diversity, systems may be more or less integrated among themselves. However, in the end, they must complement each other and serve the organization as a whole.

Accordingly, the task of system maintenance should be viewed more within the context of the nature of the portfolio taken as a whole than within that of the development life cycle of any one system taken individually. In this section we elaborate upon this concept. We consider first the portfolio context itself and then examine the types of work comprising the maintenance task, along with requisite knowledge and skills and the issue of specialization. A discussion of various tools of the maintenance trade concludes the section.

1. The application system portfolio context

Historically, application system portfolios have been established for the most part by the in-house development of their software. Across the twelve cases of our study, for example, as summarized earlier in Figure 3.22, fully 80 per cent of the systems of the portfolios were developed in-house, that is, by the IS department's systems development unit. Another 12 per cent were developed by other IS departments at other locations within the host organization, and 2 per cent by user units of the host organization. Only 6 per cent were procured through the marketplace (4 per cent on contract, 2 per cent purchased off the shelf). Figure 5.2 shows how the individual cases differ in this respect.

More recently, the development of application software has been recognized to hold promise as a major commercial market, suggesting that in-house development may not dominate in the future as it has in the past (Field, 1987). At present, however, the nature of an organization's application system portfolio both shapes and is shaped by the nature of the system development and maintenance unit with which it has been associated over the years. The portfolio reflects the unit's experience and skills directly (for example, in terms of languages employed). For this reason, the systems–staff relationship described in Chapter 1 is fundamental to maintenance. As we shall see, the effective management of this relationship also depends upon the underlying diversity among both systems and staff.

Because application system portfolios are established over time by 'growing

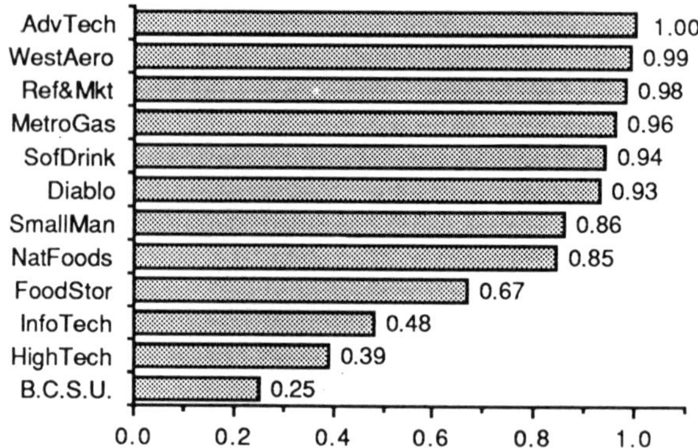

FIGURE 5.2 Percentage of portfolio developed in-house

them from the ground up', employing scarce staff and computing resources, IS departments may be usefully contrasted in terms of the maturities of their portfolios, i.e. the extent to which portfolios are fully grown. IS departments with mature, fully developed portfolios tend themselves to be older and fully grown in terms of staff size and composition, while those whose portfolios are still growing, with areas of application yet to be served, tend to be younger, with further room for staff growth.

Because host organizational change is continuous, and mature portfolios age and need renewing, the development of new systems for a portfolio is a never-ending activity, even for older IS departments. Where portfolios are mature, however, new systems tend to be replacement ones. Among our twelve cases, for example, replacement constitutes a substantial bulk of the new system development effort, as seen in Table 5.2. Among 112 new systems under development overall, 59 (52.7 per cent) are replacement ones.

The maturity of a portfolio is further indicated by its net growth rate, defined here as the number of new systems under development (including replacement ones) less the number of installed systems to be replaced divided by the total number of those installed. Table 5.2 compares our twelve cases; the range of growth rates is seen to vary between 0.242 (in one instance, West Coast High Tech Manufacturing, reflecting a major consolidation) and 0.214, and the aggregate growth rate is 0.047.

Mature portfolios may or may not involve a high frequency of replacement. In some instances, systems may simply age in place, however painful that might be for all concerned. In the case of Integrated Information Technologies, for example, such pain is all too apparent, as systems are replaced only 'when they have screamingly reached end of life', in the words of one manager. It is therefore also useful to compare portfolios in terms of their relative agedness by, for example, comparing proportions of systems over ten years old (Figure 5.3).

TABLE 5.2 Maturities of application system portfolios (12 cases)

Case	Installed systems	New systems	Replacement systems	Systems replaced	Growth rate
Ref&Mkt	51	16	4	12	0.078
SofDrink	81	22	9	9	0.160
HighTech	33	11	11	19	−0.242
Diablo	14	3	0	0	0.214
NatFoods	103	15	10	10	0.049
InfoTech	89	21	11	16	0.056
BCSU	28	5	3	3	0.071
FoodStor	33	6	3	3	0.091
SmallMan	22	0	0	0	0.000
AdvTech	30	3	2	2	0.033
MetroGas	25	10	6	6	0.160
WestAero	171	0	0	0	0.000
Totals	680	112	59	80	0.047

Note: New systems counts include replacement counts.

Portfolios also differ in terms of the variance in the ages of their systems. Figure 5.4 illustrates this for our twelve cases, in which the mean age of systems in a portfolio is 6.6 years and the standard deviation is 4.3 years. On average, older portfolios are seen to be more varied in age.

In general, the older and more established the IS department, the more varied in age will be the systems in its application system portfolio. No matter how many systems are replaced over time, every IS department seems to maintain a few which are as nearly as old as the department itself.

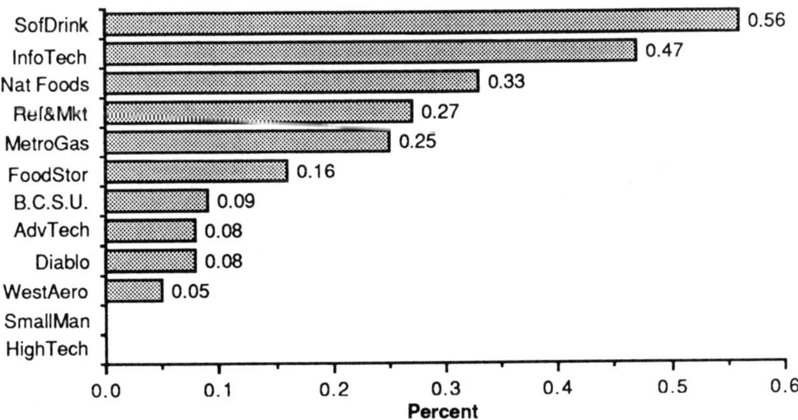

FIGURE 5.3 Proportion of portfolios over 10 years old

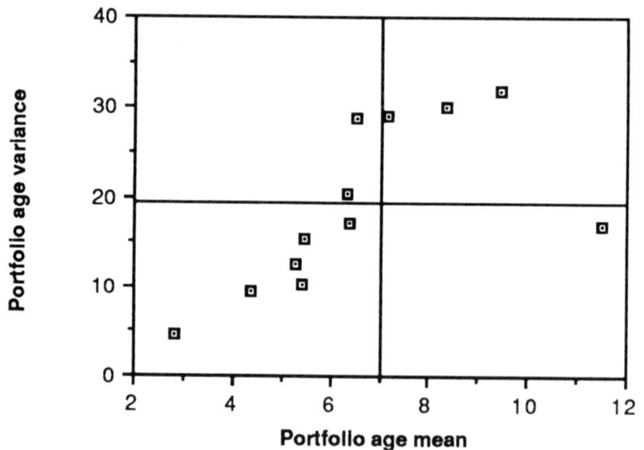

FIGURE 5.4 Age distributions of application system portfolios (twelve cases)

On average, older systems are known to require more maintenance effort, as we discussed in Chapter 2. Even more significant, however, may be the variance in system age within a portfolio. Substantial variance in age is likely to be associated with still other diversity (for example, in the underlying technology employed within the portfolio), with obvious implications for the knowledge and skill required in maintenance.

In summary, the IS maintenance task varies significantly according to the maturity of its application system portfolio. The more established and mature the portfolio, the greater should be the focus on maintenance. Moreover, new system development, because it is based largely in replacement, is itself motivated by problems in maintenance, where the firm's portfolio is mature.

2. Types of maintenance work

Broadly speaking, maintenance incorporates all task components involved in sustaining operational information systems within organizations, as we stated in Chapter 1. The basic typology of software maintenance work—that of corrective, adaptive, and perfective maintenance—suggested by Swanson (1976) was discussed briefly in Chapter 2. It will be helpful to consider again its three types, both in terms of the traditional view of maintenance and in the light of the portfolio context emphasized here.

Corrective maintenance, performed in response to processing, performance, or implementation failures, corresponds most closely to the narrow view of maintenance as keeping the system 'up and running'. Emergency fixes and routine debugging are characteristic. 'Firefighting' is descriptive of the task where an emergency prevails. Much corrective work is routine, however, involving fixes necessary to bring code into conformity with specifications or standards, for instance, where time may not be of the essence. In general, the older the systems in a portfolio, the greater will be the task of corrective maintenance (Lientz and Swanson, 1980).

Adaptive maintenance, performed in response to anticipated changes in the data and processing environments, extends the notion of keeping systems up and running. In general, the more diverse the systems within a portfolio, and the more varied their operating environments, the more frequent should be the adaptive requirement. Further, the more integrated the systems within the portfolio, the greater should be the magnitude of the adaptive task when it is required.

Perfective maintenance, performed to eliminate processing inefficiencies, enhance performance, or improve maintainability, accounts for more than half of the broadly viewed maintenance effort, as was mentioned in Chapter 2. Providing user enhancements is the major portion of the perfective task (Lientz and Swanson, 1980). Here the notion of keeping the system up and running is stretched to incorporate the requirement that it be responsive to the evolving needs of its users. That is, the provision of ongoing business support is now fundamental. In general, the perfective task should be the greater where change in the host organizational environment is characteristic. It is also likely to be greater where systems are relatively new, and users are discovering their needs through initial use.

3. Knowledge, skills, and specialization

Requisite knowledge and skills in maintenance may be partitioned into two domains—the software and the application. The software domain is that within which the programmer works, as described above. Here the system is represented in terms of instructions and data for computer processing. The application domain is that within which the system analyst works, as also described above. Here the system is represented in terms of functionality and information provided to the user. Traditional areas of specialization are thus in programming and systems analysis, as we discussed earlier.

However, this traditional approach to specialization ignores the portfolio context of the overall task. In particular, it disregards the implications of the number and variety of systems within a portfolio. Significantly, variety among a portfolio's application systems requires correspondingly different knowledge and skills among the maintenance staff. This requisite variety is associated with both software and application domains.

In general, the older and larger the IS department, the greater will be the requisite variety of staff knowledge and skills. In the software domain mature portfolios tend to be characterized by, for example, diversity in hardware and system software environments and in programming languages and tools employed. In the application domain mature portfolios tend to be associated with variety among users served. This latter variety forms another basis for specialization among staff.

Where specialization is by domain of application the individual task focuses upon one or several organizationally related applications (for example, serving a specific group of users). Emphasis is typically placed upon the development of expertise which is local to one or more user departments more than it is global for the parent organization as a whole.

Where IS departments are in their rapid growth phase, with a significant number of new systems under development, specialization by application domain may be especially useful in that it focuses upon building new application expertise. Such expertise is likely to be particularly important; new systems necessarily reflect the knowledge and skills of their original developers, for better or for worse. IS relationships with individual user departments may also be facilitated by application specialization, which lends itself in part to the development of a customer service orientation among staff.

However, such an approach may also tend toward treating these customers as if they were relatively independent, whereas the users of the typical IS department may need, in fact, to be much better integrated. Indeed, the very purpose of many operational systems is the co-ordination of organizational subunits.

Even more importantly, where the IS department has a mature portfolio it may need to focus more clearly on its overall maintenance task. That is, it may need to find a way to specialize in maintenance in particular, as distinct from the development of new systems. Specifically, it may need to focus upon its ongoing support of the business. We will return to this issue momentarily. Before doing so, however, we consider the technology of maintenance in terms of its tools.

4. Tools of the maintenance trade

Among the diverse tools of the trade of maintenance and development are: the overall development methodology and its standards and procedures; conceptual and diagrammatic methods for system analysis, specification, and design; programming languages and structured coding technique; data dictionary and database management systems; and tools for software testing, analysis, and structuring. By far the majority of these tools have been originated for new system development. However, many of these find subsequent application in maintenance as well, and ease of maintenance of systems developed with certain tools is often claimed to be among their virtues.

Among specific development methodologies is the commercial package SDM/70, marketed by Atlantic Management Systems of Philadelphia. A manual forms-driven system, it incorporates a comprehensive specification of generic tasks and required products and documentation across all stages and phases of system development as traditionally viewed. Conceived as a rigorous general framework, it is compatible with a number of widely used analysis and design methods. As with other traditional methodologies, it is not especially suited to maintenance. Its use is illustrated by Westcoast Refining & Marketing, among our twelve cases.

Conceptual and diagrammatic methods for system analysis, specification, and design are numerous. Among the tools of system analysis are document flowcharts, data flow diagrams, entity-relationship (E-R) diagrams, structure charts, and HIPO (Hierarchical and Input–Process–Output) charts. Methods for specification and design employ two major approaches: functional decomposition and data structuring. Functional decomposition focuses upon the system as the unit of analysis, and proposes a top-down, hierarchical approach to development. Data structuring concentrates on data as the unit of analysis, and derives the system structure from that of the data it processes. Included among commercially available tools for functional decomposition are Yourdan's structured analysis and design method; Gane and Sarson's Improved System Technology (IST); and SofTech's Structured Analysis and Design Technique (SADT). Included among data-structuring approaches are the Jackson design and the Warnier–Orr methods. (For reviews, see King, 1984; Colter, 1984.)

These various conceptual and diagrammatic methods have two purposes in maintenance. First, they serve as documentation for the originally developed systems. Second, they may be used as maintenance tools in their own right. With regard to the first purpose their usefulness may be rather limited in that they are not tied to the working code of the system and, because as a system ages, its documentation tends to become increasingly obsolete. With regard to the second purpose, it is worth noting that tools may not be equally useful in both new system development and maintenance. For example, functional decomposition methods are more widely used in new system development than are data-structuring ones. However, there is some reason to believe that the latter may be preferable in maintenance (Parikh, 1981).

At the most detailed level, software is often specified by means of pseudo-code, after which it is encoded in a particular programming language. The most popular commercially oriented language is COBOL (COmmon Business Oriented Language). However, many other languages have been, and continue to be, used in various contexts and situations. In Chapter 3, Figure 3.23 summarized the average distribution of programming languages employed across our twelve cases; COBOL was seen to account for a majority (63 per cent) of language use. Figure 5.5 provides a further perspective, showing the extent to which individual organizations tend to employ one dominant language (COBOL or PL/1, except for West Coast High Tech, which uses a Pascal-like language for most of its systems).

Although in four of our twelve cases one language is used exclusively within the portfolio, in the other eight a small number of applications are maintained in other than the dominant language. This poses potential problems for maintenance over the long term in that multiple-language skills must be maintained within the IS department, even where these skills are little or seldom exercised.

Perhaps the most important discipline used in coding the system is that of structured programming, in which a hierarchical structure is imposed upon the

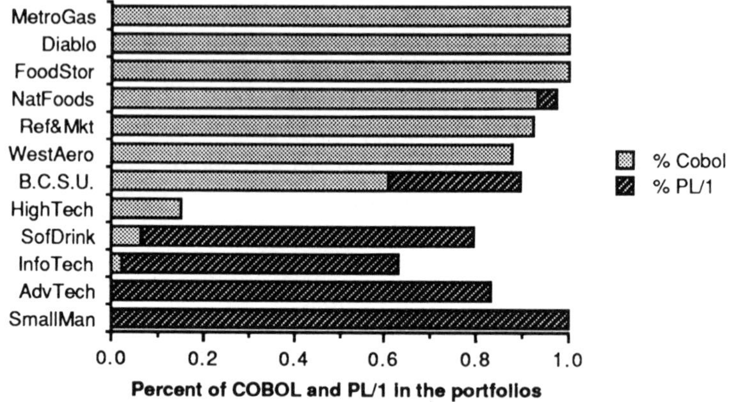

FIGURE 5.5 Language use in the portfolios

software. On average, approximately 40 per cent of the systems in the portfolios of the twelve cases studied employed structured programming. The structured walk-through, in which a program's logic is systematically reviewed and inspected by members of a design team, is also a widely used work method; for example, it is found in ten of the twelve cases. Both structured techniques tend to be highly regarded by maintainers in that they are oriented to program code which is well ordered and accessible to others, apart from the person who writes it.

The use of data dictionary and database management systems (DBMS) enable systems to be developed around common data structures and representations. Automated aid in the form of fourth-generation languages and application generators is also often available. Many organizations employ both database and fourth-generation tools; however, penetration of the application portfolios is frequently slight, perhaps because many installed systems predate these technologies. Clearly, another problem is posed here for effective maintenance; for example, limited use of a data dictionary across a portfolio tends to create barriers in communication among applications. Moreover, fourth-generation tools have been found to pose their own problems for maintenance (Tinnirello, 1985).

Several tools and techniques are aimed directly at the support of maintenance. (See Roman, 1986.) The most significant of these include automated code analyzers, restructurers, and converters. These enable older, poorly documented systems to be reworked, or 'retrofitted', extending their useful life. Gill (1986) reports the existence of 45 tools of this type for use in IBM mainframe environments. The more advanced of these make use of artificial intelligence (AI) technology (Carlyle, 1985). Surprisingly, given the maturities of many application system portfolios, these tools are not as widely used as might be expected. For example, among our cases only one organization made use of structured retrofitting.

Figures 3.13 and 3.14 in Chapter 3 summarized the frequency of use of various of these tools and techniques across the twelve cases. These frequencies overstate the use of these methods and techniques, which are often employed on only a fraction of the systems in the portfolio, as shown in Figures 3.24 and 3.25.

In general, maintenance and development tools are, of course, intended in substantial part to increase staff productivity. However, studies report only limited evidence of actual productivity gains. (See, e.g., Banker *et al.*, 1987.) The reasons for this are not well understood; however, in maintaining systems it has been suggested that labor savings in corrective work tend to be re-allocated to perfective work in the form of system enhancements. The quality of systems maintained may therefore be improved, although the overall level of effort remains the same (Lientz and Swanson, 1980).

Perhaps the most significant consideration in the use of productivity tools may be the organizational overhead involved. Particularly where tools proliferate within a portfolio over time, and are differentially used across systems, substantial knowledge and skill requirements may be imposed upon the IS staff. Thus, ironically, among the burdens of maintaining systems is that of maintaining familiarity with the tools which support them.

HOW MAINTENANCE DIFFERS FROM DEVELOPMENT

How does maintenance actually differ as a task from new system development? One might at first be inclined to answer that it does not, inasmuch as continued development in the form of user enhancements is characteristic, as we have seen. From a narrow, development life-cycle perspective, such work consists simply of recycling within the development framework, involving nothing different in kind from that which originally preceded it. Even the debugging work of maintenance may be seen to be a simple extension of the original software testing. Nevertheless, a close examination reveals a number of significant differences.

At the level of the individual task, maintenance typically requires that a programmer spend a significant proportion of his or her time in attempting to understand how the program is constructed and how it functions (Littman *et al.*, 1987). Indeed, the time spent in defining and understanding a change, reviewing documentation, and tracing program logic is likely to consume as much as implementing the correction or enhancement (Fjeldstad and Hamlen, 1979). Jones (1986) claims that '. . . the overhead costs associated with exploring existing software run so high that changing one or two lines in an existing large system may cost up to 1000 times more than creating one or two lines of code for a new system' (p. 50). Among our cases the story of the repair of a cost accounting system at Integrated Information Technologies (Case 7·1), requiring one person-year to diagnose and solve a single problem, is illustrative. The importance of prior familiarity with a system to its effective maintenance (Lientz and Swanson, 1980) is thus underscored. So, too, is the significance of certain diagnostic and system analytic skills which are not, at present, well understood.

However, our argument in this book is that maintenance is more than an individual task; it is also an organizational one. In this context, maintenance of systems is characterized by problems of unpredictable urgency and significant consequent firefighting. Requirements are likely to be presented as relatively clear-cut, based on actual system use and continuous feedback from operations. Technology is relatively familiar, especially to the user who lives with it daily. Involvement of the user is also highly motivated in that current work is directly and immediately impacted. Design is necessarily incremental, and architectural integrity of systems is increasingly difficult to maintain. Familiarity with code is also increasingly distant. User service is the dominant issue, if not the acknowledged objective.

In contrast, new system development may be buffered from the user's current task. Urgency is relatively predictable and dominated by schedules. Requirements are based more in anticipated, rather than actual, use. Technology may be new and unfamiliar to both IS and the user, whose involvement may also be weakly motivated in that impacts are not immediate. Design is systemic, often proceeding from a 'clean slate'. Code is recent and familiar. The delivery of the software product of acceptable quality, on time, and within budget is typically the understood objective.

Thus maintenance differs significantly from new system development when examined from an organizational point of view. In the language of organization theorests the two activities involve different contingencies. Most importantly, new system development is product-oriented, maintenance is service-oriented. This difference carries significant implications for specialization and for the organizational design of the IS department, as we shall see in Chapter 6.

For the present, we note simply that expertise in new system development may be distinguished from expertise in maintenance. One problem with this as a basis for specialization is, of course, the common belief among systems professionals that maintenance is a second-class activity while new system development offers the greater challenges and opportunities. Understandably, where such a belief prevails only those individuals with a low 'growth need strength' may be content to work in a maintenance role (Couger and Colter, 1985). However, we will argue that career prospects account for this belief more than any other factor, and that IS organizations may be designed in ways which upgrade, rather than downgrade, the maintenance task.

SUMMARY

The task of information system maintenance in any IS organization is shaped substantially by the installed application system portfolio. More mature portfolios are larger and grow more slowly, as new systems under development are often replacement ones. They are also more diverse both in terms of their application domain, serving a greater variety of users, and of their underlying computer and work technologies. For these reasons, more mature portfolios typically require both greater resources and more varied skills in their maintenance.

The tools of information system maintenance are, for the most part, those employed in new system development. More mature portfolios are often also characterized by variety among the tools with which they were originally developed and with which they must frequently now be maintained. These tools themselves require maintenance, or at least the maintenance of skills associated with their use, as do the systems to which they are applied.

Specialization within the IS staff may take any of three alternative forms. A first form relies upon distinguishing between programming and systems analysis skills. A second specializes by domain of application (for example, distinguishing among different groups of users). A third form emphasizes the difference between maintenance and new system development. Here the cultivation of a service orientation in maintenance is facilitated, as we shall argue further in Chapter 6.

REFERENCES

Banker, R. D., Datar, S. M., and Kemerer, C. F. (1987) 'Factors affecting software maintenance productivity: an exploratory study', *Proceedings of the Eighth International Conference on Information Systems*, Pittsburgh, 6–9 December, pp. 160–75.

Boehm, B. W. (1981) *Software Engineering Economics*, Prentice-Hall, Englewood Cliffs, NJ.

Carlyle, E. R. (1985) 'Can AI save COBOL?' *Datamation*, **31**, 18, 15 September, 42–3.

Cheney, P. H. (1988) 'Information systems skill requirements: 1980–1988', *the 1988 ACM SIGCPR Conference on the Management of Information Systems Personnel*, College Park, Maryland, 7–8 April, pp. 1–7.

Cheny, P. H., and Lyons, N. R. (1980) 'Information systems skill requirements: a survey', *MIS Quarterly*, **4**, 1, 35–43.

Colter, M. A. (1984) 'A comparative examination of systems analysis techniques', *MIS Quarterly*, **9**, 1, 51–65.

Couger, J. D., and Colter, M. A. (1985) *Maintenance Programming: Improved Productivity Through Motivation*, Prentice-Hall, Englewood Cliffs, NJ.

Field, A. R. (1987) 'The free-for-all has begun', *Business Week*, 11 May, 148ff.

Fjeldstad, R. K., and Hamlen, W. T. (1979) 'Application program maintenance study—report to our correspondents', IBM Corporation, DP Marketing Group. Reprinted in *Tutorial on Software Maintenance* (Eds G. Parikh and N. Zvegintzov), IEEE Computer Society, 1983, pp. 13–27.

Gill, P. J. (1986) 'Tools ease time-consuming tasks of maintenance, documentation', *Information Week*, 15 December, 21–5.

Jones, C. (1986) 'Software maintenance', *Computerworld*, **20**, 17, 28 April, 49–55.

King, D. (1984) *Current Practices in Software Development*, Yourdan Press, New York.

Lientz, B. P., and Swanson, E. B. (1980) *Software Maintenance Management*, Addison-Wesley, Reading, Mass.

Littman, D. C., Pinto, J., Letovsky, S., and Soloway, E. (1987) 'Mental models and software maintenance', *Journal of Systems and Software*, **7**, 4, 341–56.

Nolan, R. L. (1979) 'Managing the crisis in data processing', *Harvard Business Review*, **57**, 2, March-April, 115–26.

Parikh, G. (1981) 'Structured maintenance: the Warnier/Orr way', *Computerworld*, 21 September, 11ff.

Roman, D. (1986) 'Classifying maintenance tools', *Computer Decisions*, **18**, 14, 30 June, 36–43.

Swanson, E. B. (1976) 'The dimensions of maintenance', *Proceedings of the Second International Conference on Software Engineering*, San Francisco, 13–15 October, pp. 492–7.

Tinnirello, P. C. (1985) 'Software maintenance in fourth generation language environments', *Data Management*, **23**, 3, 38–43.

Zvegintzov, N. (Ed.) (1988) *Software Maintenance News*, **6**, 8, August, 12.

CASES

Introduction

We present here three cases, all of which involve high-technology manufacturing organizations. Case 5.1, Advanced Technologies Manufacturing, discusses information system maintenance at one of the original manufacturing sites of a large, profitable, and well-respected company. Staff work concurrently on both maintenance and new system development and a sharp distinction between the tasks is not drawn.

Case 5.2, West Coast High Tech Manufacturing, describes maintenance at a small manufacturing outpost of the parent firm. New system development is centralized in this organization, and only maintenance is performed at the location described. A small staff of seven faces the prospect of implementing a new Manufacturing Resource Planning system being developed by the parent corporation.

Case 5.3, Small City Manufacturing, also involves a high-technology manufacturing plant, operating within a principal division of one of the world's leading US-based corporations. A major reorganization of IS has recently taken place here, and jobs have been significantly redefined. New system development is also frozen during the present period of transition. Problems in maintenance are seen as substantially normal when compared to those of other organizations. However, significant concerns with the skills of staff are expressed.

Case 5.1. Advanced Technologies Manufacturing

The organizational environment

Advanced Technologies Manufacturing (AdvTech) is one of three facilities (including two plants and a laboratory) located in Central City at one of the original manufacturing sites of a large, well-respected, profitable, high-technology company. About 10 000 employees work at the two plants; AdvTech itself employs about 4000 people. Three lines of computer components are produced and shipped by AdvTech to other divisions of the parent company for use in the manufacture of computer and communication equipment.

Central City, with a population of about 200 000, is very much a company town. Situated in a valley more than two hours by car away from any large metropolitan area, it offers the advantages of pleasant surroundings and relatively low-priced housing to AdvTech employees.

As part of a company-wide move toward decentralization, the Central City facilities were reorganized about three years ago. One result of this was the split of the IS organization, which previously had serviced both plants, into four groups. As before, the data center remained separate from the plants themselves. The systems and programming staff, however, was allocated among the three user organizations it served. One of the new groups, Financial Information Systems, supports the Finance organization as a whole and reports through the Site Controller to the site General Manager. The other two groups, Products Information Systems and Technology Information Systems, support the two Central City plants, and thus each has been attached to a 'services' organization reporting to a plant manager, along with other departments providing services to the plants such as maintenance, procurement, distribution, etc.

The heads of the four information services groups continue to maintain close contact, with the data center manager acting as the central point of communications. Their strong, informal relationship helps them maintain consistency in policies, standards, and practices, in addition to improving co-ordination in the delivery of information services to the site.

Figure 5.6 illustrates the organizational location of the four information services at the Central City site.

Technology Information Systems

Technology Information Systems (TIS) has as its mission the support of the manufacturing process in the AdvTech plant. Its immediate user community numbers about 5000. In addition, a number of TIS applications are also used at as many as 24 other plants throughout the parent company, creating a substantial extended user community.

The application systems staff (those working directly on application systems, excluding managers) currently numbers 102. Eight of these are first-level managers (to whom no other manager reports). Last year the staff numbered 103

TIS is headed by P.W., the TIS functional manager. Reporting to him are three project managers, one of whom is responsible for department plans and controls. The applications staff of TIS is divided into two groups (see Figure 5.7). One, Applications Systems, develops and maintains systems that control the flow of products through the manufacturing process. These systems operate principally in a DOS/CICS environment. The other group, Data Systems, develops and maintains systems that generate data to drive the manufacturing process. Some of these systems operate in an MVS environment, and others, such as those involving numerical control of machinery, are on microcomputers.

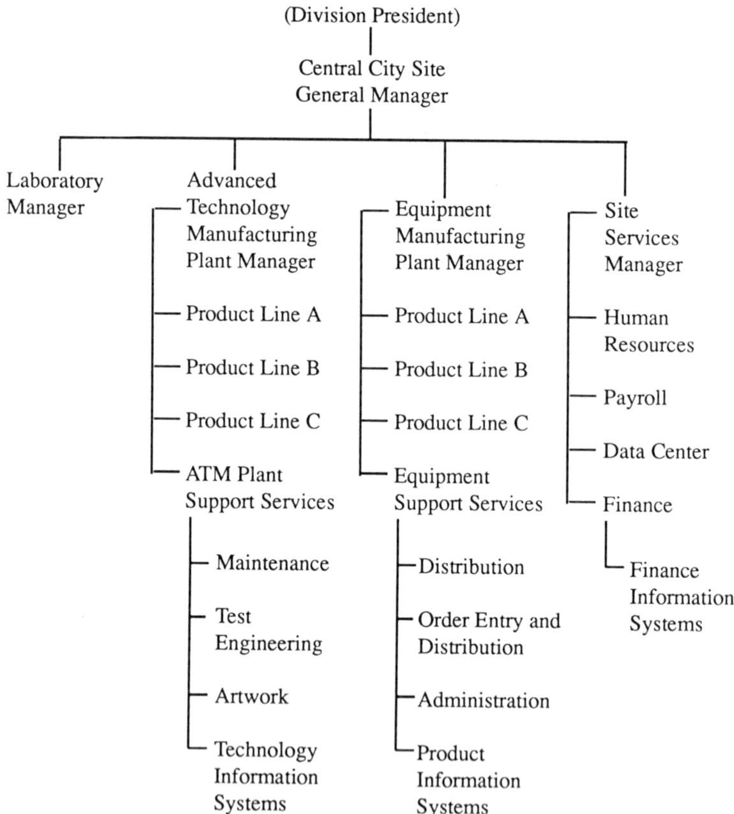

FIGURE 5.6 Information Services at the Central City Site, AdvTech

Both applications groups are broken into departments, with each department responsible for a group of systems. Within each department the staff does both maintenance and development. Each staff member allocates an average of 40 per cent of his or her effort to maintenance (program fixes and customer support) and 60 per cent to development. As a rule, maintenance assignments are made based on experience with the system. For newer personnel in particular, these assignments are viewed as useful, if not necessary, learning experiences. Maintenance work builds a working knowledge of the application portfolio and an understanding of the user environment and their use of the systems, and develops a rapport with these users. Development assignments, on the other hand, with their greater visibility, may have more impact on upward career movement but use the maintenance experience as a foundation for this success.

Contact between the TIS staff and the user community is relatively intense, as might be expected where the applications staff has been decentralized to its user

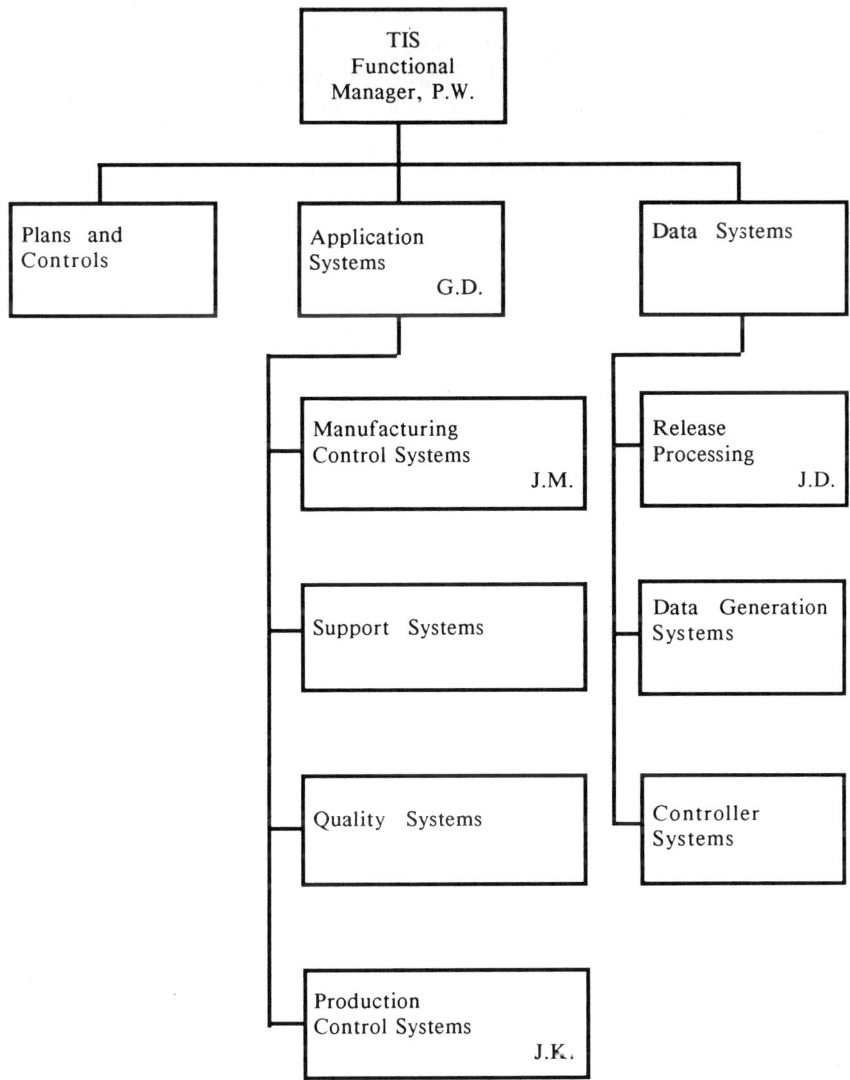

FIGURE 5.7 Technology Information Systems

community. By far the bulk of the application staff (80 people, 79 per cent) work directly (face to face) with users on a daily basis. The rest (22) work with users no less than weekly. Virtually all the staff have prior work experience at other site jobs apart from their current positions, either in the earlier information systems organization (70 people, or 69 per cent of the application staff) or in other positions at the site (30 people, or 29 per cent). Among these other positions are various manufacturing technician positions, from which non-degreed people have been successfully recruited. The data center is another source for staff. Referring to this, one project manager observed: 'This area provides some of our most effective people, because they have such a good understanding of the operating environment'.

Unlike most other information systems organizations, TIS has no applications staff who were previously employed in IS organizations outside the parent company. Most new hires come directly from school.

Reflecting the policy of the parent company, length of service with the company among the TIS application staff is typically rather high. A large part of the application staff (44 people, or 43 per cent) have been with the company over 6 years. Another 29 (28 per cent) have been with it for 3–6 years and 27 (26 per cent) for 1–3 years. Only two people were hired during the previous year.

While it is relatively unusual for members of the TIS staff to leave the company, movement from TIS to other assignments at the Central City site is not uncommon. The previous manager of TIS is now a manager in Engineering, and P.W., the current TIS manager, spent about a year as a Manufacturing manager during his otherwise TIS-oriented 15-year career. The site laboratory, a research and development facility, is another popular destination for TIS staff members.

Overall, the internal turnover rate in the IS groups is estimated to be 'significantly greater than' that of the typical non-IS group in the parent company. However, this is considered to be a healthy, not a harmful, situation. In the opinion of G.D., a project manager, IS experience is considered highly desirable in other parts of the division. He projects that eventually many of the upper management of the division will need to understand information systems.

The TIS application staff is college educated, for the most part. Two-thirds of the staff (67 people) hold a bachelor's degree as their highest degree obtained. Eleven more hold graduate degrees. Fifteen have two-year college degrees and nine hold a high-school diploma or less. Many of the staff have undergraduate degrees in computer science. Some have electrical engineering degrees, particularly those who hold the more technical programming jobs. Among the older staff members some have liberal arts degrees.

Most of the applications staff (70 people, or 69 per cent) received between one and two weeks of working-hour classroom education during the past year. Another 10 people received between one day and one week of training. Seventeen received between two and four weeks of training and five had received four or more weeks. The emphasis on training is to 'fill in the gaps', to familiarize new staff with the local environment, and to increase technical skills.

Ten of the staff are members of the Association for Computing Machinery (ACM) and three are members of the Association for Systems Management (ASM). None of the current application staff holds the Certificate in Data Processing (CDP) and none is a member of the Data Processing Management Association (DPMA).

Organizational techniques established by TIS for application maintenance include: periodic maintenance audit, user change request procedure, change request review board, formal retest procedure, and scheduled maintenance. Post-implementation reviews are carried out three months after system delivery, 'to see what errors occurred in the code', in the words of one department head. Another department head has begun to track details of maintenance expenditures in order to choose areas in which future maintenance investments might have the maximum payoff.

Development and major enhancement costs are budgeted twice each year. Maintenance costs are budgeted in 'Period Support Agreements', which basically define (and limit) the level of support that will be made available for each application. On a monthly basis users are charged for development and maintenance costs at the business unit and functional level (TIS serves three business units and approximately 20 functions).

Among work methods established by TIS for application system development and maintenance are: structured programming, top-down design, program development library, checkpoint review, benchmark testing, and test data generator. Of these, structured programming and top-down design are considered to have significant positive impacts on maintenance productivity. With respect to benchmark testing, it is interesting to note that new releases for some systems are required to continue supporting data formats associated with previous versions; a benchmark database containing data in all supported formats is used to test the new release.

Tools currently used for documentation for development and maintenance are: data dictionary, user manual, pseudo-code, data-flow diagram, and test history. Of these, pseudo-code is considered the most helpful for the maintenance programmer. 'That's where you can go to see what the program really does', says J.D., a department manager.

Programmer quality for development tasks is measured on the bases of (1) conformity to requirements, (2) timely delivery, and (3) cost. In addition, user satisfaction with the system is measured, as is programmer satisfaction with the project. Programmer quality in the maintenance area is not directly measured but is reflected by user satisfaction. The lack of an up-front agreement on maintenance costs at the task level makes conformity to cost and schedule for maintenance tasks impossible to evaluate at this time. For the future, TIS managers indicate, there is interest in improving measurement of maintenance task performance to cost and schedule.

The application system portfolio

The current application system portfolio includes 30 major installed systems, an increase of only one system over the previous year. The major operating functions supported by this portfolio are: Manufacturing, Manufacturing Engineering,

Production Control, Yield Management, Process Automation, Maintenance, Quality, and Information Systems.

Nearly half the systems in the current portfolio (14 systems, or 47 per cent) are more than 10 years old. A number of these are major systems, which were innovative when introduced and which have been adopted at other company locations. Five systems (17 per cent) are between 6 and 10 years old, five are between 3 and 6 years old, and five are between 1 and 3 years old. One system was installed within the past year. In recent years, new system development activity has been motivated primarily by changes in the manufacturing technology supported rather than by the need for new major systems.

For example, of the three major new systems currently under development, two will replace those more than 10 years old that no longer meet business needs and have become a burden to operate and use. One of the new systems will go from batch to on-line, in addition to adding new functions required by new manufacturing technology, new manufacturing processes, and a company interest in better control. The second replacement project was triggered by a system assessment which revealed that the system did not have the level of control and visibility currently deemed necessary. Both these replacement systems will be installed within the next year.

Growth of systems within the current portfolio has been substantial, as reflected by the data associated with five major systems depicted below. Of the total of 1599 programs in the five systems, 178 (11 per cent) were added during the last year.

Growth in five major systems

System (*no.*)	*Age* (*years*)	*Size* (*programs*)	*Year's growth* (*programs*)	*Maintenance effort* (*annual hours*)
1	2	111	8	1 200
2	3	96	31	570
3	3	485	70	5 200
4	7	240	30	1 000
5	12	667	39	5 000

All but one of the systems in the current installed application system portfolio were developed by the TIS organization. One was developed by an outside firm, as a package. As mentioned above, a number of TIS's applications have been adapted for use by other plants. (Typically, adapted versions are maintained at the using site.) A few applications are used at other plants in versions developed and actively supported by TIS staff. Development by outside firms, on the other hand, seems infeasible to TIS managers, both because of security ramifications and because of the complex character of the systems architecture. 'You can't just throw specs like ours over the wall', points out J.D.

Driven by the leading-edge nature of the manufacturing technology employed in the plant, ten (33 per cent) of the systems in the current application portfolio are considered by the TIS staff to be leading-edge applications in the sense of providing users with functions beyond those typically available to their counterparts in other organizations in the industry.

In addition, nine of the systems (30 per cent) provide direct service to customers of the plant, primarily in the form of information on the results of the manufacturing process or on how to do subsequent processing of the plant's products. For example, detailed test and quality control reports accompanying the products shipped.

Integration among the systems in the application portfolio is relatively high. Eighteen of the systems (60 per cent) rely on other major systems for their input data and 22 (73 per cent) are relied upon for input data by other major systems.

The operating environment for the system portfolio is IBM or IBM-compatible. The bulk of the systems (21, 70 per cent) are processed using MVS on IBM-3081 equivalent machines. Five (17 per cent) operate under a 'home-brewed' operating system that runs on IBM 370-type gear. Two use IMS, one uses DOS/CICS, and one uses VM/SQL.

The majority of the systems (25, or 83 per cent) are written in TIS's standard programming language, PL/1. Two of these also use Assembler language and one also uses REXX, an interpretive language. The five remaining systems (17 per cent) are written in Assembler. One application was developed using an off-line application generator.

It is TIS policy to use structured code, and eleven (37 per cent) of the current systems (primarily the most recently developed ones) now conform to this policy. Nine of the systems (30 per cent) use one of several database management systems, some of which were internally developed. Two use a data dictionary, two an interactive report generator, and another two an off-line report generator. One employs a user query language, one system includes a tutorial function (an on-line help function) and one has re-usable program code.

The management problem set

The Problem Awareness Questionnaire was complete by J.M., a department manager, to provide an overall perspective on the extent of various problems experienced at TIS in maintaining the application portfolio. Among 26 possible problem items, five were considered to be major: lack of user understanding of the application system, adequacy of application system design specifications, meeting scheduled commitments, inadequate training of user personnel, and user understanding of their responsibilities in the development phase. Eight items were considered to be a somewhat major problem: quality of application system documentation, user demand for enhancements and extensions to application system, competing demands for maintenance programming personnel time, lack of user interest in application system, motivation of maintenance programming personnel, system hardware and software reliability, unrealistic user expectations, and adherence to programming standards in maintenance.

Statistical analysis of the problem item responses and comparison of the results with a reference survey population produces the following problem profile:

User knowledge	1.11	Substantially above normal
Programmer effectiveness	0.63	Normal
Product quality	1.13	Above normal
Programmer time availability	0.57	Normal
Machine requirements	−0.20	Normal
System reliability	1.15	Substantially above normal

That is, problems of programmer effectiveness, programmer time availability, and machine requirements at TIS are equivalent to those experienced among the reference survey population; however, user knowledge, product quality, and system reliability are more problematic at TIS. These results may reflect a greater sensitivity to these last three issues at TIS rather than the existence of genuine problems. We discussed these issues with TIS management.

With respect to the user-knowledge problem, J.D. says he feels that TIS is 'still evolving to high user involvement particularly in helping users understand what is involved in development'. In the case of maintenance, another manager points out that 'the biggest chunk of maintenance is answering user questions'. In the absence of detailed budgets and charges for maintenance tasks, problems further arise from users' ignorance about the costs of their requests. P.W., the functional manager, is philosophical about this issue. 'It's a fact of life, a situation that exists. More and more people are getting involved [with systems]. Sometimes they don't want to change their ways. Sometimes they need pushing a little.' The resolution, as he sees it, is being worked out jointly between TIS and the company managers.

On the issue of product quality, P.W. and J.D. both note that maintenance of many of TIS's systems is made more difficult because of the age of the systems, their complexity and size, and the fact that several of them are in Assembler language. P.W.'s goal for maintenance costs is that each department should spend 10 per cent or less of its time doing basic maintenance ('fixing something that is wrong, or answering questions'). 'We should be doing things right the first time, and doing them in ways so the user doesn't get confused. That's how we can best support the manufacturing plant.'

With respect to system reliability, J.D. points out that they have had some data-integrity problems with one of the systems, but for the most part the data-processing center provides them with 'the resources they need to get the job done'. Response time may be more of a problem than reliability, in his experience. P.W. agrees. He points out that the data center meets its service level agreements, and believes that there is more of a reliability problem in the applications supported than in the systems software and hardware.

Overall, P. W. does not consider maintenance to be a TIS problem area. 'I don't think I've had a conversation just about maintenance before this', he said. He believes that maintenance is not as challenging as development, and he is concerned that the people doing maintenance maintain good morale. He believes it is workable to have newer people start in maintenance, moving to development as they mature.

Questions

(1) What is the basis for the division of labor in application system maintenance and development in Technical Information Systems (TIS) at Advanced Technologies Manufacturing? What are the apparent consequences?
(2) What is the level of effort in maintaining installed systems compared to that in new system development? Does maintenance appear to be a significant problem area at Advanced Technologies Manfacturing?
(3) TIS at Advanced Technologies Manufacturing has no staff who were previously employed in IS organizations outside the parent company. What are the ramifications for system development and maintenance? (See Chapter 7.)

Case 5.2. West Coast High Tech Manufacturing

The organizational environment

West Coast High Tech (HighTech) is a manufacturing facility for a large, US-based international computer and peripheral manufacturing company. Other manufacturing facilities are located across the United States, Canada, Mexico, and South America, as well as in the United Kingdom and Europe. Sales and service are international in scope. An older, somewhat conservative, organization, HighTech's parent company has recently gone through a major series of reorganizations and made new acquisitions to improve its ability to compete in the current marketplace.

The changes to HighTech's parent corporation have been reflected by similar changes at the HighTech plant. During the past five years, the 400 000 square foot facility, located on a 30-acre site, has gone from a staff of 1700 people to as few as 700. The staff currently has stabilized at 1200. The product mix at HighTech has undergone major changes as well. Two years ago, all products manufactured at the facility were non-industry-compatible, used only as part of systems sold by its parent corporation. Currently, its products are also sold in the plug-compatible peripheral market and the plant's volume has increased greatly.

The basic organizational structure of HighTech is shown in Figure 5.8. It consists of nine major departments, including: Product Engineering, Product Assurance, Controller's Office, Manufacturing Engineering, Purchasing, Human Resources, Manufacturing Control, Management Systems, and Manufacturing. It should be noted that there are no marketing responsibilities at the plant level.

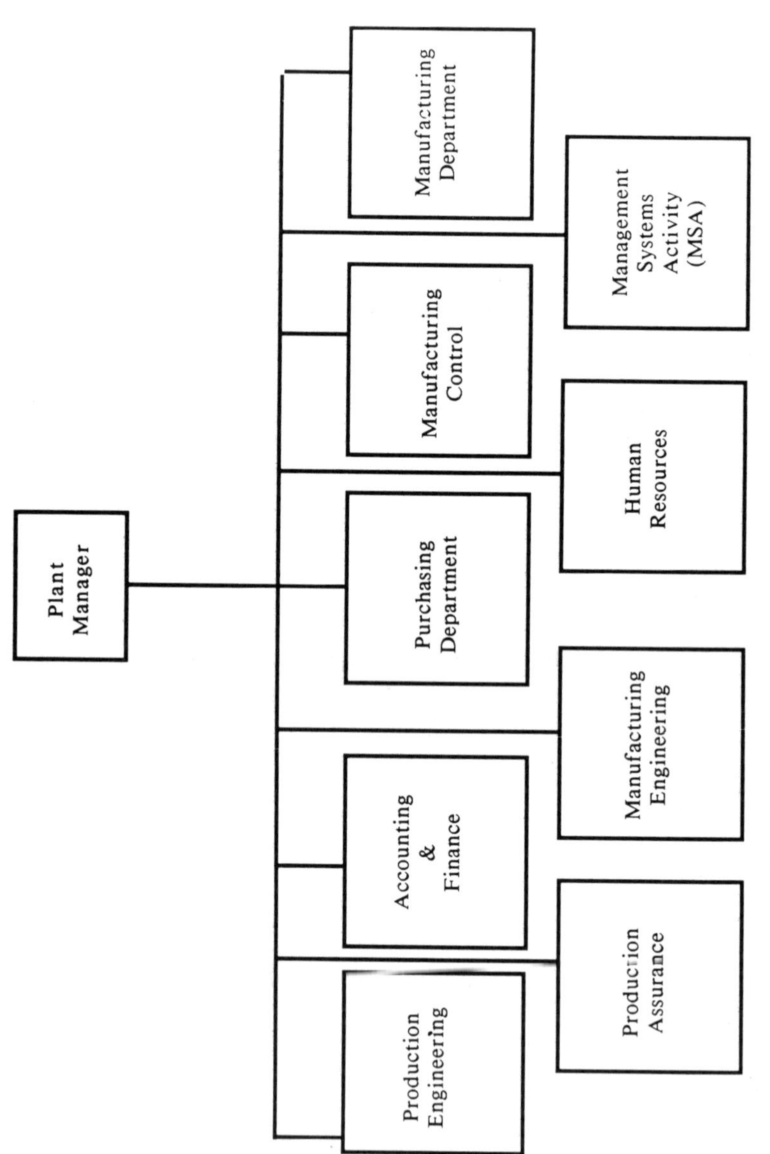

FIGURE 5.8 Organization structure of HighTech

The Information Systems Organization

The current (1984) Management Systems Activity (MSA) budget is $1 231 000 for all categories of expense. The current personnel budget is $553 000 (45 per cent of the total). The annual budget for 1983 was $1 062 000. Of this, about $406 000 (38 per cent) went to personnel.

Reporting to the plant manager (Figure 5.8), MSA consists of two major areas, Systems Analysis and the Data Center (Figure 5.9). A new development this year (1984) is the Information Resource Center, which currently reports to the Data Center Manager. It is planned in the next year to place the Information Resource Center on the same level as Systems Analysis and the Data Center. Operations are conducted by the Data Center while the development and maintenance of the Applications Systems Portfolio is the responsibility of Systems Analysis.

C.M., the MSA Manager, has held his position for approximately one year. He previously had a variety of positions in the IS area with the parent corporation, and his last was also as MSA Manager in an overseas plant that was closed during the reorganization noted earlier. He is in his mid-thirties and is especially interested in moving MSA into step with today's data-processing environment.

C.M. noted that 'the mission of MSA is to optimize the basic manufacturing functions of the business by means of data processing'. He added that 'the charter

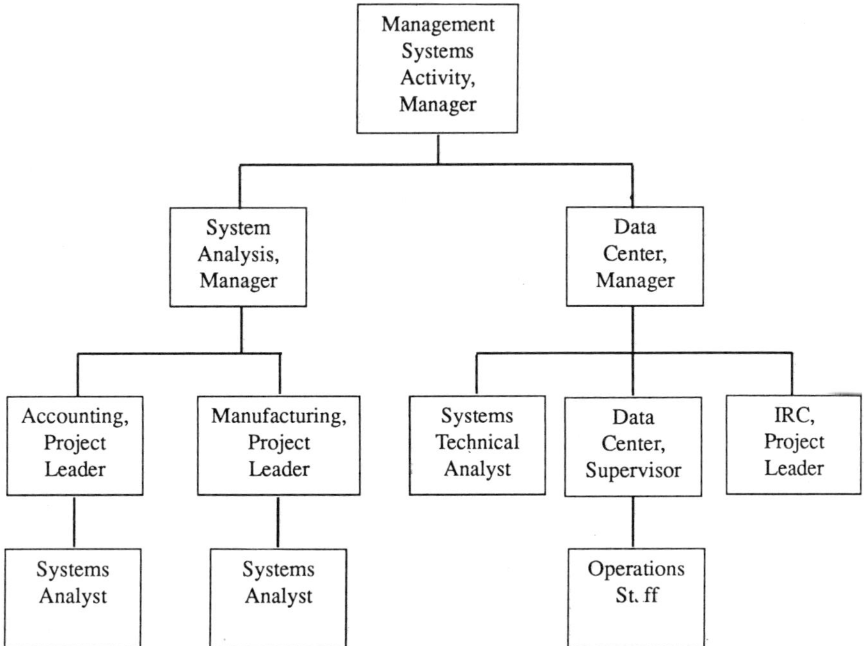

FIGURE 5.9 Organization structure of MSA

of MSA is to provide a professional, reliable, data processing function with the attendant data security, reliability, and accessibility. MSA also must provide programmer/analyst support to the user community to solve problems, develop systems solutions where appropriate, and act as an advisory body to plant operational personnel'. C.M. wants to establish a new area with several analysts to do 'Business Systems Analysis' and take an increasingly pro-active role in the operations of the plant.

The position of Systems Analysis Manager is currently unfilled and the MSA Manager has no plans to fill it. He is currently co-ordinating the activities of the Systems Analysis Department himself along with two project leaders, P.S. and T.J. The Systems Analysis staff, including the project leaders, consists of seven full-time employees. T.J., one of the two project leaders, has been with the parent corporation for over 30 years and at HighTech for 14 years. She is an experienced applications support analyst who knows all current plant systems in detail. P.S., the second project leader, has been at HighTech for 4 years. This is his first position following school.

The Data Center Staff consists of 10 people, including the Data Center Manager, R.J., who has been with HighTech for 7 years. He has been Data Center Manager for 4 years and previously was a systems analyst for 3 years. The Data Center is organized into three areas (Figure 5.9), Operations, Technical Analysis, and the Information Resource Center. R.J. manages the technical analysts directly while Operations is supervised by C.F., a 23-year veteran with the parent corporation. C.F. has been Operations Supervisor since HighTech opened 16 years ago.

The Information Resource Center, a relatively new (1 year) portion of the Data Center, currently has no manager but is co-ordinated by P.H., who has been at HighTech for 4 years. The Information Resource Center was P.H.'s idea and C.M., the MSA Manager, asked him to join the MSA group to build the center. Working with him is B.A., who has been with the parent corporation 10 years and at HighTech for the last 5 years. B.A. previously was the senior technical analyst in the Data Center.

It should be pointed out that the longevity of the MSA staff is unusual, especially for the geographic location of HighTech. The MSA Manager noted that annual turnover was less than 25 per cent. In Systems Analysis all but one of the analysts has been with HighTech for more than 1 year and three of the seven have been there for 3 years or more. The Data Center staff is similar in experience levels. Key players such as the Data Center Manager, Operations Supervisor, and project leaders have all been at HighTech for 4 years or more. In the current analysis staff, four joined HighTech right after school while the rest (three) held IS positions either within or outside HighTech.

The largest portion (86 per cent) of the Systems Analysis staff is college trained. Four (57 per cent) hold bachelors' degrees while two (29 per cent) hold advanced ones. One member of the group does not have college training. Three members of

Systems Analysis are members of a professional society (ACM) but none hold a Certificate of Data Processing (CDP). The bulk of the staff (86 per cent) received at least two weeks of working-hour classroom education during the past year.

All the Systems Analysis staff spends more than two-thirds of their efforts on maintenance activities. Most major plant systems have been in place for more than 6 years with some as old as 10 years. Also, all major plant systems are supplied by the parent corporation and are locally supported. Because of the age of the systems, a great deal of maintenance effort is required. All analysts are assigned several 'primary' systems to support plus a number of 'backup' ones for which they are also responsible. A conscious effort is made by the MSA Manager to see that there is as much cross-familiarization as possible because of the small number of analysts. Also, analysts are routinely switched between financial systems and manufacturing systems to broaden their experience base. All analysts work directly (face to face) with the users they support. They often take an active role in training new system users.

There is very little use of specialized work methods for application development and maintenance since most systems are corporate supplied. Top-down design is used when local systems are developed and there is also increasing use of application generating systems both for creation of report programs in COBOL and entire database applications. There is, however, only one current plant system in use that was developed entirely by an application generator.

User requests for changes are all acted on as time and workload permit. No prioritization or review of the requests is made. Minimal acceptance review is practiced to transfer software from development to maintenance status. The only documentation provided for systems are user manuals and system-maintenance journals located in the actual code of the system.

The application system portfolio

The current application system portfolio consists of 33 major systems serving a user population of 84 administrative and managerial staff. Three new systems have been implemented since last year. Twenty-one (64 per cent) are over 6 years old while three are more than 10 years old. Seventy per cent of the systems are over 3 years old.

Eleven new systems are currently under development by the parent corporation and will be implemented at HighTech within the next year, replacing most of the manufacturing and material control systems at the plant. One project leader, P.S., is currently working full-time to become familiar with the new systems. Nine of the 11 new applications will use a single, unified database replacing nine applications with nine separate databases that have had to be updated simultaneously. Together, these 11 new applications will constitute a state-of-the-art Manufacturing Resource Planning System (MRP II). This represents a major undertaking for the parent corporation.

Of the current applications implemented at HighTech, 13 (39 per cent) were developed by MSA, 19 (58 per cent) by other MSA organizations within the parent corporation, and one (3 per cent) by a user organization within the parent corporation. No packages were purchased from outside the corporation. None of the current applications can be considered to be leading edge and none of the current systems provide direct services to customers or suppliers.

The current domain of the systems maintained by the MSA organization are in the financial control and material control areas. Systems for General Ledger, Payroll, Accounts Payable, and Asset Control are among the major financial applications. Major material control applications include Bill of Material, Parts Ordering, Inventory Control, Floor Picking, Receiving Control, and Shipping Control. A major area of weakness is floor work-in-process control. However, major applications currently exist to assist Product Engineering. Twelve applications that are part of the material control system of the plant rely interdependently on each other. All of these 12 (plus seven more) will be replaced shortly by a more integrated series of 11 applications using one major database and two smaller systems. A total of 19 systems (16 of which are 10 or more years old) will be replaced by the new MRP II system.

The major programming language in use at HighTech is a powerful one similar to Pascal (28 systems) while the rest of the applications (five systems) use COBOL. Twenty-five per cent of the major plant systems contain at least 20 000 executable source statements while 50 per cent have at least 10 000 lines. Seventy-five per cent of the applications contain at least 5000 lines of code. All applications run on the plant's dual-processor mainframe system.

Six of the current HighTech systems utilize a DBMS while five employ a user-query language (DM Inquiry). Eight systems provide interactive report generators while two supply off-line report-generation facilities.

The management problem set

How does management view the problems of application software maintenance? To provide an overall perspective, C.M., MSA Manager, completed the Problem Assessment Questionnaire. Statistical analysis of the problem item responses and comparison of the results with a reference survey population produced the following problem factor profile:

User knowledge	0.64 Above normal
Programmer effectiveness	0.48 Normal
Product quality	1.18 Above normal
Programmer time availability	1.15 Above normal
Machine requirements	0.55 Normal
System reliability	0.32 Normal

The problems of maintenance in the Management Systems Activity, as assessed by C.M., are thus interpreted as normal to above-normal when compared to those of other IS organizations.

Discussions with C.M., MSA Manager, reveal a number of concerns for his department. First and most urgent is the advanced age of the majority of existing plant systems. The bulk of the work done by the Systems Analysis staff revolves around critical maintenance tasks required simply to keep the systems running on a daily production basis. On the horizon is an even more serious problem. The next generation of hardware planned for acquisition will not support many of the critical plant systems. Additionally, the staff of seven is too small to accomplish the tasks needed and still be able to create new systems as required by the user population.

Another serious problem is lack of adequate documentation for existing systems. The often-patched plant systems have numerous capabilities that have been 'lost' since users are no longer aware of them. Often, when these are 'rediscovered' they no longer function because of earlier patches with which they were not tested. A final concern is poorly maintained and documented workflows control programs (equivalent to IBM Job Control Language), which run series of jobs and control batch application flow.

The MSA Manager noted that efforts were being made to address all these issues. As noted earlier, a large number (19) of older plant systems are slated for replacement in the next year. However, the resources required for putting the systems into production have not been acquired. Project Manager P.S. is currently spending two weeks per month at the pilot implementation plant for the new MRP II system in order to gain advanced experience with the software.

The remaining problems of documentation and up-to-date workflows are being addressed as part of a plant-wide quality program. In MSA all new systems must be fully documented and workflows are also being audited on a regular basis and upgraded as needed to meet the current standards.

C.M. says he feels that application generators and the Information Resource Center will help relieve the workload of MSA by cutting the time necessary for generating new systems and maintaining them. He is actively pushing the implementation of these ideas in his department.

Questions

(1) How does the system maintenance and development task at West Coast High Tech Manufacturing differ from that at most other organizations? What are the likely implications?

(2) What are the implications of the small Systems Analysis (SA) staff size for specialization at West Coast High Tech Manufacturing?

(3) What are the likely career advantages and disadvantages of working as an analyst at West Coast High Tech Manufacturing? (See Chapter 7.)

Case 5.3. Small City Manufacturing

The organizational environment

Small City Manufacturing (SmallMan) is a high-technology manufacturing plant, operating within a principal division of one of the world's leading US-based corporations. Established in the late 1950s, the plant is located on the perimeter of a small midwestern city of about 75 000 citizens. Surrounded by rolling

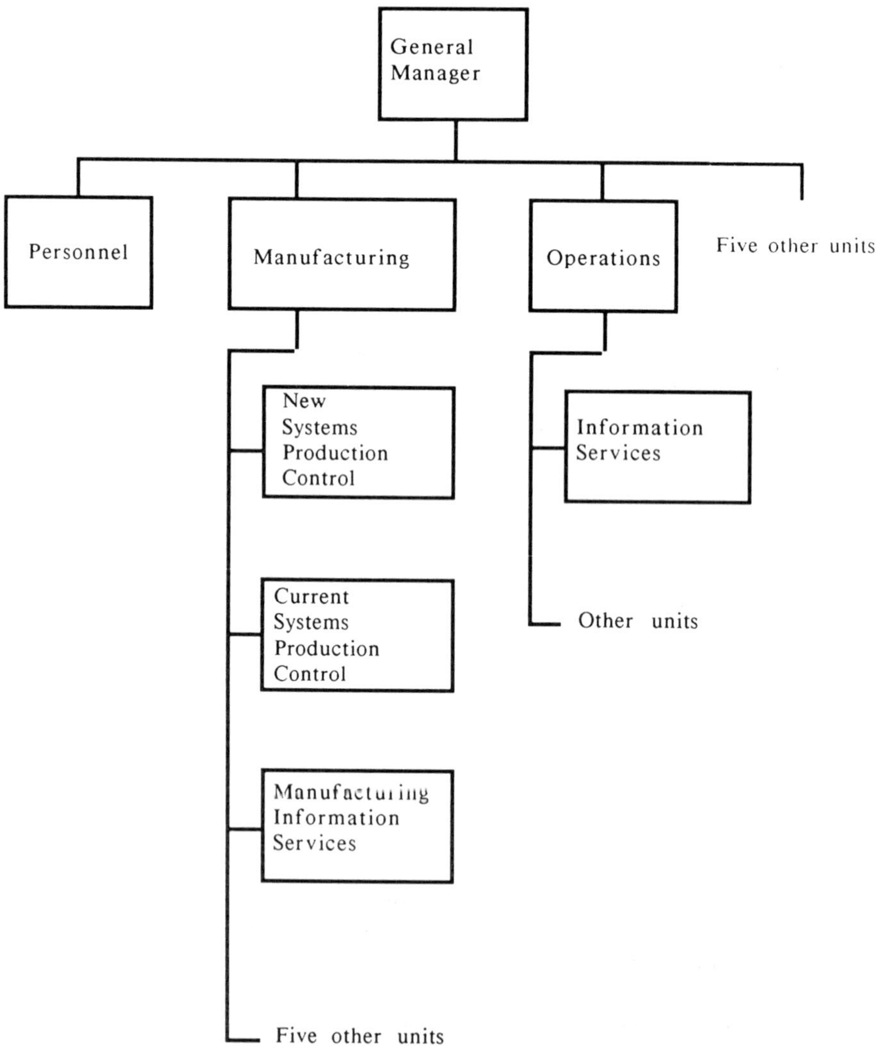

FIGURE 5.10 Organization structure of SmallMan

countryside and spreading suburbs, the plant shares its 500-acre site with a development laboratory which serves it.

SmallMan is one of the city's two major employers. Both contribute much to the pleasant character of the city, which is substantially middle-class and prosperous, and possesses an excellent public school system. Within the parent corporation, which is known for its general security of employment, SmallMan has the lowest turnover and absenteeism rates among all US manufacturing locations.

The product lines of SmallMan are several. These consist of low- to medium-priced commercial equipment, within the full range of products of the corporation.

Recent years have seen substantial organizational change at SmallMan, reflecting a new emphasis on decentralized profit responsibility within the corporation. The recent result is a 'vertical organization' in which product lines are managed independently to the extent possible in place of the previous integrated functional one.

This new organization has brought profound change to the Information Services function within the manufacturing plant. In general, the costs of its manufacturing applications have become increasingly 'visible', with the result that some product managers are said to have come to the conclusion 'You [IS] guys are expensive; I can't afford you'.

The most significant change occurred one year ago. The Manufacturing Information Services (MIS) department was formed by spinning off a major portion of the existing 'Mother IS' unit (as it is referred to by those born of the move). The revised organization structure is shown in Figure 5.10. As is seen, the break between MIS and IS is substantial, with common management two levels removed.

The newly created MIS Department assumes full responsibility for development and maintenance of applications directly supporting the manufacturing function. Information Services retains responsibility for data-processing operations and for the development and maintenance of indirect applications, such as site facilities and services, personnel, and payroll.

In addition to the programming staff taken from IS, the new MIS unit also includes systems analysts who formerly worked in the user departments. In this regard, 'synergism in the programmer/analyst activity' is mentioned by one manager as a principal objective of the new organization.

Recent months have seen further efforts to bring the work of the MIS Department into close alignment with the new decentralized profit orientation at SmallMan.

Manufacturing Information Services (MIS)

Manufacturing Information Services (MIS) at SmallMan is organized as shown in Figure 5.11. Three departments report to B.D., Manager of MIS. Two of these, Manufacturing Systems I and II, are responsible for development and

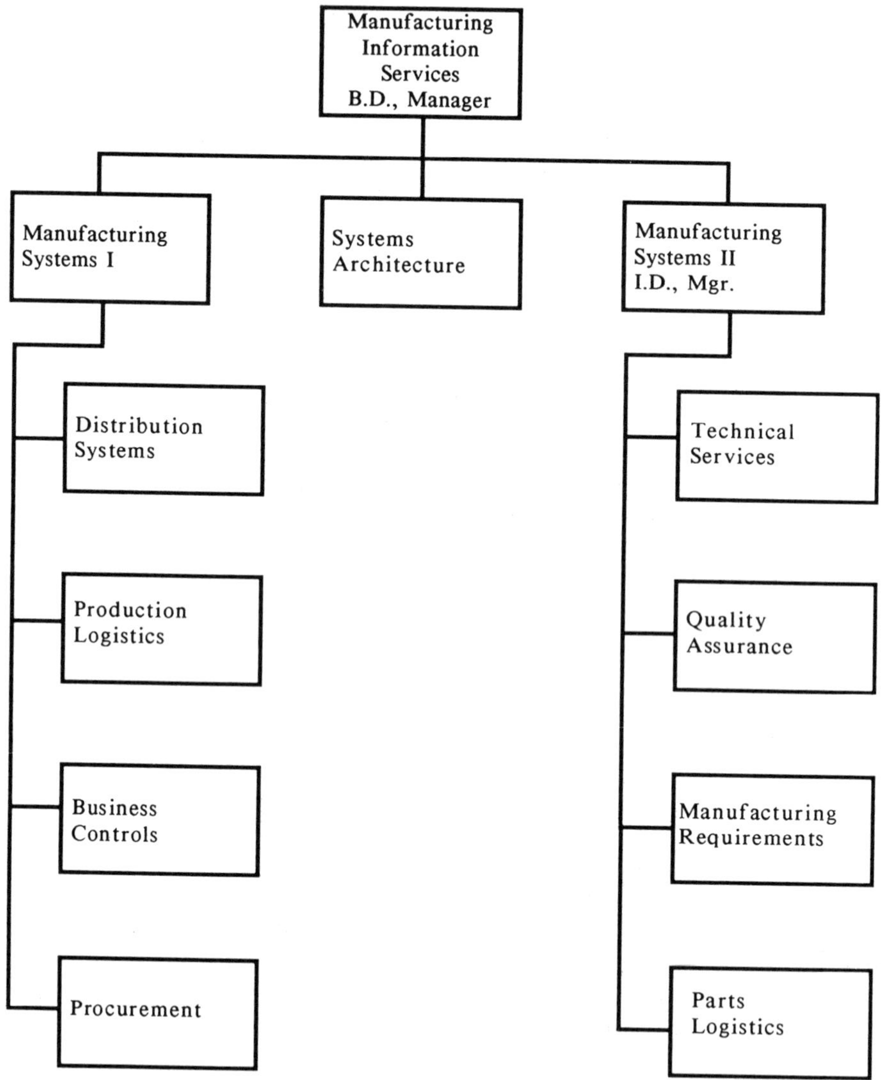

FIGURE 5.11 Manufacturing Information Services

maintenance of the application system portfolio. The third, Systems Architecture, is responsible for co-ordination of the overall effort.

B.D., who has been with SmallMan for more than 17 years, became MIS manager upon creation of the organization one year ago. He began his career at SmallMan as a computer programmer and, with the exception of one or two short-term assignments, had worked exclusively in Information Services prior to the recent change.

The MIS application staff currently numbers 117 employees organized into nine departments at the working level. As indicated in Figure 5.11, organization is by application area.

As mentioned above, included among the application staff are 36 employees who were formerly systems analysts in user departments. These analysts come to their present positions in MIS as the result of a two-decade evolutionary process associated with their role at SmallMan. The original analysts were simply those 'with a flair for using systems', who could work with programmers in the development process. Training was strictly on the job. Eventually, user departments began to hire individuals with computing backgrounds for these positions, which spread throughout the plant, and acquired career paths that paralleled those of programmers. More recently, user departments began to think of further extending their computing competence, and the words 'let's get our own [programmers]' began to be heard. The subsequent creation of the MIS department has, however, short-circuited this notion.

I.D., manager of Manufacturing Systems II, is among those who came to MIS from user departments. A former systems analyst, he thus represents the perspective of this career group within the new organization.

A substantial majority of the MIS staff (estimated at 70, 60 per cent), has been with Small City for more than 10 years. Only 16 individuals have been with the organization 3 years or less; of these, only five are new within the last year.

The staff is largely college educated. A two-year or four-year college degree is possessed by about 100 (85 per cent) of the membership. However, there are few, if any, graduate degree holders. (Summaries of the educational backgrounds of the staff are not generally made available to its management. One manager guessed that some staff member probably held a graduate degree but knew of no one in particular who did.) New staff have historically been recruited primarily from undergraduate computer science programs in the region. No applications staff member holds the Certificate of Data Processing (CDP). Professional society memberships, if any, are not generally known.

The average staff member received at least two weeks (but less than four weeks) of working-hour classroom education and training during the past year. A few (estimated at seven) received four weeks or more.

One-third of the staff members works daily with users of the application systems maintained. Another third works directly with users at least once weekly. The balance works directly with users less frequently.

A number of organizational techniques have been adopted for the management of the maintenance process. The initiative for the adoption of these techniques originated with T.R., a former first-level department manager, who has since taken on a new assignment outside the MIS department. His successor, M.S., has continued to build upon the foundations established, a number of which were in place prior to the reorganization of one year ago.

Among the organizational techniques adopted are: maintenance escorts (developers assigned to temporary maintenance responsibility); acceptance reviews (in transferring software from development to maintenance); user change request procedure; scheduled maintenance; formal retest procedure (in implementing changes); operation and maintenance cost charge-back; and periodic maintenance audits. In the case of the chargeback system, a product line is charged for applications costs on the basis of the proportion of part numbers it possesses within the total plant inventory.

Also implemented is a reporting system for maintenance management, which came about as a result of a 'productivity push' at SmallMan. Measuring the productivity of programmers was the recognized problem. As recalled by T.R., management's charge was 'You tell me how good we are, and how we measure it'. The reporting system was developed in response to this charge. Among the reports are: a report of the maintenance responsibilities of individual programmers, with programs documented as to size and complexity, and one of the processing time of the 'overnight series' of programs, a time series reported graphically. (The reduction of the average processing time of the series from 6 to 3 hours is attributed to the emphasis given by the new reporting system.)

Among the work methods established by the MIS department are: top-down designs; structured walk-throughs; structured programming; checkpoint reviews; and a program development library. An in-house application generator, experimentally adopted, is no longer in use.

Among the documentation tools used are: data model diagrams; data dictionary; HIPO diagrams; data-flow diagrams; system development and maintenance journals; operations error history; and user manuals.

The application system portfolio

The MIS Department maintains a current portfolio comprising 22 major application systems serving several hundred principal users. No new systems are currently under development, while the newly created department adapts to its unique organizational position.

Production control and distribution constitutes the principal domain of application. Included are systems in support of material requirements planning, inventory control, procurement, warehousing, logistics, labor claiming, and quality assurance. Support of certain administrative and technical functions (including distributed data processing) is also provided.

The application systems range in size from the very small (less than 1000 executable source statements) to the very large (in excess of 500 000 statements). The average system is about 20 000 statements in size.

Fifteen of the systems in the portfolio are maintained by Manufacturing Systems I and seven by Manufacturing II. Of the seven systems maintained by Manufacturing II, three are 1–3 years old and four are 6–10 years old. Six of the seven systems were locally developed. The seventh was developed elsewhere in the corporation and adapted locally.

Three of the Manufacturing II systems are considered 'leading edge' in terms of functions provided to the user. Included is a demand management application with 'what if' planning capability.

The systems maintained by Manufacturing II are fully integrated. All rely upon others for their input data, and are in turn themselves relied upon for data by other systems. The hardware and system software operating environment is IBM and IBM-compatible. The principal processor is the IBM 3081 or the equivalent, making use of IMS. System/38s are also employed for distributed data processing. Mainframe applications are written in PL/1. In the case of the System/38, RPG is used. The use of a data dictionary and structured code is standard across the applications.

The management problem set

The Problem Assessment Questionnaire was completed by I.D., as manager of Manufacturing Applications II. Among the 26 candidate problem items, I.D. evaluated three as being 'somewhat major problems': turnover of maintenance personnel; quality of application system documentation; and user demand for enhancements and extensions. Four additional items were mentioned as 'minor problems': quality of original programming of application system; lack of user understanding of application system; adequacy of application system design specifications; and turnover in user organization.

Statistical analysis of the problem item responses, and comparison of the results with a reference survey population, produced the following problem factor profile:

User knowledge	−0.03	Normal
Programmer effectiveness	−0.54	Normal
Product quality	0.49	Normal
Programmer time availability	−1.19	Below normal
Machine requirements	−0.59	Normal
System reliability	−0.32	Normal

The problems of maintenance in MIS, as assessed by I.D., are thus substantially normal when compared with those of other organizations surveyed. An exception is the problem of programmer time availability, which is significantly less of a problem in MIS, reflecting perhaps the current commitment of MIS staff to maintenance and enhancement of existing systems rather than the development of new ones. The related problem of programmer effectiveness also scores on the low side of normal, which may also reflect satisfaction with the present deployment of the staff to the maintenance task.

Over the longer term, however, I.D. recognizes the problem of integrating the formerly separate systems analyst and programmer staffs, brought together with the creation of the MIS department. The work role of the future is seen by management as the combined programmer/analyst position, and this poses understandable difficulties for current personnel comfortable with one or the other of the two tasks but not both. Among the former user analysts are a number of '45-plus year olds [without programming skills]' who now 'look at their careers as going nowhere', I.D. admits. Similarly, among the former programmers are those who may have problems in working face to face with users, preferring instead their accustomed communication with computers. These former programmers must nonetheless face the fact that 'now you're going to have to talk to people who talk funny', I.D. warns.

Staff attrition has also created some problems for the new MIS department. Prior to the reorganization, 167 employees worked in positions now staffed by less than 120. Pressure to reduce staff was (and is) significant, according to B.D.: '[We are] getting beaten over the head on headcount'. The difficulty, he notes, is that 'What happens when you squeeze the tube is you lose a lot of cream off the top'.

The reorganization of one year ago, and its continuing aftermath, has posed particular problems for management strategy and planning, according to B.D., who adds, '[We are] trying to build a systems strategy on quicksand ... What is it that provides the bedrock?'

An illustration of this difficulty occurred in the initial months following the reorganization. With encouragement from users, one of the eight MIS work units was given the lead to independently innovate in applications, making use of purchased, off-the-shelf software. The idea was to move away from the complex, integrated personnel-intensive systems of the past. It developed, however, that smaller-scale application solutions could not be so easily purchased. The complexity of the needed solutions was inherent in the problems being addressed. Thus the realization sank in that 'multiple complex solutions are more expensive than a single complex solution', and users were advised to 'get your mind off this functional off-the-shelf stuff'.

The revised strategy has all eight work units involved in setting the future MIS direction. A joint solution to the application problems of various users is recognized to be necessary. '[Now we have] all eight departments pulling the sled,' B.D. remarks.

The MIS department is thus moving to a matrix form of project management, with emphasis on both functional and customer elements. Among the current initiatives are: an effort to eliminate the less useful systems ('lower the water, expose the rocks') and the development of a customer-satisfaction index ('see ourselves as users see us').

Increased staff professionalism is also now being encouraged in an attempt to facilitate the desired organizational transition. Included is an emphasis on improved knowledge of the basic manufacturing business. 'We want to get out of the systems analysis business, into the business analysis business,' B.D. states.

Thus several staff members have begun attending American Production and Inventory Control Society (APICS) conventions. Two individuals have begun company-sponsored programs of study at a university offering an innovative curriculum in manufacturing engineering. Also, 20–40 hours of business education is now given staff members as part of a company-offered course in business requirements planning. Reflecting upon future hiring policy, B.D. adds in conclusion, 'I would take some MBAs now'.

Questions

(1) How is the origination of Manufacturing Information Systems (MIS) at Small City Manufacturing related to management's business strategy? (See Chapter 4.)

(2) Does the relocation of systems analysts from user departments to MIS imply any changes in the overall task of system development and maintenance?

(3) What are the implications of B.D.'s statement, 'We want to get out of the systems analysis business, into the business analysis business', for the overall MIS task? How does the integrated programmer/analyst job position serve this objective?

(4) What apparently accounts for the low rate of staff turnover at Small City Manufacturing? What are the implications for the MIS department? (See Chapter 7.)

Postscript

Cases in other chapters further illustrate alternative approaches to the maintenance task. At Western Aeronautics (Case 4.2) a freeze on new system development dictates a 'maintenance-only' policy at present. However, an 'elite' Information Systems Support Department is being formed in anticipation of an eventual return to an environment dominated by new system development. At National Foods (Case 6.2) management draws a sharp distinction between maintenance and new system development and assumes the requisite skills and preferences among its staff to similarly differ. Metropolitan Gas Company (Case 7.2) defines jobs in terms of the traditional distinction between programming and systems analysis work.

Chapter 6

MAINTENANCE ORGANIZATION AND MANAGEMENT

INTRODUCTION

The management of the development function receives much attention in the IS literature, and the implicit assumption seems to be that maintenance can and should be managed more or less the same way (e.g. see Cash *et al.*, 1988). Maintenance work, however, presents unique management problems and opportunities.

In Chapter 4 we argued that the IS department's maintenance philosophy is expressed in its choices of departmental policies regarding maintenance. We concluded that a long-term view is an important foundation for the management of maintenance. In Chapter 5 we examined the maintenance task itself and showed how it is intimately related to the portfolio of application systems. We argued that the maintenance task is different from the development task in many important dimensions. We will now argue in this chapter that the need for a long-term view for maintenance and the fact that the maintenance task differs significantly from the development task mean that to properly manage maintenance it must be separated from development. The degree of separation, of course, varies, as will be seen below.

Irrespective of whether or not maintenance is separated from development, there are other issues regarding the management of maintenance that must be considered. Maintenance must be planned and monitored, for example, and many policies related to the management of maintenance analysts and programmers must be established. We discuss some of these maintenance management issues in this chapter.

THE DEPARTMENTALIZATION QUESTION

Organization structure—the definition of responsibilities and reporting relationships among individuals and subunits—is an important tool of strategy implementation. The departmentalizing of a staff is motivated by a desire to aggregate meaningful groups of workers who can work productively toward a goal. Several bases for making meaningful groups have been suggested, such as function, process, product or purpose, market, geography, time orientation, etc. (Galbraith, 1977). The variety of options for designating groups reinforces the idea that not all ways of organizing are equally effective in any particular situation, nor is there any single best way to organize.

Choosing an organization structure involves making trade-offs, frequently involving emphasizing the elaboration of one kind of skill over another or to elect tight control in one area at the cost of loose control in another. For example, when all the people serving one market work together for a period of time their group knowledge of that market and their skills and innovativeness in dealing with it will become more elaborate. This increased skill is then available to be leveraged by management, if it chooses to do so. Control of this group can further emphasize its market orientation. Visibility of effort made to serve the market enhances planning and monitoring; cohesiveness within the group makes control more effective and efficient.

The trade-offs in choosing a single-market focus for the group include the facts that the group may lose, or fail to develop, knowledge of other markets and that integration across markets will be more costly and harder to motivate among the staff. Innovations found to be effective with one market will be less likely to diffuse to groups serving others. Departmentalizing along product or geographical lines involves similar trade-offs, in which gains due to specialization within one area are balanced against increased costs of integration between areas.

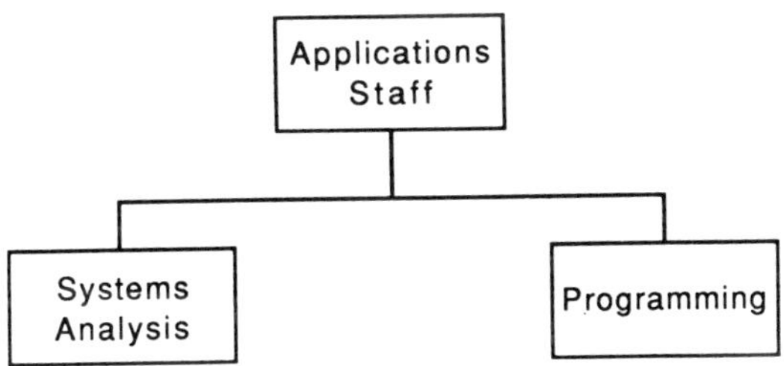

FIGURE 6.1 Responsibility for development and maintenance separated according to technical skills

IS managers seem to use three basic approaches to departmentalizing their systems and programming staffs: dividing the staff on the basis of (1) technical skills (see Figure 6.1), (2) application skills (see Figure 6.2), or (3) life-cycle phase, or development versus maintenance responsibility (see Figure 6.3).

Multiple-level departmentalization allows the staff to be divided first on one basis and then, at a lower level, on the other. In some of our cases (National Foods and Westcoast Refining & Marketing are examples) the application staffs are departmentalized first on the basis of application and then, within the application area, maintenance and development are assigned to separate groups. Davis and Olson (1985) suggest another possibility, a matrix structure, in which both users and IS managers have responsibility for managing an applications development staff, but we have not yet seen any firm using this approach, either in the twelve cases or in our other experiences.

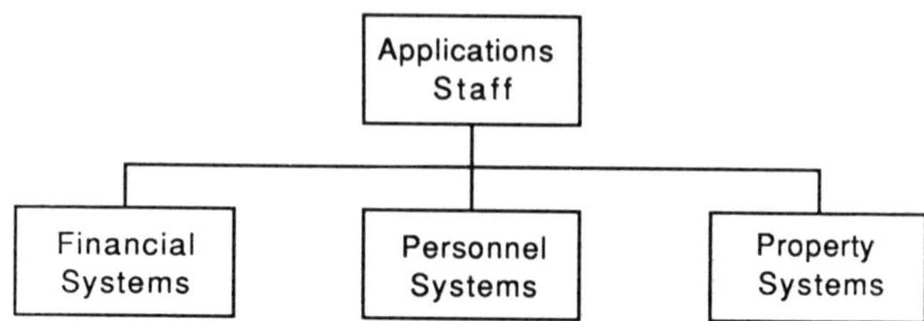

FIGURE 6.2 Responsibility for development and maintenance separated according to application skills (similar to Diablo National Laboratories, Case 6.3)

In this section we discuss the advantages and disadvantages of each of the three basic approaches. We describe the three approaches first and then consider the implications of combining them.

1. Three ways to departmentalize

Departmentalizing on the basis of technical skills is less common these days than it was when analysts could be found in one department and programmers in another (Davis and Olson, 1985; Zmud, 1984). Among our cases, only Metropolitan Gas Company still separates analysts from programmers, although many others probably did at some time in the past. These days a more frequently observed way of departmentalizing on the basis of technical skills is to create clusters of people specializing in some technology. Metropolitan Gas Company, for example, has a subdepartment developing and maintaining CICS programs. In other firms the division is along language lines—COBOL versus Assembler or FOCUS—or along the lines of specific systems analysis skills—'decision support systems' or 'strategic systems' groups can be found. The strength of departmentalizing on the basis of technical skills is that the skills being isolated can be enhanced and exploited. This specialization should result in systems of higher technical quality.

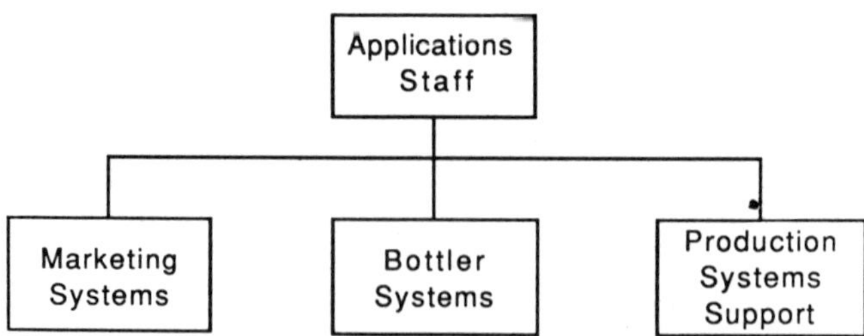

FIGURE 6.3 Responsibility for development and maintenance separated according to life-cycle stage (similar to Nationwide Soft Drink, Case 6.1)

Departmentalizing on the basis of application knowledge can be done in many different ways, but the most common approach is to mirror the main user areas, assigning to each IS subdepartment those applications that support each main user area. In some of our cases, such as at Westcoast Refining & Marketing, even the names of the subdepartments in the application staff area are the same as those of the user functional areas. The strength of departmentalizing on the basis of application seems to be the potential for involving users in the resource allocation and planning process, both for maintenance and development. Typically, a user area implicitly 'has a claim on' the staff members assigned to the IS subdepartment that bears its name. The resource-allocation process for that user area is thus somewhat simplified. Development versus maintenance priority trade-offs can be resolved in the user department instead of the IS department. The IS manager can say to the user manager, 'These are the people who support you. What do you want them to work on?'

Among our cases, when department lines are drawn on the basis of technical skills or application knowledge, a single sub-department becomes responsible for both the maintenance and development of a system throughout the system's life. Consequently, most people in the subdepartment do both maintenance and development. However, more often than not, we noted, with either of these types of departmentalization the skills emphasized are development ones; maintenance skills are de-emphasized.

Departmentalizing on the basis of life-cycle stage—separating development from maintenance—is the third basis. With this design one subdepartment is responsible for developing the system, which then gets turned over to another subdepartment for maintenance. Some authors have suggested that a maintenance subdepartment could be located in the data-processing or operations department (Embry and Keenan, 1983) or in the user organization (Boehm, 1983), although we did not observe these specific options in the twelve cases. At Western Aeronautics something like a maintenance 'swat team' is being formed that has some responsibilities traditionally located in the operations group, such as controlling the libraries of production software and providing the first line of operational support (corrective maintenance in the event of abnormal terminations and related operating difficulties).

The principal advantage arising from departmentalizing on the basis of the life-cycle stage is that distinct management techniques can be employed in the two very different life-cycle phases. Of particular interest to us, of course, is the opportunity presented by this separation for the maturation of techniques for managing maintenance, as noted at the beginning of this chapter.

2. Choosing a departmentalizing approach

Like all organization designers, IS managers face trade-offs when choosing among these three ways to departmentalize their application staffs. For example, when considering a departmentalization based on technology they have to decide whether a particular technology can or should be mastered by all their staff or if it is more sensible to have a small group specialize in that technology. Of course, IS organizations often attempt to standardize on technologies, using only one operating system and a single language, for example, to avoid this problem.

In considering a departmentalization based on application the IS managers must consider whether the application portfolio can reasonably be divided along user lines, and whether this will improve or subvert their planning process. Many applications, sometimes the most important ones, support multiple users. Where an application provides the information linkage between two co-operating user areas—such as a production planning and control system provides between marketing and manufacturing—giving control over application staff resources to just one of these groups can create more planning problems than it solves. Moreover, reinforcing 'information boundaries' between components of the value chain can undermine opportunities to develop strategic linkages within the value chain.

Separate maintenance departments present some problems of their own. Separate maintenance and development subdepartments may involve additional co-ordination costs between users and the application staff and additional costs in transferring systems between groups. With separate groups, knowledge about the development history of a system, crucial to maintenance, may be less easily available to maintainers; knowledge about installed applications, crucial when developing systems that will be integrated with those applications, may similarly be unavailable to developers. In addition, separated maintenance groups are sometimes suspected to be unmanageable maintenance ghettos, with low morale and low levels of technical expertise (Couger and Colter, 1985).

Separating maintenance from development can also present political problems. When a single subdepartment offers a user area both maintenance and development support there is a tendency to use the 'maintenance' budget as a 'slush fund' for development overruns. Or, an unfinished system can be officially designated 'complete' and moved to maintenance status. Thus both IS and the user can effectively shift resources between maintenance and development with limited accountability. Eliminating this slush fund may be politically hazardous.

3. Hidden advantages of the life-cycle approach

Nevertheless, we believe that separating maintenance from development has some advantages that may not be well recognized, such as the following:

- Better visibility of maintenance expenses is an obvious advantage. The benefits of investments in maintenance-supporting tools—such as for restructuring or testing software—are thus easier to evaluate and justify.

- Better visibility may be expected to motivate more creative management of maintenance. (The next section of this chapter provides more detail on this topic.)
- Buffering of the development staff from the intermittent demands of maintenance reduces the amount of interruption of development and thus contributes to the increased efficiency of developers.
- The maintenance staff will learn much about how *not* to write programs; given the opportunity, they can be expected to make a strong contribution to the development of department standards.
- A larger maintenance unit will be headed by a higher-level manager, will have more levels of hierarchy, and will offer more career options.
- Communications within a maintenance subdepartment are more effective than those among several maintenance groups; good communications among staff are an important antecedent for the development of specialization and professional practice regarding maintenance.
- Better software quality may also be expected where maintenance and development are separated, as the maintenance work unit will be motivated to require a meaningful acceptance test or other demonstration of maintainability prior to assuming responsibility for a new system.
- As suggested by the preceding, the development of formal acceptance criteria is more likely to be supported where maintenance is separated from development. These acceptance criteria provide a critical avenue for the assimilation of end-user developed and purchased software.
- A unit with responsibility for the entire portfolio is more likely to value a firm-wide data dictionary and more likely to see opportunities for potentially strategic cross-functional, value-chain, or data-sharing applications.
- A separate maintenance unit encourages a focus on an improved level of service to users. Development is, by its nature, buffered from the day-to-day operations of the business and concerns the future delivery of a product. Maintenance, on the other hand, is at times the user's partner in assuring correct day-to-day operations, and thus is more concerned with a service point of view.

This list of advantages of a separate maintenance group is formidable. Moreover, we believe that many of the 'difficulties' presented by separating maintenance are, in part, red herrings. The so-called 'low motivating potential' of maintenance (Couger and Colter, 1985) may be more a consequence of management disregard of maintenance than of the nature of the maintenance task itself (Lientz and Swanson, 1980; Canning, 1981). If IS management views maintenance as low-value work, the maintainers are unlikely to be so enlightened as to see it as high value work.

Increased co-ordination costs, another alleged problem with separate maintenance departments, may be offset by improved efficiency resulting from specialization. Similarly, increased costs of quality assurance may be compensated by the benefits of improved quality in the application portfolio.

In summary, there is no 'one best way' to departmentalize the application staff. However, certain contingencies may cause one approach to be obviously superior to another. When the portfolio is mostly still under development, and the systems are mainly new and unfamiliar to the entire application staff, an application-based departmentalization may be the best choice. This may also be preferred where the application portfolio is not highly integrated and where the applications are of low day-to-day strategic importance. On the other hand, when the portfolio is mature, or the firm is dependent on some part of the application portfolio, or the information architecture does not correspond closely to the host organization's structure, a departmentalization based on the life-cycle stage may be more appropriate.

As mentioned earlier, the IS managers in many of our cases dealt with the problem of making organization design trade-offs by using combinations of departmentalization schemes, dividing the application staff, for example, first on the basis of application area and then, within the application groups, separating development staffs from maintenance ones. The reverse approach, with the separation on the basis of life-cycle phase at the first level and, at the second level, the development unit subdivided by development project and the maintenance unit subdivided by technology or application area, is also feasible.

Among our twelve cases, nine organizations currently do both maintenance and development. In six of these most of the staff is in application-oriented subdepartments in which maintenance and development are not formally separated. Thus many individuals split their time between maintenance and development tasks, though even in these firms some people spend more than two-thirds of their time on maintenance and others are similarly dedicated to development projects. The other three IS departments separate their maintenance and development staffs, either at the first level within the application staff organization (Nationwide Soft Drink) or at the second (National Foods and Westcoast Refining & Marketing).

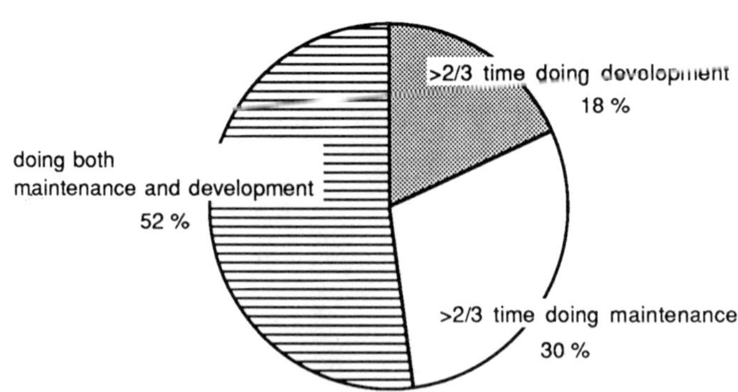

FIGURE 6.4 Allocation of effort: maintenance shared (N = 6)

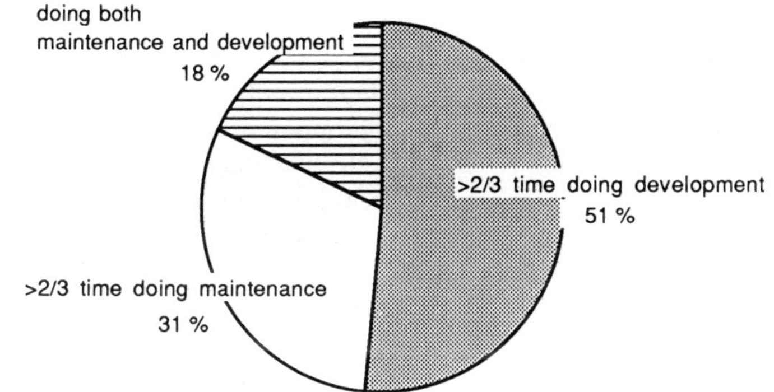

FIGURE 6.5 Allocation of effort: maintenance separated (N = 3)

In all three of the firms separating maintenance and development we were told that the maintenance staff was formally separated from the development one in order to buffer the development staff from the demands of maintenance, allowing the developers to concentrate on their projects. This goal seems to have been achieved. As can be seen in Figures 6.4 and 6.5, there are significantly more human resources devoted to development work in the IS departments separating their maintenance and development staffs (Student's t-statistic = 4.613, significant with probability = 0.002). A similar result was found by Lientz and Swanson (1980); in that study it was found that departments separating maintenance from development spent relatively less time on maintenance (reported significantly different with probability = 0.02). We believe that this can be interpreted as an increased efficiency in the maintenance unit due to:

(1) The elimination of the habit of using maintenance resources as a slush fund for development;
(2) The development of expertise among the maintenance staff regarding the portfolio of applications and techniques of maintenance; and
(3) The elaboration of maintenance management techniques by the managers of maintenance groups.

That is, departmentalization on the basis of life cycle, even when motivated by a need for improvement in development productivity, results in increased professionalism in the maintenance group. In the next section we turn to a discussion of techniques for managing maintenance.

MAINTENANCE MANAGEMENT TECHNIQUES

Maintenance management techniques appear and are institutionalized not only in separate maintenance departments but wherever managerial attention is focused on the maintenance function. In this section we describe some specific techniques for managing maintenance that we think are particularly effective. Elsewhere in this book we discuss management techniques such as articulating a maintenance strategy (Chapter 4), adoption of work methods suited to maintenance (Chapter 5), employing an appropriate scheme for departmentalization (this chapter, above), and designing effective human resource management systems (Chapter 7). In this section the discussion focuses on formal and informal techniques for planning, monitoring, and controlling maintenance work.

Some of the techniques described in this section are key supporting mechanisms for a separate maintenance unit; many are useful to maintainers irrespective of the approach taken to departmentalization. At Big City State University, for example, the 45-member application staff is organized by application, but maintenance is the object of substantial managerial attention. The IS department is guided by what we have called a long-term view, and many of the organizational or managerial techniques for managing maintenance described below are used there.

1. Monitoring techniques

The first step in monitoring is measurement. Knowing how much work needs to be done, what resources are needed to carry out the work, and what the work will cost starts with measuring things. First and foremost for managing maintenance is measuring certain characteristics of the portfolio (Swanson and Beath, 1986). Application complexity, size, age, and technology contribute to the amount of corrective maintenance and to the effort involved in making enhancements. The development of a database describing the portfolio in terms of these characteristics is a good first step in defining the maintenance burden.

Application (or module) complexity can be measured subjectively (by a committee of local experts, for example), or more formally by using simple measures such as McCabe's Cyclomatic complexity number (McCabe, 1976) or lines of code or more complex measures such as McClure's Control Flow Metric (McClure, 1978) or Henry and Kafura's Information Flow Metric (Henry and Kafura, 1981). Kafura and Reddy (1987) describe these and several other complexity measures and compare their use on a single system. (See also Curtis *et al.*, 1979.)

Complexity metrics generally measure size, unique operators and unique operands, unique inputs and outputs, complications in data structure or data flow, and processing complexity. The simpler measures examine the code itself and the more complicated ones consider also the data and procedure structures implied by the code. More important than the precise nature of the measurement, however, are consistency of measurement across the portfolio and the use of a measure that seems relevant to the local application staff. Gremillion (1984) found, at the site he studied, that size alone was a better predictor of bugs than was a complexity measure.

Application size can be measured with almost any simple lines of code measure. Jones (1986) discusses a number of ways to measure size. In addition, many librarian software or version control packages track and report lines of code. Whether or not comments are included does not make much difference in the long run; the important thing is to measure size consistently at the local installation.

Applications that have been around the longest are generally also the hardest ones to maintain. They have little or very poor documentation, they use old technologies with which no one is familiar (McNurlin, 1983), and the mental models underlying their design may be unfathomable for the maintainer. Application age seems easy to measure, although partial replacements and major enhancements may cloud the age issue. However, earliest installation date is a reasonable measure of age. Application technology—batch or on-line, use of a DBMS, access methods, languages—can usually be determined by inspection. Many other characteristics of the portfolio can also be measured (see Chapter 3 for those we considered important). Users and operators of the systems can also be polled for their subjective evaluations of the systems (Ives *et al.*, 1983; Goodhue, 1987).

Periodic maintenance audits are carried out in some IS departments, either of all major systems or of a few apparently problematic ones, in order to anticipate demands for maintenance or to identify applications that could be made more maintainable, so that the inevitable enhancements can be more easily applied. Maintenance audits might include user evaluations of ease of use or coverage of needed functions. They might also include user predictions of business changes likely to trigger requests for enhancements.

Measurement of past maintenance activity helps in predicting future maintenance requests. The maintenance managers we talked to found this to be more true than one might expect, especially if enhancements are tracked over a few years and for more than one or two systems. At Advanced Technologies Manufacturing one of the department heads tracks maintenance expenditures and uses them to choose areas in which future quality investments might have the maximum payoff. Complexity measures can help determine which systems or which parts of them are most difficult and most costly to enhance. Analysis of changes can reveal where regression errors (errors in corrections), a sign of difficult-to-maintain code, are occurring (Bowen, 1983). A charge-back or cost accounting system can be used to collect the most elementary information about maintenance expenditures, but in our experience charge-back figures on maintenance are much too general to be useful. Information as to the *nature* of the maintenance work is needed:

- Was it corrective, adaptive, perfective, or a little of each? (The 'informative' role of maintenance—answering or diagnosing questions, providing supplementary training—might well be added to this list, as it comprises a substantial body of work for many maintainers).

- How much time was spent in diagnosis, programming, and testing?
- Did the request require disruption of other work or not?
- What was the source of the problem? Did the change originate from a development project, the computer center, daily operations, management, customers, or a regulatory body?
- What were the descriptive characteristics of the system or module—size, complexity, age, technology—before and after the modification?

Tracking the sources of maintenance requests is important for some systems. Helms and Weiss (1985) found that 30 per cent of the maintenance requests they studied were a function of externalities of the organization. On the other hand, Chapin (1985) notes that, from his survey of 260 information systems personnel, the greatest source of problems in maintenance was 'not user requests, but the circumstances or conditions under which software changes must be made'. That is, the stumbling block for maintainers is not the fact that enhancements are requested but that the amount of time to make an enhancement may be unpredictable or uncontrollable, due to difficulties in diagnosis and execution.

Establishing a baseline profile of the portfolio, a history of maintenance work, and an analysis of the environment from which maintenance requests arise are the foundation for managing maintenance. The establishment of a set of records describing the ebb and flow of maintenance requests can help to alleviate the victimization mentality to which maintainers are sometimes subject, due to their lack of control over the rate of arrival and volume of work requests. Local data on the effect of size and complexity, programmer effectiveness in maintenance, and the sources of requests for change are necessary to provide a foundation for local investments in maintenance support tools and techniques and for maintenance planning.

2. Planning for maintenance

By far the bulk of the literature on planning for information systems is devoted to planning for development (e.g. King, 1978; King and Cleland, 1975; Kriebel, 1968; McFarlan, 1981; McLean and Soden, 1977). Thus most IS managers have well-developed planning skills when dealing with projects or identifiable, bounded systems and programming objectives. In the maintenance area, however, much of the work arises as small, imprecise, equivocal requests. The most common approach to planning for maintenance is simply to plan to spend about the same amount of effort next year as last year, irrespective of changes in the size of the portfolio, improvements in maintenance productivity, or other exogenous events. As one of our respondents told us, his organization assumes that it will obtain improvements in maintainer productivity equal to the portfolio growth rate. Hence, each year the organization's annual plans show no change in the budget for maintenance staff resources. However, no effort is made to measure maintainer productivity rates.

With reliable information about the portfolio and prior maintenance activity, more disciplined planning for maintenance is possible. As is true with development work, it is reasonable to expect requests for maintenance work to be written down (even if after the fact), logged, and reported. In addition to the backlog of maintenance requests that accumulates from this process, two other related elements are needed for maintenance planning: estimates of as yet unidentified requests and plans for major maintenance projects.

Estimates of undisclosed requests are not impossible to make, given reasonable experience with the portfolio and frequent communications with the user community. Corrective maintenance, in particular, can be roughly estimated from size, complexity, and prior history of bugs. Corrective maintenance, however, is typically a small part of the maintenance effort. Vessey and Weber (1983) report repair rates of between 0.6 and 2.3 repairs per hundred production runs. Estimating undisclosed adaptive and perfective requests is a matter of having a service request policy and good user communications. One maintenance manager told us that proactive planning sessions by the maintenance staff was helping to unearth the invisible backlog.

Under the category of 'major maintenance projects' we include renovation projects (McNurlin, 1983), scheduled maintenance work, and the budgeting of discretionary funds for perfective maintenance (Boehm, 1983). Proactive renovation strategies arise with the practice of performing maintenance audits. In performing scheduled maintenance or using a release concept (McNeil, 1979) work requests are batched and carried out on a specified schedule. Efficiency gains result from being able to make several changes and then perform a single system test prior to re-installation, instead of a series of tests. However, some additional complexity in diagnosis and programming may result. Scheduled maintenance is particularly important for systems with extensive or dispersed user communities. Finally, budgeting discretionary funds for perfective maintenance, to simplify complex modules, to insert re-usable code, and to attach data dictionary entries yields higher-quality code that is cheaper, faster, and easier to maintain.

Finally, we note that good maintenance plans are a product of co-operative efforts between IS and users, and that a change request review board can help reduce the slush fund factor in utilization of maintenance resources.

3. Maintenance policies

The nature of the IS department's system acceptance policy has a strong impact on the ability of the maintenance unit to manage its workload. Strong acceptance policies lead to manageable maintenance; weak ones leave maintainers with little control over their work.

The most effective regime for turnover from development to maintenance starts well before the moment of turnover, early in development (Martin and McClure,

1983; McClure, 1981). As described in Chapter 5, there are many techniques and work methods employable in the development process that eventually enhance maintainability. (It should go without saying that systems should also be maintained for maintainability.)

However, development projects can include other maintenance-enhancing ingredients beyond just having a maintainability objective. A vision of the life cycle of the system is a good start. Will scheduled maintenance be appropriate? What kinds of modifications are most likely? What kinds of bugs are most common? What approach will be taken for removing the old system from service and re-installing the new one? Development audits also reduce the need for later maintenance (Wu, 1987), probably by improving the quality of the completed systems.

Built-in modifiability is a good objective for systems with volatile segments; tax tables were an early example of this. Testability can also be built in; test facilities and test support tools can be included among the development objectives, even though they increase the investment required for the system.

The need for documentation geared toward maintenance goes almost without saying, but there is surprisingly little literature describing what good documentation might be. Program listings, input–output charts, and comment lines in programs are the most useful, say maintenance programmers (Guimaraes, 1983); this is probably because most other documentation is much more unreliable. Maintainers need documentation and program analysis tools to help them find system parts and the interconnections between those parts, or, in other words, to find the structure and flow of procedures, control, and data. Data dictionaries reveal structure of data. Cross-reference tools can be used to trace the flow of data in and out of procedures. Code analyzers can be used to reveal the structure and flow of procedures and control.

The use of maintenance escorts—programmers who participate in system development and then 'escort' the system into the maintenance unit—was suggested by Lientz and Swanson (1980) to help bring knowledge from the systems development team, which is important to the efficiency of the maintenance unit. Formal training for maintenance personnel regarding the new system is another way of sharing system knowledge that transcends the limits of written documentation.

Finally, specific formal acceptance criteria for all systems stand guard at the gateway to the maintenance unit. These criteria might be the same for all systems or agreed upon during systems design. Quality reviews usually include participation in system and acceptance testing, visual or automated inspection of code (using a code analyzer, for example), and review of documentation. Where maintenance personnel have not participated in development, quality reviews might also include design reviews. Post-development complexity analysis can be used to choose candidate sections for rewriting (Markusz and Kaposi, 1985). Well-worked-out acceptance criteria are also useful when purchasing application packages and when taking over maintenance for user-developed applications or those developed in other IS departments.

SUMMARY

In this chapter we have discussed issues of direct interest to those who manage maintenance workers—the departmentalization of the maintenance staff and maintenance management techniques, including monitoring, planning, and policies. We have argued that separating maintenance is a very important way to insure that maintenance work gets the visibility it deserves. Separate maintenance groups also have an opportunity to develop relevant skills, while the managers of separate units develop skills at managing maintenance.

We have also discussed some maintenance management techniques that we think are important to maintenance managers, irrespective of whether or not such work is separated from development. The most important thing, we suggest, is simply to begin to measure maintenance work and the application portfolio in as many creative ways as can be devised. An information system about maintenance is the foundation for good maintenance management.

In the next chapter we consider the management of human resources for maintenance. In the final analysis, maintenance is professional work, and the skills and motivation of the maintainers are key to successful maintenance.

REFERENCES

Boehm, B. (1983) 'The economics of software maintenance', *Proceedings of the Software Maintenance Workshop*, Naval Postgraduate School, Monterey, California, 6–8 December, pp. 9–37.

Bowen, J. B. (1983) 'Software maintenance: an error prone activity', *Software Maintenance Workshop*, Monterey, California, 6–8 December, pp. 102–5.

Canning, R. (1981) 'Easing the software maintenance burden', *EDP Analyzer*, **19**, 8, August, 1–14.

Cash, J. I., McFarlan, F. W., and McKenney, J. L. (1988) *Corporate Information Systems Management: The Issues Facing Senior Executives*, Dow Jones-Irwin, Homewood, Ill.

Chapin, N. (1985) 'Software maintenance: a different view', *AFIPS Conference Proceedings*, **54**, National Computer Conference, pp. 509–13.

Couger, J. D., and Colter, M. A. (1985) *Maintenance Programming: Improved Productivity Through Motivation*, Prentice-Hall, Englewood Cliffs, NJ.

Curtis, B., Sheppard, S., Milliman, P., Borst, P., and Love, T. (1979) 'Measuring the psychological complexity of software maintenance tasks with the Halstead and McCabe metrics', *IEEE Transactions on Software Engineering*, **5**, 2, March, 96–104.

Davis, G. B., and Olson, M. H. (1985) *Management Information Systems: Conceptual Foundations Structure and Development*, 2nd edition, McGraw-Hill, New York.

Embry, J. D., and Keenan, J. (1983) 'Organizational approaches used to improve the quality of a complex software product', *Proceedings of the Software Maintenance Workshop*, Naval Postgraduate School, Monterey, California, 6–8 December, pp. 87–9.

Galbraith, J. (1977) *Organization Design*, Addison-Wesley, Reading, Mass.

Goodhue, D. (1987) 'IS attitudes: toward theoretical and definitional clarity', *Proceedings of the Seventh International Conference on Information Systems*, San Diego, California, 15–17 December, pp. 181–94.

Gremillion, L. (1984) 'Determinants of program repair maintenance requirements', *Communications of the ACM*, **27**, 8, August, 826–32.

Guimaraes, T. (1983) 'Managing application program maintenance expenditures', *Communications of the ACM*, **26**, 10, October, 739–46.

Helms, G. L., and Weiss, I. R. (1985) 'Application software maintenance: can it be controlled?' *Data Base*, **16**, 2, Winter, 16–18.

Henry, S., and Kafura, D. (1981) 'Software structure metrics based on information flow', *IEEE Transactions on Software Engineering*, **SE-7**, September, 509–18.

Ives, B., Olson, M. H., and Baroudi, J. J. (1983) 'The measurement of user information satisfaction', *Communications of the ACM*, **26**, 10, October, 785–93.

Jones, C. (1986) *Programming Productivity*, McGraw-Hill, New York.

Kafura, D., and Reddy, G. R. (1987) 'The use of software complexity metrics in software maintenance', *IEEE Transactions on Software Engineering*, **SE-13**, 3, March, 335–43.

King, W. R. (1978) 'Strategic planning for MIS', *MIS Quarterly*, **2**, 1, March, 27–37.

King, W. R., and Cleland, D. I. (1975) 'A new method for strategic systems planning', *Business Horizons*, **18**, 4, August, 55–64.

Kriebel, C. H. (1968) 'The strategic dimensions of computer systems planning', *Long-Range Planning*, **1**, 1, September, 7–12.

Lientz, B. P., and Swanson, E. B. (1980) *Software Maintenance Management*, Addison-Wesley, Reading, Mass.

Markusz, Z., and Kaposi, A. A. (1985) 'Complexity control in logic-based programming', *Computing Journal*, **28**, 5, November, 487–95.

Martin, J., and McClure, C. (1983) *Software Maintenance: The problem and its solutions*, Prentice-Hall, Englewood Cliffs, NJ.

McCabe, T. J. (1976) 'A complexity measure', *IEEE Transactions on Software Engineering*, **SE-2**, December, 308–20.

McClure, C. (1978) 'A model for program complexity analysis', *Proceedings of the Third International Conference on Software Engineering*, Atlanta, Georgia, May, pp. 149–57.

McClure, C. (1981), *Managing Software Development and Maintenance*, Van Nostrand Reinhold, New York.

McFarlan, F. W. (1981) 'Portfolio approach to information systems', *Harvard Business Review*, **59**, 4, July-August, 142–50.

McLean, E. R., and Soden, J. V. (1977) *Strategic Planning for MIS*, John Wiley, New York.

McNeil, D. H. (1979) 'Adopting a system release discipline', *Datamation*, January, 110–17.

McNurlin, B. C. (1983) 'Replacing old applications', *EDP Analyzer*, **21**, 3, March, 1–12.

Swanson, E. B., and Beath, C. M. (1986) 'The demographics of software maintenance management', *Proceedings of the Seventh International Conference on Information Systems*, San Diego, California, 15–17 December, pp. 313–26.

Vessey, I., and Weber, R. (1983) 'Some factors affecting program repair maintenance: an empirical study', *Communications of the ACM*, **26**, 2, February, 128–34.

Wu, C.-F. (1987) 'Information systems development audits and software maintenance', *Proceedings of the Conference on Software Maintenance—1987*, Austin, Texas, September, pp. 190–97.

Zmud, R. W. (1984) 'Design alternatives for organizing information systems activities', *MIS Quarterly*, **8**, 2, June, 79–93.

CASES

Introduction

The three cases that follow present very different pictures of how maintenance work can be organized and managed. In each, the influence of both the 'maintenance philosophy' (Chapter 4) and the dimensions of the maintenance task (Chapter 5) can be observed in the choices that have been made regarding management of maintenance.

In Case 6.1, Nationwide Soft Drink, maintenance is organized separately from development, but most of the focus in the IS department is on development. The manager of the maintenance unit is very sensitive to morale problems associated with maintenance and has taken steps to forestall these.

In Case 6.2, National Foods, maintenance is separated from development but at the second level of organization, so that there is a maintenance group within each of the two development groups. A short while before we prepared this case maintenance was done in a single group, not two. Signs of this former incarnation can still be seen at National Foods.

In Case 6.3, Diablo National Laboratories, most of the application staff members do both maintenance and new system development work. Diablo's application portfolio is young and still growing, and as a result their maintenance burden is quite different from those in many of the other cases, which tend to be more mature. This difference is perhaps significant in evaluating how maintenance is managed at Diablo.

Case 6.1. Nationwide Soft Drink

The organizational environment

Nationwide Soft Drink (SofDrink) is the flagship division of Worldwide Beverage, an international consumer product company operating principally in the soft drink industry. SofDrink is marketing oriented, emphasizing increases in unit volume, market share, and earnings. According to a recent annual report, company strengths include an 'impeccable and positive image with the consumer', complex and innovative distribution systems, and aggressive marketing strategies. Introduction of new products, packaging, and distribution channels are considered essential to increases in unit sales and market share in an industry plagued by increasingly smaller sales growth rates.

SofDrink manufactures soft-drink concentrate and syrup, which sells to franchise-holding bottling companies, company-owned bottlers, and wholesalers. The bottling companies bottle or can soft drinks and sell these, in turn, to food chains or other food retail outlets, the fountain trade, or directly to the consumer through vending machines. Wholesalers service mainly fountain outlets, particularly in the rapidly growing fast-food market.

In recent years SofDrink's business data-processing needs have reflected the dynamic changes occurring in the soft-drink business. The number of different soft drinks that the company sells has grown from two to 15, partly as a result of the increased demand among consumers for caffeine-free and diet drinks. The number of packages has also grown, from two to 20. Intensified marketing has increased the number of customers tracked (100 000 to 250 000 over 7 years) and the monitoring of activity at retail sites (0 to 8000 in only 2 years). When changes such as these are linked to competitive strategy, the data-processing response must frequently be swift, accurate, and complete, even though that organization may be, as its Manager laments, 'the last to know'. 'Nevertheless,' he says, 'We meet critical deadlines.'

The Management Information System Department (MISD), which is part of SofDrink Administration, supports all other major areas in the company, with the exception of a Human Resources unit, which looks to Worldwide Beverage's corporate Human Resources group for its systems support.

The Management Information Systems Department

The Management Information Systems Department (MISD) 1984 annual budget was about $12 million, a 15.4 per cent increase over the $10.4 million budget of 1983. Application Systems and Programming wages for 1984 were budgeted at $4.2 million, a 16 per cent increase over 1983.

The Manager of MISD reports to the Vice-President of Administration, who reports in turn directly to the President of SofDrink. As shown in Figure 6.6, MISD is composed of six groups. Four of these (Marketing Systems, Operational Systems, Bottler Systems, and Production Systems Support) are responsible for development and maintenance of the application system portfolio. Planning and Technical Support assists in MISD planning, and provides quality assurance, database administration and technical support to the other groups. The Computer Production Services (CPS) group interfaces with the mainframe computer facility, which is organizationally and physically located in Worldwide Beverage's corporate headquarters. (SofDrink accounts for 80 per cent of the mainframe's use.) CPS offers data entry, data control, report printing and distribution, and a microcomputer center where SofDrink employees can obtain advice on use and purchase of personal computers for business or home use.

Currently there are 102 application systems analysts and programmers in MISD and nine openings. Twelve of the 102 application staff are first-level supervisors. Staffing levels have been fairly constant over the last 4 years.

Median length of service of the applications staff is approximately 3 years, but over a quarter (28 per cent) of the staff has been with MISD for over 6 years. Turnover is low; only six of 180 people departed MISD las year. The heads of the MISD groups are all career MISD and SofDrink employees. K.R., the Manager of MISD, had been at SofDrink in the MISD for 15 years and has been the

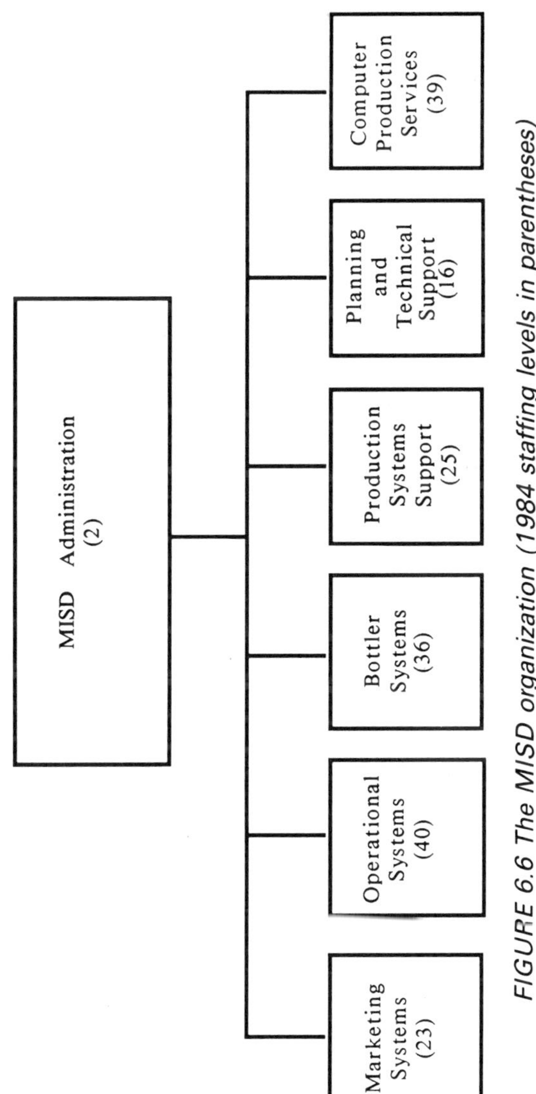

FIGURE 6.6 The MISD organization (1984 staffing levels in parentheses)

Manager for 4 years. Previous MISD managers were also career MISD/SofDrink employees. Typically, they have stayed at the company, moving up the management ladder with success.

The great majority (85 per cent) of the application staff have no job experience in SofDrink, apart from their current positions in MISD. Thirty-seven people (36 per cent) were students when hired. Forty-five (44 per cent) held positions in IS organizations outside SofDrink. Of those with prior SofDrink experience (15 per cent), three people held positions in other of the company's IS organizations and twelve came from other SofDrink units.

The application staff is substantially college educated. A total of 87 people (85 per cent) have a four-year college degree, and 10 of these (10 per cent of the 102 total) have an advanced one. Professional association memberships, however, are not extensive. Only eight people (8 per cent) are members of ACM of DPMA, and only one holds the Certificate of Data Processing (CDP). Education heads a list of 'staff issues' at MISD. This emphasis on education is reflected in the amount of working-hour classroom education and training received by the applications staff at SofDrink. Sixty-seven people (66 per cent) received between two and four weeks of training during the last year, and no one had less than one week.

Virtually all the applications staff (99 per cent) work face to face with users at one time or another.

Throughout the application staff, work assignments are primarily for either maintenance or new systems development. Twenty-nine of 102 applications staff members (28 per cent) currently allocate more than two-thirds of their effort to maintaining and enhancing applications. Ten people (10 per cent) more nearly balance their effort between maintenance and development and 63 (62 per cent) devote more than two-thirds of their time to new system development.

To a large extent, maintenance and new systems staff are organized as separate departments in MISD. Of the four groups within MISD responsible for the applications portfolio, Production System Support provides maintenance only. Marketing Systems and Operational Systems primarily develop systems but also have limited maintenance responsibilities. Bottler Systems both develops and maintains a group of common systems.

While these four groups are described by MISD principally on the basis of the clients they serve, they may also be differentiated on the basis of type of work done. The Bottler Systems group, for example, develops and maintains a set of common systems for administration of the company-owned bottling companies. These systems run on medium-sized computers (moving to a network of IBM 4341s), rather than the mainframe, and are programmed in RPG, rather than PL/1, the standard MISD language.

The Marketing Systems group develops systems for Franchise Bottler Operations, Marketing Research, and the Planning Department. It also supports (including maintenance responsibility in this case) timesharing and 'decision support' systems (some of which employ SAS, a statistical language), which are used primarily by marketing people. The group's work may be characterized as having a short-term horizon, in terms of either system or development life cycle. Typical in this area are 'artificial deadlines', or deadlines chosen according to the demand for service, rather than by summing and projecting all the hours required to complete a task.

The Operational Systems group develops systems for the Financial, Purchasing, Fountain Sales, Manufacturing, and Technical departments. As the name 'Operational' suggests, this group works mostly on systems that tend to have longer useful life cycles and development periods. It also has maintenance responsibility for two order-entry systems that operate on minicomputers.

The Production System Support (PSS) group is responsible for maintenance and enhancements for the systems developed by Marketing Systems and Operational Systems, with the exception of the timesharing, decision support, System/36, and SAS systems mentioned above. In essence, PSS maintains all the PL/1 and FOCUS programs (which constitute the bulk of the application portfolio and which run on the mainframe computer) and a few other applications, such as those running on the System/32s, for which some economies of scale can be achieved by having PSS handle the maintenance. PSS spends about 5 per cent of its time dealing with abnormal program terminations, 20 per cent making quick changes, and 75 per cent providing system enhancements. Within the PSS group there are two main subgroups:

(1) Financial and Manufacturing, where the staff tend to specialize in a particular application; and
(2) Marketing and Fountain, where they work with retrieval languages applied to a large number of smaller dynamic systems.

Priorities for maintenance tasks are established jointly by PSS managers and their four main client areas, with whom they meet monthly. Work assignments are mainly based on expertise, although each programmer/analyst has at least one system for which he or she is the primary person responsible.

F.H., the manager of PSS, is keenly aware of the differences between PSS and the two development groups. For example, whereas in these groups many of the college graduates have Computer Science degrees, in PSS there is more variety. People have come to PSS from computer operations or other SofDrink groups with no degree or a Liberal Arts one. The maintenance people also tend to work longer hours, with no additional compensation, and they all carry beepers and have TSO terminals at home. There is more time pressure in maintenance, and the tasks are smaller and have more externally set deadlines. While there are advantages to working in PSS that K.R. can point to, such as the customer contact, the quick mastery of a variety of technical skills, rapid promotions, and an informal 'team leader' title, the main incentive is to move 'up' to the development groups. In four years 100 per cent of the applications staff has left PSS, with all but seven moving to development. (Four of the seven who did not move to development left the company.) Perhaps, for some people eager to break into systems development but lacking a Computer Science credential, the PSS experience offers a chance to demonstrate their natural abilities. Both F.H. and K.R. understand that the advantages of the PSS experience are unappreciated 'among the troops'. Says K.R., 'They consider it a 24-hour job'.

F.H. is particularly sensitive to the morale of the PSS staff. He is disappointed that the MIS literature does not deal adequately with what he considers the most pressing problem for any maintenance organization, the 'stigma of maintenance'. He believes that if MISD cannot mitigate this problem it may have to recombine the maintenance and development groups.

Organizational techniques established by MISD for application maintenance include: periodic maintenance audit, user change request procedure, and acceptance review (in transferring software from development to maintenance). On occasion, maintenance escorts (maintainers who participate in systems development) are used, and sometimes maintenance is scheduled in a release, although F.H. notes that for the marketing systems, where responsiveness is much more important than cost, the release concept is unacceptable to the user. It has more potential, in his opinion, with systems in the more stable financial area. Users are not currently charged for maintenance or development costs but they *are* charged for TSO computer costs, and they will be charged for MISD costs in the next year or so. This promises to be a major change for MISD. Apparently the motivation for implementing a MISD charge-back system is to reduce costs, but K.R. does not think 'there is much fat in the maintenance budget at this time'. Maintenance budgets change very little from year to year. (The maintenance staff has grown by five people over the past 4 years.) Department staff increases are usually for development work.

Among work methods established by MISD for application system development and maintenance are: structured programming, structured walk-through, top-down design, program development library, checkpoint review, and use of an application generator. F.H. notes that he has seen no clear productivity improvement from the use of structured code. While there may have been a quality of work life impact in that the code is less uncertain to deal with, it is not at all clear that real maintenance costs have been reduced.

Tools currently used for documentation are: data model diagram, data dictionary, user manual, Warnier diagrams, and an operations-error history. Method/1, a document-oriented development methodology from Arthur Anderson, was implemented last year, with mixed results. PSS uses Method/1 much less than do the development groups, in order to complete projects more quickly.

The application system portfolio

The current application system portfolio includes 81 major installed systems, serving a user population of 10 000. Eight major new systems were installed last year and 22 major new ones are currently under development. Twenty of these are scheduled for installation within the next year. Of the total number of new systems under development, nine will replace those currently in the application system portfolio. On average, the systems being replaced are 7 years old; the average age of the 81 currently installed ones is also 7 years. Replacement is most frequently due to changes in the business, and because of maintenance problems, rather than usage problems, in the opinion of the MISD managers.

One of the replacement systems under development is a new billing system. The original system was written for an IBM 1401, to bill two products in two sizes with a single billing logic. Current requirements are to bill 15 products in 20 sizes, with a large variety of billing logics. There is little documentation on the existing system, which consists of several hundred PL/1 programs running in batch and TSO. Included are sections of code to print a particular message on a single bill on a single occasion. The two full-time maintainers are reluctant to remove such code as the system is considered extremely fragile. It is worth noting that the replacement system is justified with a safety argument (that is, SofDrink's ability to produce bills automatically is in jeopardy with the current system), not on the basis of cost savings or some other dollar advantage.

Two leading-edge applications are the Key Account and the Sugar systems. The Key Account system tracks sales visits to 200 000 major customers. The salesmen use hand-held data-entry devices to record information about these important customers, giving Marketing important and timely information about product movement. The system's ability to accommodate changes in the information recorded is considered key to its success.

The Sugar system supports purchases of sugar, SofDrink's largest input item, from the planning stages through its high-hygiene delivery. The system is unique to the industry. Soon after it was implemented SofDrink began buying liquid corn syrup in addition to dry sugar. The Sugar system accommodated this change well, partly because the development team learned in advance of its likely occurrence.

Flexibility to environmental changes is a key ingredient of successful systems at SofDrink. The Accounts Receivable system has been in production for 5 years, during a time of rapid and sometimes unpredictable change in the company. Nevertheless, this system, of which MISD is justifiably proud, has required only one database change during its first year of operation and no changes to the database in the last four years.

The application system portfolio operates in an IBM environment using a variety of hardware and system software. Most of the systems (90 per cent) run in IBM 3081 OS/MVS environments. A few run on machines in the IBM System/32-36 series and one on an IBM 8100, under DPCX. The company-owned bottlers share a network of three IBM 4341s. PL/1 is the predominant, but by no means exclusive, application system language. Fifty-nine (73 per cent) of the major application systems are written in PL/1, four in COBOL, two in Assembler, three in RPG, 12 (15 per cent) in FOCUS, and one in Natural (an Adabas retrieval language). Application size information is not available.

Almost all the major applications were developed by MISD. Only five were developed outside MISD, two on custom-build contracts (the two Assembler systems) and the other three as purchased packages. The packages are written in COBOL.

One of the COBOL packages is the Accounts Payable system. Over the last 5 years SofDrink has installed upgraded versions of this package several times, but Accounts Payable is still a maintenance problem. Part of the difficulty is that the system is written in COBOL (and MISD is a PL/1 shop), part is that the package owner retains some maintenance responsibilities (fixing serious bugs), and part is that this system is both tightly integrated with other systems and is very sensitive to input errors. Eight other systems pass data to the Accounts Payable system, and with the magnitude of business changes at SofDrink, data 'errors' are inevitable. Unfortunately, the package halts completely (OC7) with every data error. SofDrink plans to install the next upgrade when it is available, but relief is not guaranteed or expected.

Interdependence among the major systems is quite low. Only 10 major systems (12 per cent) rely on others for input data, and only 20 (25 per cent) pass data to other major systems.

Thirty of the 81 major application systems are written in structured program code. Eight (10 per cent) use a database management system and a data dictionary. Twelve (15 per cent) are written in FOCUS, an interactive application generator, and three (4 per cent) are written using an off-line report generator (either RPG or the SofDrink built report generator).

The management problem set

To provide an overall perspective on the extent of various problems experienced at SofDrink in managing the application portfolio, F.H., manager of PSS, completed the Problem Assessment Questionnaire. Among 26 possible problem items, seven were considered by F.H. to be 'major problems': changes made to hardware and software; user demand for enhancements and extensions to application systems; number of maintenance programming personnel available; competing demands for maintenance programming personnel time; forecasting of maintenance programming personnel requirements; unrealistic user expectations; and meeting scheduled commitments.

Statistical analysis of the problem-item responses and comparison of the results with a reference survey population produced the following problem profile:

User knowledge	−0.03	Normal
Programmer effectiveness	1.70	Substantially above normal
Product quality	0.52	Normal
Programmer time availability	1.15	Above normal
Machine requirements	0.55	Normal
System reliability	−0.12	Normal

The problems of maintenance at SofDrink, as assessed by F.H., are thus interpreted as above normal in the two factors related to programmers: programmer effectiveness and programmer time availability. This reflects, perhaps, F.H.'s sensitivity to his domain of responsibility: the maintenance programming group. Potential sources of maintenance problems outside this domain, e.g. the development group (who would be responsible for product quality), users, or the computer operations group (who would be more closely connected with system reliability), are seen by F.H. as problematic in about the same degree that other managers of IS organizations see them.

K.R. the manager of MISD, on the other hand, does not count PSS among his major problem areas. According to him, 'PSS costs are relatively low. It functions well. It's responsive.' In a department where 'responsiveness' to a dynamic business environment is a key goal, K.R.'s endorsement of PSS is strong indeed.

One issue that does command attention from K.R. is the confusion over division of responsibilities between MISD and its users. 'This is a daily problem,' he says. With more PC use, more user-friendly languages, and more inherent expertise in the user community 'the user will be doing more of our tasks'. Sorting out the implications of this change and smoothing the transition to the new state of affairs are considered critical to MISD success.

The impending move to charge-back does not particularly worry K.R. He does not see charge-back as an indictment of MISD's responsiveness or its professionalism. 'We do those things that have to be done when they have to be done,' he says, 'Responsiveness is more important than cost around here, except at budget time.'

Questions

(1) What is the manager of Production Systems Support, the maintenance group at Nationwide Soft Drink, doing to combat the threat of a maintenance 'morale' problem?
(2) Nationwide Soft Drink separates maintenance from development. Does this indicate a long-range maintenance philosophy? In what way?
(3) What changes would you predict that charge-back will have on the maintenance environment at Nationwide Soft Drink?

Case 6.2. National Foods

The organizational environment

National Foods (NatFoods) is a diversified, international food and beverage company which markets products in more than 60 nations from production facilities and sources in 15 countries. It has enjoyed a reputation for quality and value among its customers for well over half a century. The company markets more than 175 varieties of canned fruits, vegetables and tomato products; various fruit beverages and soft drinks; fresh and dried fruits; about a dozen specialty grocery products; and a selection of frozen convenience foods and beverages. Its product lines are the most diverse in the industry and are stocked in virtually every American supermarket. Substantially all the company's canned and dried good operations are seasonal in nature and all its products are subject to intense competition.

NatFoods was formed in the early part of this century by the merger of several fruit and vegetable packers and distributors. Over time, the company expanded across the nation and around the world, building on the strength of its brand name and its reputation for premium-quality products. In the late 1970s it was acquired by a worldwide consumer product company. The food businesses held by the parent at that time, together with others acquired by it shortly thereafter, were combined with NatFoods, broadening its product line but (by outside estimate) increasing its volume only slightly. Industry analysts surmised at the time that the parent company intended to leverage the traditional strengths of NatFoods, agricultural and production knowhow, and consumer recognition by giving the company added marketing strength.

Following the merger and subsequent consolidations and reorganizations, NatFoods went through a difficult four-year period of restructuring, during which 12 sideline businesses with almost no earnings were dropped, 38 plants were closed, and many employees were offered early retirement. These austerity measures improved the company's production efficiency and boosted earnings. More recently, NatFoods has also become increasingly market sensitive, e.g. in emphasizing low-sugar, low-sodium, or nutritional products through more aggressive advertising. This emphasized consumer orientation is expected to increase profits by increasing sales of high-margin, value-added, and differentiated products. For the future, NatFood's major focus is on developing more high-margin, value-added lines and on maintaining the company's high level of productivity and accompanying operating efficiencies in the long-standing high-volume, high-quality lines of processed fruits and vegetables.

NatFoods is organized principally on the basis of product lines. Reporting to the president and CEO of NatFoods are six group vice-presidents heading up the six main product lines: Dry Grocery and Beverage Product (DGBP), International Grocery Products (International), Frozen Foods, Specialty Grocery Products, Fresh Fruit Operations, and Franchise Beverage Products. Also reporting to the CEO are the Chief Financial Officer (a Senior Vice-President), and four other Vice-Presidents, of Planning, Legal, Human Resources, and Corporate Relations. The Vice-President of Information Resources reports directly to the Chief Financial Officer, along with the Controller (also a Vice-President) and the Directors of Tax, Auditing, and Corporate Purchasing.

Information Resources (IR) considers its client base to include the Corporate offices, including principally the Financial departments, but also Planning, Legal, Human Resources, and Corporate Relations; the Dry Grocery and Beverage

Products Group (DGBP); and the International Group's home office operations. DGBP is responsible for processing, distribution, marketing, and sales of the bulk of NatFoods' fruit and vegetable products at more than 20 plants located throughout the nation. The products are sold by about 450 sales representatives working out of 30 offices across the United States and distributed from a network of 12 computer-linked distribution centers.

Together, the Corporate and DGBP groups represent the core of the original NatFoods operations. DGBP is estimated to account for about 60 per cent of IR's total activity, Finance for about 30 per cent, International for about 5 per cent, and the other corporate offices for the rest.

International is also supported by several overseas data-processing facilities. Similarly, the Fresh Fruit Group has data-processing operations both overseas and on the east coast, where they are headquartered. The Frozen Foods and Specialty Grocery Products Groups, both of which when acquired had some data-processing operations, currently are supported by separate, small data-processing operations, distant from the NatFoods home office.

The Information Resources organization

The 1984 budget for Information Resources (IR) is approximately $10.4 million, a 7 per cent increase over the $9.7 million budget for 1983. Of the $10.4 million total, 38 per cent is for equipment and facilities and 60 per cent for personnel, about the same as the previous year.

IR consists of four departments organized as shown in Figure 6.7. The development and maintenance of the application systems portfolio is the responsibility of the Development department. Operations, data entry, production control, and customer services (a help desk) are offered by the Support Services department. The Office Systems and Telecommunications department develops and supports the decision-support and management science systems in the application portfolio. The Planning department provides technical support.

C.K., Vice-President of Information Resources, came to NatFoods from a food-service division of NatFoods' parent company a little over a year ago. He is the first head of Information Resources to have vice-president rank. His predecessor was with NatFoods for 18 years, during which time he followed a career path within IR, from analyst to Director of IR.

The organization of the Development department is shown in Figure 6.8. The Information Systems (IS) and Logistics groups are reponsible for development and maintenance of application systems. The Logistics group supports NatFoods' DGBP division and the IS group does the same for NatFoods' Corporate and International offices. A third group offers database support to the programmers and analysts in the Logistics and IS groups. The fourth is concerned with planning for the Development department.

M.T., Director of Development, has been with NatFoods since 1957. His 27

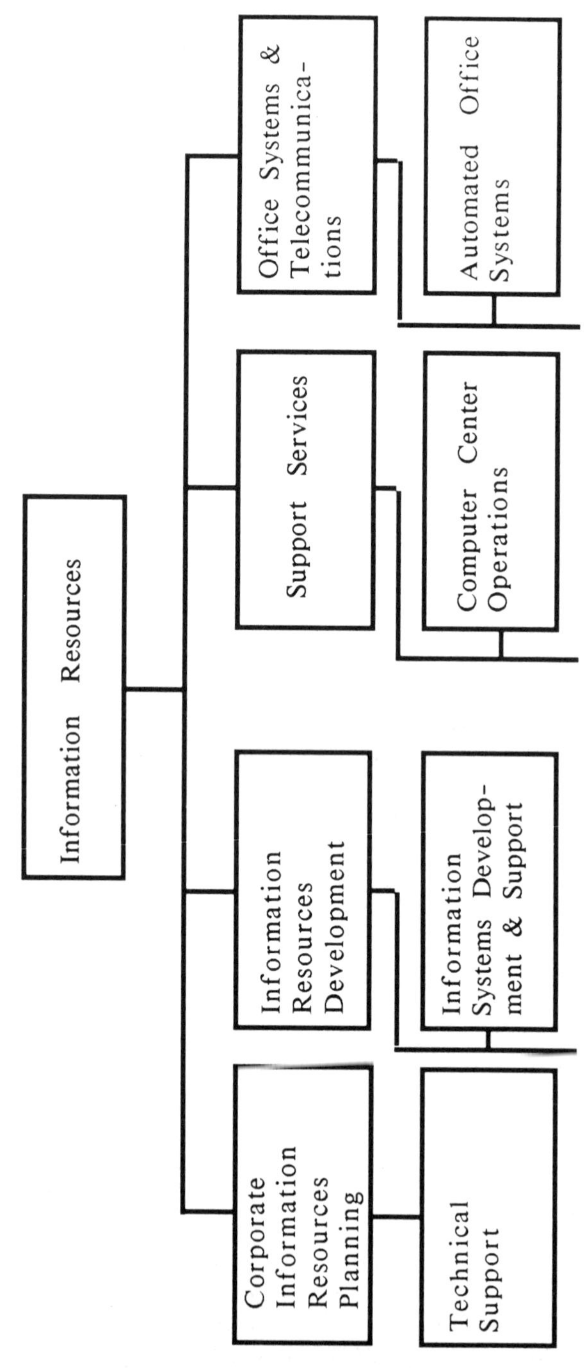
Information Resources
Corporate Information Resources Planning
Information Resources Development
Support Services
Office Systems & Telecommunications
Technical Support
Information Systems Development & Support
Computer Center Operations
Automated Office Systems

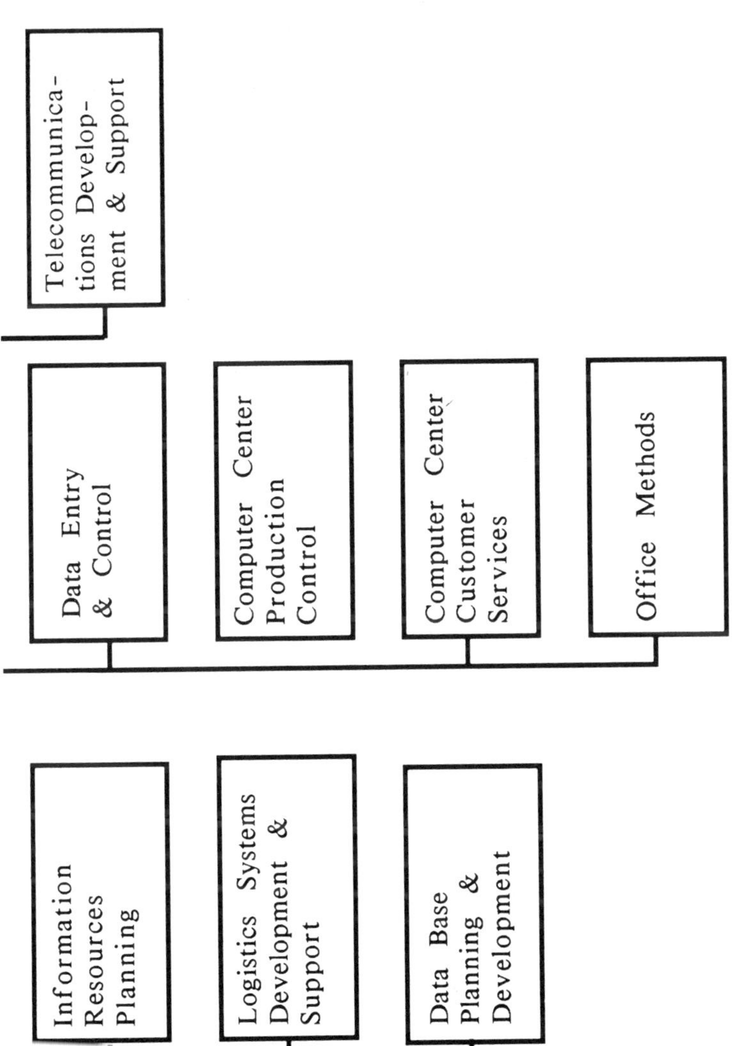

FIGURE 6.7 Information Resources organization chart

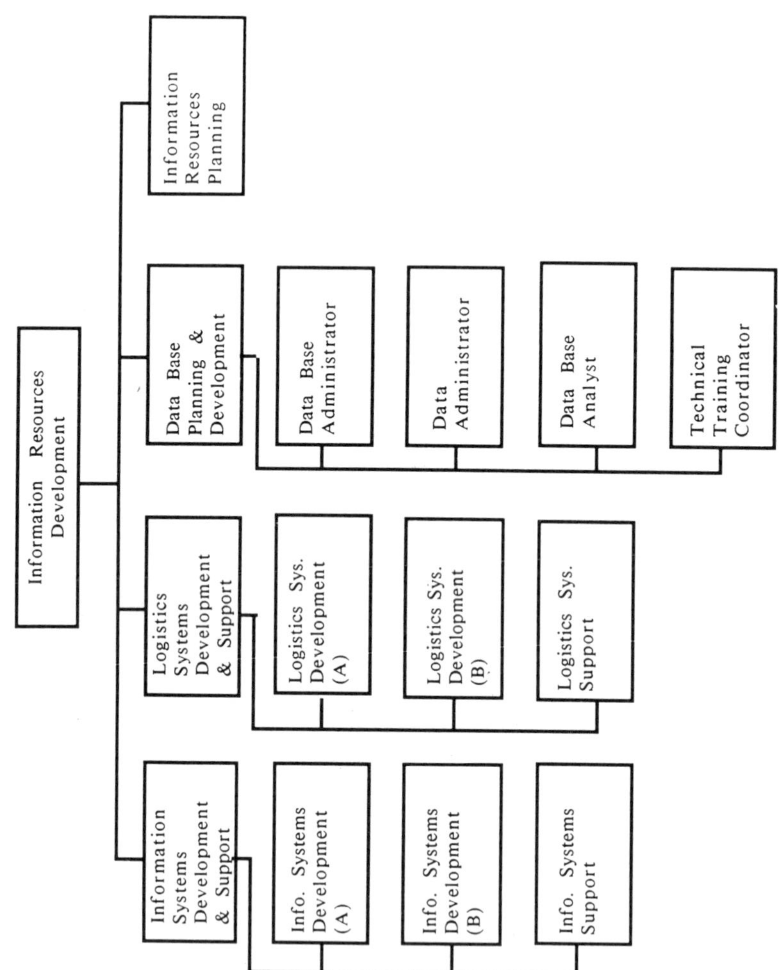

FIGURE 6.8 Information Resources Development organization chart

years have been spent mostly in the systems development area, during which time he has seen the area reorganize several times.

The total application systems staff (those working directly on application systems in both the Development and the Office Systems departments) is 46 full-time employees (17 in DGBP, 21 in Information Systems, and eight in Office Systems), of which seven are first-level supervisors. Last year there were 42 application systems staff members. Median length of service in the applications staff is approximately four years. Sixteen staff members (35 per cent of the total) have been with the IR organization for more than 10 years.

Before coming to NatFoods' Information Resources department nearly half (22) of the current applications staff held positions within NatFoods, either in other NatFoods IS departments (12) or in an operating department (10). Many of the latter group are currently supervisors or managers who initially came to IR as part of a rotation scheme that exposed high-potential individuals to many facets of NatFoods. About a third of the current application staff (15) came to NatFoods from IS organizations outside NatFoods and seven (15 per cent) were previously students.

The applications staff is substantially college educated. A total of 38 individuals (82 per cent) possess a four-year college degree and eight of these (17 per cent of the 46 total) an advanced one. Professional association memberships are significant, possibly because a few managers, among them the previous Director of IR, have been active in their local and national chapters of these organizations. Six of the current application staff are members of ASM, two belong to ACM, and one to DPMA. Four (9 per cent) hold the Certificate in Data Processing.

All the applications staff received at least one week of formal training during the past year. Over half (24) received between one and two weeks of training and another third (17) between two weeks and four weeks.

From about 1970 until quite recently most maintenance was done by an Applications Support group reporting to the Director of Development. The motivation for creating a separate group was threefold:

(1) It was felt that maintenance activities were interfering with development (80 per cent of the programming group was doing maintenance);
(2) There was a need to retain a declining number of staff members with pre-IBM/360 operating systems experience; and
(3) It was perceived that the skills involved in maintenance were different from the skills involved in development.

With no small fear that everyone would quit, the organization formed a 'Support' group, headed by an experienced 7074/1401 programmer. This supervisor was very influential in the success of the Support group, according to M.L., a 29-year IR veteran who now heads up the Operations department. 'He put on the quality stamp,' says M.L., 'Their motto was, "never leave it worse than it was." If a problem occurred, they would fix it fast, but then they would back up and make the system right.'

Developers would turn over completed systems to the Support group, but not until after these had been in operation for some time. Originally it was expected that these turnovers would be sooner but this was found to be unworkable. The early turnovers involved, says M.L., 'a lot of nit-picking'. However, as time went by, the development groups improved their compliance with standards and the support group, on the other hand, gained a better understanding of which standards were really important to them. Eventually the turnover process was reduced to training on the general data flow of the system as opposed to a detailed documentation review.

IR management is still firm in its belief that development and support work appeal to different types of people. For the most part, it hires staff for one type of work or the other, not both or either. There is very little movement of staff between the groups. To M.L., the difference is that support types prefer solving many small problems with quick feedback. 'They like the big in-basket, big out-basket,' he says. To M.T., Director of Development, support types like more variety, and prefer to work at their desks, whereas development types are more patient, have a longer-term view, and like to work with people.

Recently the Support Staff was split in two, according to area of service (Logistics or Information Systems), and merged with the concomitant development staff, so that now in each of these services areas there exist separate staffs for development and maintenance. Thus the applications staff members in Development generally allocate most of their effort to either development or maintenance. Those in the Office Systems department, and a few in Development, divide their time more equally between development and maintenance. In both groups, 12 people (26 per cent) allocate most of their time to maintenance, 22 (48 per cent) to development, and 12 (26 per cent) more nearly balance their effort between the two.

Applications staff members work face to face with users quite frequently. Over three-quarters of the group works with users at least weekly. Only three (6 per cent) work with users less than once a month.

Organizational techniques supporting application system maintenance include: periodic maintenance audit, user change request procedure, change request review board (for requests over 30 man-days), operation and maintenance cost charge-back system, maintenance escort (participation of support staff toward the end of development), acceptance review (as part of their turnover procedure), formal retest procedure (on a few critical systems), and scheduled maintenance (although, as M.L. says, 'spaced stalls' might be a better description).

Among the work methods established by the IR organization for application system development and maintenance are: structured programming, structured walk-through, top-down design, program development library, test data generator, application generator (MANTIS, a product of Cincom), use of report writers, and prototyping. Documentation tools used include: data model diagram, data dictionary, user manual, and system-maintenance journal. Standards are proposed by temporary committees and are circulated for review subject to a 15-day concurrence window. If there are no dissenting opinions the proposals become standards.

The application system portfolio

The current application system portfolio consists of 103 major installed systems serving a user population of 1100 in the NatFoods headquarters and additional personnel at 36 plants or distribution centers, 24 sales offices, 60 brokerage offices, four regional offices of the International group, three offices of other NatFoods business units, and four independent product distributors linked to NatFoods through the grocery industry's UCS (Uniform Communication System).

The application domain of the current major installed systems is as follows (numbers of systems in each category are indicated in parentheses):

Multiple-user systems (22)
Corporate (12)
DGBP—general, or multiple DGBP users (13)
DGBP—finance, accounting, sales accounting (17)
DGBP—marketing and sales (14)
DGBP—operations, distribution (14)
International (8)
Other (3)

(Included in the Multiple-user category are a number of data-processing support systems.)

Six major new systems were installed within the last year and 20 more are scheduled for installation within the next, of which 15 are currently under development. Ten of these are replacement systems. The median age of the systems being replaced is over 10 years and that of those currently installed is about 4. Replacement is most frequently due to users' desire for on-line systems and the systems being a burden to use rather than to maintain, in the opinion of the IR managers.

Twenty of the installed application systems are considered by IR management to be leading-edge applications in the sense of providing users with functions beyond those typically available to their counterparts in other organizations in their industry. Examples of these cited by M.T., Director of Development, include: the order-entry and invoicing systems, which interface with UCS, and a grocery industry system, which provides direct services to NatFoods' customers; a plant-breeding system that R & D uses in the development of new seed; a nutrient-analysis system that supports nutritional labeling of canned or processed foods; and an accounts receivable system, which does cash application automatically.

Most of the application system portfolio (87 of 103 systems) was developed by the IR organization. Ten systems were developed by an outside firm on custom-build contracts, and four were purchased as off-the-shelf parameterized packages. Two systems were developed by user organizations within NatFoods.

All but two of the 103 systems in the application portfolio operate on an IBM 3038 under MVS. In addition, eight of these application systems and the two remaining ones run on a network of 38 IBM Series 1s under EDX that serves NatFoods' plants and distribution centres. One application system also runs on a network of 24 Mohawk Data Systems Series 21s at NatFood's sales offices and another on 5 Datapoint 1500s.

The principal programming language employed within the current installed application system portfolio is COBOL, but it is by no means the only one with which the IR staff works. While 93 per cent of the systems use COBOL, a dozen other languages are represented in the portfolio. The second most frequently used one is Mark IV, which is operated on 40 (39 per cent) of the systems, mostly for report writing from systems that are otherwise written in COBOL. MANTIS, T-ASK, Answer-DB, and FOCUS are also used for report generation. A few systems use Assembler (5 per cent), PL/1 (4 per cent), Fortran (4 per cent), Basic (2 per cent), EPS (2 per cent), or SAS (3 per cent). Programs running on the Series 1/EDX network are written in EDL or PXS; those on the Mohawk Data Systems Series 21s are in COBOL.

Interdependence among the major systems is significant. Fifty (48 per cent) of the systems rely on other systems for input data. Twenty (19 per cent) systems provide data to other systems. Twenty-four of the 104 application systems use a database management system, TOTAL. A few of these and most of the rest of the application system portfolio (90 systems in all) are supported by a data dictionary. Because IR encourages its programmers to use high-level languages, nine systems employ a user-query language; 16 an interactive report generator, such as MANTIS; 40 Mark IV, an off-line report generator: 12 an interactive application system generator; six employ modeling languages, such as EPS, SAS or GPOS/P1-1; and three a graphics language. Forty (39 per cent) of the systems use structured program code and 20 are partly written with re-usable program code. Four systems employ a tutorial function.

The management problem set

To provide an overall perspective on the extent of various problems experienced at NatFoods in maintaining the application portfolio, M.T., Director of Development, completed the Problem Assessment Questionnaire. Among 26 possible problem items, only one was considered by M.T. to be a 'major problem': user demand for enhancements and extensions to application system. Three items were considered to be 'somewhat major problems': lack of user understanding of application system, unrealistic user expectations, and budgetary pressures.

Statistical analysis of the problem item responses and comparison of the results with a reference survey population produced the following problem profile:

User knowledge	0.44 Normal
Programmer effectiveness	0.19 Normal
Product quality	−0.04 Normal
Programmer time availability	−0.02 Normal
Machine requirements	0.57 Normal
System reliability	0.73 Above normal

The problems of maintenance at NatFoods, as assessed by M.T., are thus interpreted as normal in the five factors relating to user knowledge, programmer effectiveness, product quality, programmer time availability, and machine requirements. In the case of the sixth factor, system reliability, the problem is judged above normal in comparison to the reference survey population.

On the whole, the separate maintenance organization at NatFoods has been a plus, in the view of M.T., who counts it among ten IR department success factors (along with a senior management steering committee, the charge-back system, a feasibility presentation process, the use of an integrated programmer/analyst job position, an emphasis on usability in the selection of hardware and system software, user participation on project teams, the guideline issuance procedure, the process of system turnover, and a supportive auditing function).

All these factors have evolved over a time period of relative stability, M.T. admits, adding 'that's changing now'. A new dynamism in the company's business provides one source of this change. The introduction of new software tools and techniques in the marketplace, presenting users as well as IR with changes in opportunities, provides another.

New directions for the IR department are thus under consideration, under the new leadership of C.K. Issues of centralization and decentralization of the IR function are among those leading the current management agenda.

Questions

(1) Not long before this case was written, National Foods' Information Resources department divided their single maintenance group into two and attached these smaller groups to the two development groups. What residual effects of the previous experience with a single maintenance group can you identify in this case?

(2) National Foods' application portfolio is quite varied. What organizational techniques for its management (see Figure 3.12 for a list) would be useful under this circumstance? What is National Foods doing, and what do you think the consequences might be?

(3) How well is National Foods' Information Resources department positioned to take advantage of new information technologies?

Case 6.3. Diablo National Laboratories

The organizational environment

Diablo National Laboratories (Diablo) is one of the nation's largest research and development engineering facilities and a member of the national laboratory system. It is operated by its parent organization as a service to the US Government on a no-profit, no-fee basis. Major responsibilities are concentrated in national defense and energy programs.

The total number of Diablo employees is stable at about 8000. Of this number, more than 2500 constitute the core technical staff. This staff is highly and technically educated, with in excess of 1000 possessing doctorates in engineering, physical science, and mathematics. It is supported by an equivalent number of technical aides. Administrative personnel also number in excess of 2000.

The financial scale of operations may be described in terms of total payroll (nearly $275 million in 1983), plant assets (approximately $625 million), and purchases (more than $150 million). Diablo engages in no product manufacturing and thus produces no revenues as such. (It does, however, provide technical support to Federal contractors responsible for production to Diablo designs.)

Diablo's technical staff employs substantial scientific computing facilities, composed of CDC-6600, CYBER-172 and -76, CRAY-1, and other equipment. Plans also exist to 'attain full CAD/CAM/CAE capabilities by 1988'. The general computer culture at Diablo is thus a relatively sophisticated one.

The strategic opportunities and constraints at Diablo are shaped largely by the ebbs and flows of Federal priorities and budgets. For this reason, management has in the past been wary of short-term growth opportunities and has emphasized retention and enhancement of its basic technical expertise. During the recent, but temporary, boom in energy program funding 'We could've doubled [in size], but didn't,' notes one observer. Diablo budgetary expenditures in excess of $400 require approval as line items in the Congressional budget, a condition that influences acquisition decisions at this level.

The overall organizational structure of Diablo National Laboratories is a functional one. Administrative Information Services (AIS) is organized as a directorate, one of five reporting to a Vice-President, who is one of three who report in turn to one of two Executive Vice-Presidents reporting directly to the President.

The Information Systems organization

The current (1984) annual budget of Diablo Administrative Information Services is approximately $12 million for all categories of expense. Of this amount, approximately $4.4 million (38 per cent) is allocated to equipment and facilities and $7.2 million (60 per cent) to personnel. The balance (2 per cent) is allocated to other related expenses. The current budget represents an increase of approximately 13 per cent over the previous year.

The internal organizational structure of Administrative Information Services is portrayed in Figure 6.9. Four functional departments constitute the organization: Applications Development, Facilities Development, Operations, and Services. A Planning and Administrative unit provides staff support to J.R., AIS Director. J.R. was promoted to his current position upon the retirement of his predecessor and was formerly manager of Applications Development. His replacement was D.E., whose own career with Diablo spans more than 30 years.

The Applications Development Department consists of four units, organized according to application domain: Financial Systems, Personnel Systems, Property Systems, and Procurement Systems. Common Systems, considered a fifth category of applications, is the responsibility of the Services Department. (See next section.)

Total applications staff number 67 full-time equivalents, the same number as last year. Six first-level managers (including two in the Services Department) manage the efforts of the applications staff. Median length of service of the staff is approximately 3 years. However, 16 individuals have 6 or more years of experience in AIS/Diablo.

The applications staff also represents a diversified set of experience from prior job positions. Twelve held positions in other information systems units within Diablo or its parent organization, prior to joining Administrative Information Services. Fourteen held other positions within Diablo, 19 came from positions in organizations other than Diablo or its parent organization and 22 were students.

Educational backgrounds are also varied, though the staff as a whole is highly educated. Thirty-four individuals possess a graduate college degree and another 15 have a four-year one. Eight have a two-year college degree and ten have, at most, a high-school diploma.

A technical background is also emphasized, consistent with company culture. A recruiting booklet indicates the type of candidate sought: 'Masters in Computer Science, Math, Business, or closely related fields with emphasis on Management Information Systems'. Those with a Bachelor's degree in the same subjects are also considered, providing they also have 5 or more years of MIS experience. Six staff members hold the Certificate of Data Processing (CDP) but only three are members of the ACM, DPMA, or ASM professional societies. The average staff member received between one and two weeks of working-hour classroom education and training during the past year.

The typical individual staff member is assigned both maintenance and new system development work. The proportion varies according to area of application. Twenty-three individuals (34 per cent) allocate more than two-thirds of their efforts to maintenance and 11 (16 per cent) more than two-thirds to new system development. Twenty-eight (42 per cent) spend no more than two-thirds of their efforts on either maintenance or new system development, balancing their work evenly between the two. Five individuals work in general support of the others.

Thus the maintenance function is generally not organized separately from that of new system development. An exception is in the Procurement unit, where a staff of five individuals maintains the Integrated Procurement System. Even here,

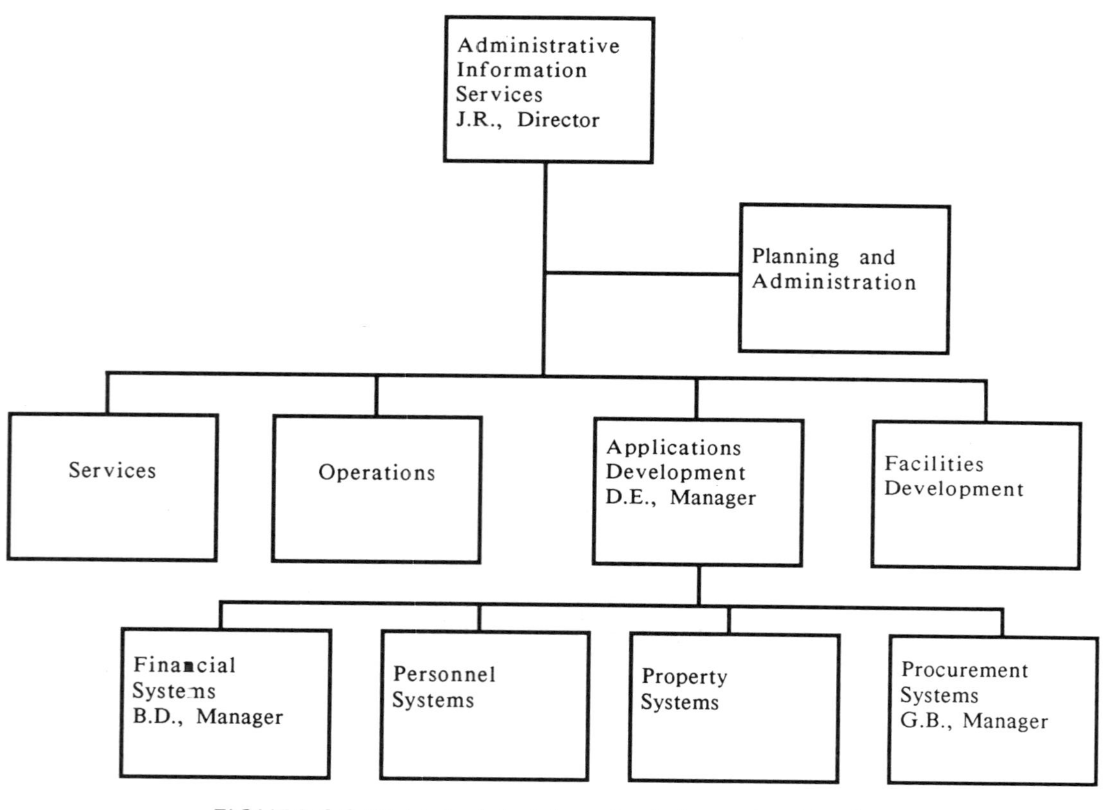

FIGURE 6.9 Diablo's Administrative Information Services

however, the term 'maintenance' is not applied to the group. Rather, the group is termed a 'production support' unit, although its manager, G.B. admits, 'We recognize it's just a nice name'.

The applications staff maintains frequent contact with users and 22 individuals are in daily contact. Another 38 are in contact at least weekly and only seven have less frequent contact.

Among the organizational techniques established for the management of maintenance are: periodic maintenance audit; user change request procedure; change request review board; operations cost charge-back; maintenance escort; acceptance review; and formal retest procedures. Maintenance costs are, however, not charged back, nor is scheduled maintenance employed, although changes are sometimes batched for implementation convenience.

The user change (service) request is the principal vehicle for communicating the needs of users to Diablo Administrative Information Services. Evaluation of a request results in one of three outcomes:

(1) The request is approved and added to the work backlog;
(2) The request is considered significant enough that a new project must be proposed for approval; or
(3) The request is rejected.

A 'tremendous' backlog has accumulated through this process. For example, the Financial Systems group reports approximately 3000 hours of approved work ahead of it. Nevertheless, D.E. recognizes that a certain portion of this work will never get done. "Some [requests] keep falling to the bottom of the stack,' he admits.

Among the work methods employed are: structured programming; structured walk-throughs; top-down design; program development library; benchmark testing; and test data generator. SDM/70 is the development methodology employed, having been adopted about 5 years ago. B.D., manager of Financial Systems, regards it favorably, and considers it particularly suited to getting IS and users to work together. It breaks down the 'us–them syndrome', he feels.

Documentation tools used include: data model diagram; data dictionary; user manual; HIPO diagram; pseudo-code; data-flow diagram; system development journal; system-maintenance journal; automated code analyzer; and operations error history.

The application system portfolio

The application system portfolio serves the administrative function of Diablo. Approximately 2000 users (25 per cent of the laboratory population) are directly involved.

Fourteen major systems comprise the current application system portfolio, three of these having been added to the portfolio last year. Another six of the systems are

3 years old or less and only one is more than 6 years old. Three additional systems are currently under development and two of these are scheduled to be installed during the coming year.

The current portfolio is largely the consequence of a major database effort undertaken in the late 1970s, which is now substantially complete.

The application domain of the portfolio is described as follows (numbers of systems in each major category indicated in parentheses):

Procurement systems (three)
  Purchasing Document Production
  Integrated Procurement, Accounts Payable, Receiving
  Automated Receiving
Personnel systems (two)
  Personnel and Education
  Employee Retirement Benefits
Property systems (three)
  Property Management Systems
  Inventory Control Systems
  Special Material Systems
Financial systems (three)
  Payroll
  Financial Reporting
  Accounting
Common systems (three)
  Data Dictionary/Directory
  Common Data Input and Retrieval
  Accounting Master Index

The five Financial and Personnel systems are considered to be leading-edge applications in terms of user functions provided. Two of the Procurement systems provide direct services to suppliers.

The operating environment is Univac 1100/80 with Executive Level/38. Dual systems are employed, with computing in support of development isolated from operations. Two application systems also are served by an HP 3000.

COBOL is the programming language, although there is minor use of Assembler and FORTRAN (the latter in subroutines written originally for systems now replaced). The median size of an application system is estimated at 40 000 executable source statements. The quartiles of the size distribution are estimated at 12 000 and 130 000 source statements (lines of code).

Thirteen of the application systems employ structured program code and 10 of them use the common database management system (which extends DMS-1100), with a data dictionary and user query language (see above). Re-usable program code is also employed by these systems. Off-line report generators are used by eleven systems and interactive report generators by three. The two systems operating on the HP 3000 use a graphics language.

The portfolio is highly integrated, with 13 of the major systems relied upon for input data by others. Nine of the systems rely on others for inputs.

All but one of the application systems were developed in-house. The exception is the payroll system, which was purchased off the shelf (from Cyborg).

The management problem set

B.D., manager of Financial Systems, completed the maintenance problem assessment questionnaire. Among 26 candidate problem items, 10 were considered by B.D. to be 'somewhat major': quality of application system documentation; changes made to system hardware and software; quality of original programming of application system; number of maintenance programming personnel available; competing demands for maintenance programming personnel time; lack of user understanding of application system; system hardware and software reliability; unrealistic user expectations; inadequate training of user personnel; and turnover in user organization.

Statistical analysis of the problem item responses, and comparison of the results with a reference survey population, produced the following problem factor profile:

User knowledge	0.62	Above normal
Programmer effectiveness	−0.32	Normal
Product quality	0.73	Normal
Programmer time availability	0.57	Normal
Machine requirements	−0.59	Normal
System reliability	1.15	Substantially above normal

It is seen that two problem factor scores exceed the normal ranges established by the survey population: user knowledge and system reliability.

The system reliability score undoubtedly reflects historical difficulties with upgrades of AIS hardware facilities. 'When they put in a new piece of gear, heaven help us,' says one manager. However, the problem is not now so severe as it was earlier, in B.D.'s opinion.

Interestingly, the 'user knowledge problem' is currently receiving substantial management attention. This stems in part from a major AIS strategy now being pursued: the transition to a distributed processing environment. This environment envisages an IBM 4341-based network for the functional gathering and distribution of information to and from the corporate database. The accompanying decentralization of function will entail the development of more sophisticated user skills, e.g. for the local development of applications by means of fourth-generation languages, it is understood. The result should be a 'whole new customer base', in the view of D.E., manager of Applications Development.

User-developed applications will not result in eventual loss of AIS control over the distributed system, in D.E.'s opinion. Company policy will require that these applications be approved by AIS prior to implementation at the system nodes.

It is also recognized that personal computers will be increasingly widespread among users. An AIS office has been opened to provide support to this acquisition process and the applications staff is being encouraged to educate itself so as to 'know as much[about personal computers] as users'. As one means to this end, applications staff are encouraged to find PC-based solutions to problems posed by user-service requests.

In support of the move to an environment where users will assume more direct computing responsibilities, user skills are being developed in part by rotation of job assignments between AIS and the user departments. 'We're the feeder for the line organizations,' D.E. remarks, looking ahead.

Justification for the move to distributed processing is based substantially on arguments of administrative efficiency. The additional computing expenditures implied must therefore promise to generate administrative savings elsewhere. Reduction of headcount is the obvious target, since this is the point of most frequent budgetary pressure.

The successful database strategy of the late 1970s was 'a tremendously high-risk effort', in D.E.'s view. The current strategy promises to be no less risky, he recognizes.

Questions

(1) The Administrative Information Services' application staff at Diablo National Laboratories is highly educated. Would you expect this to make the management of maintenance staff harder or easier?

(2) One of the ways AIS 'manages' service requests is to put them in the backlog. How does this work?

(3) Diablo's AIS department seems to have a system-reliability problem. How might that affect the management of maintenance?

Postscript

Other cases in other chapters provide additional illustrations of maintenance organization and management. In Case 7.3, Big City State University's Administrative Information Systems department appears to have a long-term maintenance philosophy but it does not organize maintenance separately from development. At Westcoast Refining & Marketing (Case 4.1) a separate maintenance department was tried for a year or two but management did not value the experience. Unlike the management at National Foods, they did not think a separate maintenance organization 'worked'. At West Coast High Tech Manufacturing (Case 5.2), a small staff size sharply constrains the organizational options.

Chapter 7

BUILDING THE MAINTENANCE STAFF

INTRODUCTION

In Chapter 6 we examined the organization and management of information system maintenance. We argued that departmentalization of maintenance, such that it is separated from new system development, offers significant advantages. We also proposed a number of management techniques in support of monitoring, planning, and the setting of maintenance policy. In this chapter we consider the management of the human resources for maintenance, and examine issues of staff selection, staff development, and the establishment of professional career paths.

We recall that problems in maintenance are hypothesized to result in part from a lack of fit between the IS staff and the application systems for which they are responsible. In earlier chapters—Chapter 5, in particular—the important features of application system portfolios were the focus of our attention. Here we consider corresponding staff characteristics and how they vary and interact with those of the portfolio, with important consequences for maintenance.

The principal strategy suggested for building the maintenance staff is the establishment of responsibility for the maintenance of strategic systems as a major stepping stone along the career path of the IS professional. Several supporting policies are also suggested relative to staff selection and development.

STAFF SELECTION

Among the most important policies of the IS organization is that which governs the recruiting and hiring of new staff for system maintenance and development.

The immediate prior job experience of new staff may vary greatly from one organization to another. In one case, new staff may be recruited directly out of school for the most part, with little prior work experience. Here selection may be based substantially upon educational preparation and achievement. In another case, new staff may be hired on the basis of significant prior IS work experience, with little regard for educational background. Here selection may focus in particular upon product-specific knowledge and skills. For example, staff may be sought who are experienced in an IBM MVS programming environment.

New staff may further come from other units within the parent organization. Where this organization is large (for example, with multiple IS units at multiple locations) staff may move among IS units as different organizational opportunities arise, where local staff expansions and contractions occur. In these circumstances, one unit's gain may be another's loss, but IS experience may continue to accumulate for the parent organization as a whole.

Employees of non-IS units within the parent organization may also be recruited for transfer to the IS department. In many cases these employees will bring important IS-user experience to the IS department, even though sometimes the short-term motive may be to retrain those whose skills are no longer needed elsewhere.

In Chapter 3, Figure 3.8 summarized the immediate prior job experience of the IS staffs of our twelve cases. On average, substantial diversity was seen to exist. However, this diversity represents significant differences among the cases more than it does common diversity across them. For example, individual organization frequently emphasizes selection of new college graduates, or those with significant work experience. At Integrated Information Technologies, for instance, the majority of IS staff (61 per cent) were hired directly out of school, while a significant minority (35 per cent) came from other positions within the parent company. Few staff have significant IS experience outside the company. In contrast, at United Food Stores almost all staff (84 per cent) worked previously in the IS departments of other organizations.

In general, smaller organizations, such as United Food Stores, tend more to seek experienced professionals, probably to avoid the diseconomies of individual training. However, availability also has a bearing. For example, Big City State University, also a smaller organization, hires more students than is typical.

We consider next the implications of differences such as these and examine issues of educational preparation, expertise gained from working in other organizations, and internal transfers within the business.

1. Raw recruits—educational preparation

Many IS departments hire a substantial proportion of their employees directly out of school on the basis of their educational preparation, with no expectation of significant prior work experience. At least two questions arise with regard to this educational preparation. How many years of college, if any, should the prospective IS employee have? What types of coursework should be emphasized?

The typical IS employee has about four years of college (the equivalent of a BA or BS degree), with coursework often focused in computer science. (See Table 7.1, which summarizes the education, training, and professional associations of IS staffs across the twelve cases.) A significant number of IS employees do not have four-year college degrees; however, many of these are older employees who began their careers elsewhere in the parent organization. Only a small fraction have graduate degrees at present but this number may grow somewhat as IS assumes a more prominent place in the parent organization and as graduate degrees become more commonplace within the workforce.

TABLE 7.1 Education, training, and professionalism of the IS staff (12 case sample)

	Mean	Std dev.	Range
Years of college education (case mean)	3.49	0.64	2.30–4.31
Annual days of on-the-job classroom education and training (case mean)	10.45	3.62	4.19–14.80
Proportion of staff with professional memberships or certification	0.13	0.13	0–0.43

Computer programming is frequently perceived to be the core task of system maintenance and development and computer science is seen by many to be the appropriate form of educational preparation. Among our cases, Small City Manufacturing is illustrative; its staff have historically been recruited primarily from nearby undergraduate computer science programs. However, some organizations look for a business orientation. Sometimes, where the technical aspects of an entry-level task are emphasized, this may involve nothing more than a familiarity with the COBOL business programming language. Increasingly, however, more substantial business preparation, e.g. an MBA, is expected, especially for those aspiring to leadership positions and management careers within the parent organization (Hartog and Rouse, 1987).

The educational preparation sought may be broad or narrow. In some instances, again where the technical aspects of an entry-level task are emphasized, students may be recruited on the basis of product-specific training received. Canning (1980) describes the popular certificate program of one private school which features 875 classroom hours of mostly computer programming instruction, almost all in an IBM hardware and software environment. In contrast, in other situations a broad technical education, in engineering, for example, may be expected, particularly where the parent organization is in a highly technical business and places emphasis on such preparation for all its professional employees. (See, for example, Diablo National Laboratories.)

In older IS organizations with mature portfolios, committed to maintenance and to user service, problems of staff fit may arise where the staff is narrowly educated in computer technology more than it is broadly so with a business orientation. Those oriented toward computers may be the least satisfied with their maintenance roles in that they are not working with the state-of-the-art technology employed on new systems. Those with a business orientation may, in contrast, orient themselves most readily to the domain of application and hence to the problems of users. Indeed, some may anticipate management careers within the user organization.

In summary, two considerations should perhaps be kept uppermost in mind with respect to the educational preparation of applications staff:

(1) The specific knowledge and skills imparted, and the consequent match with maintenance requirements, in particular; and
(2) The longer-term career opportunities and expectations established for the individual.

To a certain extent, a trade-off between these considerations is probably unavoidable. Those trained specifically and narrowly may offer a good job match, especially in the short run; however, their longer-term career prospects may be limited. Those more broadly educated may provide greater returns over the longer term; on the other hand, with better career prospects they may eventually choose to provide these returns elsewhere.

On balance, where the commitment is to maintenance, longer-term career opportunities and expectations should be the dominant consideration and a broad and business-oriented education should be preferred. However, career paths in support of this longer-term perspective are required. These paths must provide in particular for mobility between IS and its user organizations, and we discuss this further below.

2. Imported expertise—looking to the outside

Organizations often look for experience and expertise among the staffs of other IS departments of other parent organizations. Over time and among businesses, turnover among IS staffs generally varies widely. Where and when it is relatively high this typically reflects significant opportunities for staff to move from one organization to another.

These opportunities often arise because of new or additional demand for staff in selected larger organizations. Large IS departments, particularly those that work in part on contracts, have occasional panicky expansions (Withington, 1987). Such expansions, typically associated with new system development projects, may require ready skills which must be obtained in the marketplace. In such circumstances a premium may be offered the experienced IS worker, whose current employer may or may not be willing to match the offer.

IS departments also periodically introduce new technologies—new hardware and system software, new applications, and changes in work methods—where the IS departments of other organizations have preceded them in the same or comparable innovation. The staffs of these early innovators may thus be recruited by those who follow in their footsteps. Accordingly, the diffusion of an innovation among IS organizations is sometimes accompanied by a corresponding migration of staff, with long-term negative implications for maintenance across these same organizations. Having successfully developed a new and innovative system in one organization, staff may stay 'one step ahead' of maintenance by moving on to another organization to develop a new and better version.

On balance, then, maintenance staff are more likely at present to be lost to other organizations through turnover processes than they are directly gained. Experienced new hires are more likely to be assigned initially to new system development than they are to maintenance. Nevertheless, indirect gains to maintenance can be substantial where new hires are assigned to new system development and current staff can be simultaneously retained. Maintenance often suffers when its staff is pulled suddenly onto new system development projects. Where new hires are employed to meet these project needs, the investment in maintenance experience can be preserved.

In general, perhaps the most important characteristic of outsiders with significant IS experience is the diversity of professional view they inevitably bring to the organization which hires them. Insularity is always a risk for the IS department whose staff knows little of other ways of doing their work. The hiring of experienced outsiders mediates against this risk and broadens the professional perspective. While this perspective is most likely to be brought first to new system development, over time it can be carried forward to maintenance.

3. Internal transfers—looking to the inside

IS departments also recruit transfers from elsewhere in the parent organization. Where the parent organization is large, with multiple IS units at multiple locations, such transfers may involve those with substantial IS experience as well as familiarity with the organizational culture. Otherwise, prior IS experience may be very limited.

A primary source of transfers are the IS users within the parent organization. Among these users are those who work actively with IS staff in liaison roles and who thereby develop significant application expertise. Some are accordingly attracted to an IS career. Because they are often intimately familiar with existing systems in their areas, and understand well the user point of view, they are especially good candidates for maintenance work.

Another source of transfers with useful experience is data-processing operations. Many of these employees lack the educational preparation to have been hired directly into systems maintenance and development. However, through their work in operations they demonstrate their capacity for advancement as IS professionals. As with users, they also may bring useful experience to maintenance assignments in that they are familiar with the operational issues associated with installed systems.

Finally, transfers may also arise where there is dislocation elsewhere in the parent organization and workers with unneeded skills seek to be retrained. Such transfers may bring little or no prior IS experience to their jobs, although they may possess related technical skills. Nevertheless, in the event of a hiring freeze, which may be imposed when there are general pressures upon costs, such transfers may be the only recourse. During such a freeze new IS staff may have to be obtained internally.

On the whole, the most significant virtue of the internal transfer may be that the overall business values of the parent organization are reinforced within the IS department. This is especially true where transfers take place at the management, as well as the staff, level. On the whole, this is healthy to the maintenance process. It mediates against any tendency of IS to become a department of technical isolates, and gives leverage to the view that IS performance is based first of all in ongoing services to the host organization.

STAFF DEVELOPMENT

IS departments must make significant investments in the development of their staffs. Even where employees are hired on the basis of relevant product-specific experience they must learn local work methods and procedures. More importantly, current technology is typically supplanted by new technology within a very few years. Continuous training and retraining is therefore characteristic of IS departments.

Important issues in staff development include: first assignments for new hires; in-class versus on-the-job training; job expansion and rotation; and turnover and retention. All carry significant implications for maintenance.

1. First assignments—maintenance as a training ground

New employees, particularly those without prior experience, must usually be trained in the local IS work technology. This typically involves in-class training in the specific hardware and system software used as well as in the local system development methodology and tools employed. On-the-job experience begins with the first assignment to maintain or develop a particular system. The question which commonly arises is whether it is preferable to begin with a maintenance assignment or with the development of a new system. Many IS professionals believe that maintenance is a good 'training ground' before one moves on to more challenging work. Others believe that it is best left to veterans who are comfortable with the older technology and slow in adapting to that which is new.

Both beliefs place maintenance at a systematic disadvantage in relation to new system development and underscore the traditional view that new system development is the primary task of the IS department. Also, both make IS maintenance and its management more difficult than it need be.

In general, the policy for first assignments should be tailored to career paths established with the view that maintenance and new system development are of equal overall importance to the organization. A mixed strategy might thus be followed in first assignments. An individual might be assigned to either maintenance or new system development. However, initial responsibility would be limited. In the case of a maintenance assignment the system worked on would probably not be of critical strategic importance to, for example, day-to-day business operations. Responsibility for the enhancement of a small and stable off-line reporting system would be more likely.

2. In-class training—keeping current

In-class training is not only for the new and inexperienced. With continued change in IS technology, periodic in-class instruction in new hardware and system software is typically provided all staff members. However, not all organizations allocate the same resources to in-class training. Substantial variation exists, as is illustrated in Table 7.1 for the twelve cases of our study.

Larger IS departments often organize their classroom training in-house. This makes sense, in particular, where the technology employed is not widely available in the marketplace and training services cannot be economically purchased. Smaller IS units, lacking advantages of scale, must, in contrast, purchase such training services as are obtainable.

Few organizations use classroom training to familiarize staff with their application system portfolios. For IS organizations with mature portfolios, committed to maintenance, this would seem to be an oversight. Application training can be a good vehicle for building an important common body of knowledge and should probably be more widely employed. Such a program might also be extended to include the user population.

3. Job expansion and rotation

On average IS staff are known to have a high personal growth need strength, which is typical among career-oriented professionals (Couger and Zawacki, 1980; Bartol and Martin, 1982). They accordingly seek to further their own professional skills and expertise. In the current vernacular, they seek to build their own human capital.

Five core job dimensions have been identified as central to meeting an employee's personal growth needs:

(1) Skill variety—the degree to which a job involves the use of a number of different skills and talents;
(2) Task identity—the degree to which a job requires the completion of a whole and identifiable piece of work;
(3) Task significance—the degree to which a job has a substantial impact on the lives or work of other people;
(4) Autonomy—the degree to which the job provides individual freedom and discretion in scheduling and carrying out the work; and

(5) Feedback—the degree to which carrying out the job results in information about the effectiveness of the individual's performance (Hackman and Lawler, 1971; Hackman and Oldham, 1975).

All five of these dimensions are important to individual motivation, performance, and satisfaction in the maintenance task, and all may be targeted in the design of the maintenance job (Couger and Colter, 1985; Couger, 1988).

For instance, lack of skill variety in maintenance is sometimes a complaint, perhaps because maintenance staff must frequently work with older hardware and software technology while their counterparts in new system development may work with the very latest equipment. As professionals, most maintainers understandably value new technology because it provides them with opportunities for learning significant new skills (Baroudi and Ginzberg, 1986). The purposeful infusion of new tools and techniques into the maintenance task may therefore be very useful. Such tools and techniques can significantly increase the variety in maintenance work, impacting many, not just a few, jobs. Automated code analyzers, restructurers, and converters, discussed in Chapter 5, are illustrative.

Apart from such job enhancement, staff may further be rotated among job assignments to good effect. Not only are new skills learned; substitutabilities are created which may cover subsequent staff loss and turnover. Such rotation is particularly important in the case of maintenance, where older systems are otherwise exposed to the loss of the one or two individuals who are knowledgeable about them. Equally importantly, rotation may be used to underscore the overall significance of the maintenance task, ensuring that all staff share in the commitment.

4. Turnover and retention

Turnover in the IS organization has long been recognized as a frequent problem. A 1978 survey reported the IS annual turnover rate in the United States to be 28 per cent (McLaughlin, 1979). For our own case sample the mean service length of IS employees averaged slightly more than 4 years, consistent with a turnover rate of approximately 15 per cent, a smaller but still significant figure. More importantly, there were wide differences in turnover rates within the sample.

In general, differences in turnover among organizations and over time are likely to reflect corresponding differences in job opportunities, more than job dissatisfaction. Geography plays an important role here (Ginzberg and Baroudi, 1988). Where a large firm dominates a small town, for example, turnover may be low. (See Small City Manufacturing.) In contrast, in a large metropolitan region, when there is a labor shortage, starting-wage rates may rise more rapidly than internal salary scales, in which case incentives to 'job jump' are created and turnover may surge. During such a period, paying a competitive wage may be the best defense.

When is turnover too high in an IS department? When, for that matter, is it too low? The question is perhaps badly put, for it is not the turnover rate itself upon which attention should be focused; rather it is the organizational demographics of the phenomenon which must be understood.

The demographics of the IS department refer to its composition in terms of basic member attributes such as age, sex, education level, and length of service (Pfeffer, 1983, 1985; Swanson and Beath, 1986). Length of service reflects turnover most directly. Every IS organization may be described in terms of the service length distribution of its staff, i.e. of the distribution of service lengths of its individual staff members. Any such distribution may further be summarized not only by its central tendency (e.g. mean) but by its dispersion (e.g. variance) and other attributes such as skewness and lumpiness. Together, these attributes convey information which may be tracked over time and compared both within the IS department and among IS departments. For example, in Chapter 3, Figure 3.7 portrays the means and variances of the service length distributions of the staffs of the twelve cases studied here. Note the striking differences among the twelve organizations.

Where average length of service is unusually long, as in the case of Small City Manufacturing, questions of staff effectiveness may reasonably be raised, just as such questions may be raised where average service is unusually short, as in the case of Big City State University where the IS organization is relatively new. Professional groups responsible for innovation can be too old for maximum effectiveness just as they can be too young (Pelz, 1967).

Note also in Figure 3.7 that, on average, the greater the mean length of service, the larger the variance. Older staffs, in terms of length of service, tend to be more diverse, with a greater spread between young and old. This diversity may be useful (e.g. in terms of the range of different knowledge which can be called upon) or it may be problematic (e.g. when it reflects a significant gap between cohort groups).

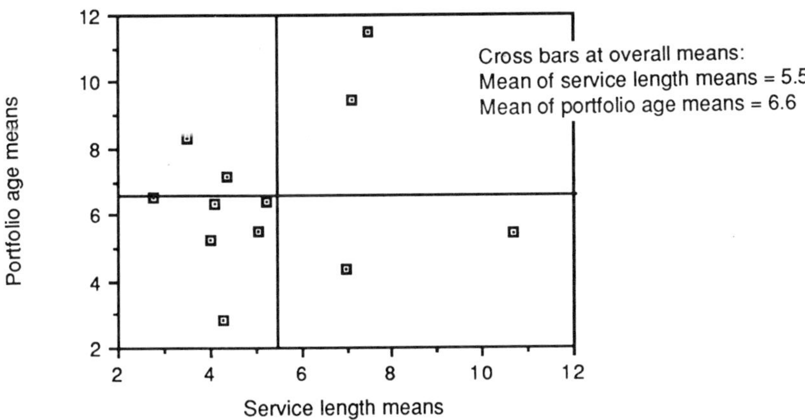

FIGURE 7.1 Mean service length versus mean system age

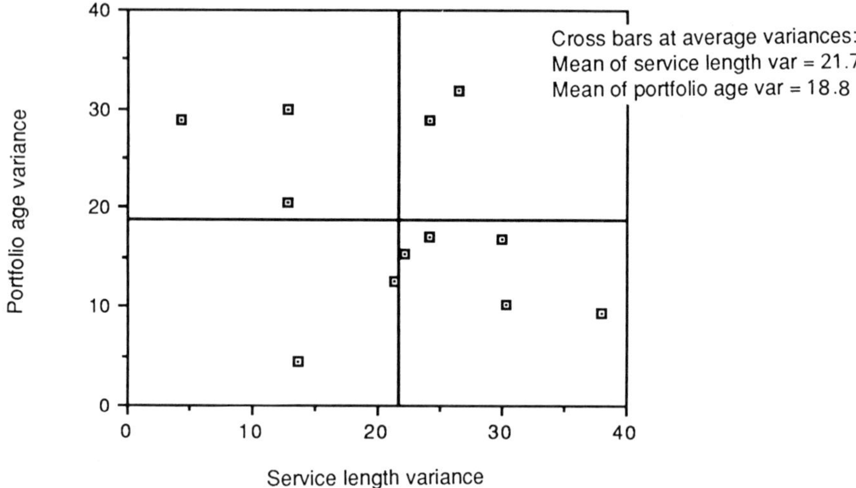

FIGURE 7.2 Service length variance versus system age variance

Note in Figure 3.7 that in the case with the greatest variance, National Foods, the mean length of service is only about average. This might signal a potential problem should it reflect a significant gap between young and oldtimers.

Demographics of staff may be usefully compared to certain characteristics of the application system portfolio in the diagnosis of problems of organizational fit, especially in maintenance (Swanson and Beath, 1986). Of particular interest is the distribution of staff tenure, when compared to that of system age. Figures 7.1. and 7.2 relate means and variances among the twelve cases. Where the mean and variance of system age substantially exceed those of staff service length the staff may lack the requisite experience for maintenance of the portfolio and problems of organizational fit may perhaps be signalled. United Food Stores, where the mean service length is less than half the mean system age, provides a case in point.

STAFF CAREER PATHS

It is also helpful to view IS staff from a longitudinal perspective, in terms of individuals engaged in personal careers, rather than from a static one, in terms of personnel matched to the organization's present job positions. A longitudinal view gives insight, in particular, into individual job satisfaction, commitment to the organization, and the choice to continue or quit.

The concept of the career path reflects this longitudinal perspective. Typically, career paths are seen as established routes within the organization. Individuals follow them by design and prearrangement. However, individual choices are not limited to such routes within the organization; job choices often span organizations, and whether a path within one organization is attractive or not is assessed by the individual in terms of other opportunities available.

In general, the IS staff member confronts two major professional career options. The first is that of the IS professional, the second is that of a career in the business of the parent organization. As an IS staff member, an individual ostensibly pursues both; however, he or she is likely to face one or more choices between the two over the long term.

Among the eventual choices faced may be that of promotion to a management position, either within IS or elsewhere in the parent organization. Where a 'dual ladder' exists, in which individuals choose between technical and managerial career advancement, this choice may occur at an important career junction. (See Allen and Katz, 1986.) However, from our point of view promotion to management within IS does not disqualify one as an IS professional. Many IS careers involve the assumption of managerial responsibility.

1. The IS career option

The true IS professional seeks a career in IS. Job assignments are valued for the IS knowledge and experience which may be gained in carrying them out and for the doors which are opened to still more responsible IS work. When the IS professional finds a better career opportunity he or she is likely to move to another IS department, perhaps in another parent organization, which may or may not be in the same business. Allegiance is to doing good IS work more than to the particular business served.

More than other IS staff members, the IS professional would be expected to associate with formal professional organizations such as ACM (Association for Computing Machinery), DPMA (Data Processing Management Association), SIM (Society for Information Management), or ASM (Association for Systems Management). He or she would also be expected to seek formal accreditation of skills by means of a CDP (Certificate of Data Processing).

Table 7.1. summarizes the professional IS associations of the staffs of the twelve cases studied. On average, the level of these associations is seen to be low. Only 13 per cent hold a CDP or are members of ACM, DPMA, or ASM. We do not know whether this is typical. It may reflect lack of maturity of the IS profession overall or IS staffs with comparatively weak professional ties. In either case, it compares poorly with other professional groups, such as engineers, for example, two-thirds of whom reportedly belong to a professional society (Kerr *et al.*, 1977). It suggests that rather weak professional values prevail among the IS staffs of the organizations studied.

2. The business career option

Not all IS employees will be oriented toward IS careers. Some will identify themselves primarily with the parent organization and its business. These individuals will value job assignments for the business knowledge and experience gained and for opportunities created within the parent organization and its industry, not necessarily in IS.

The business-oriented individual will therefore seek career mobility within the parent organization itself. This will necessitate the development of knowledge and skills unrelated to IS, which may or may not transfer easily to other businesses. Thus while greater mobility within the parent organization may be secured, IS professional mobility may be lost.

3. Maintenance as a career stepping stone

The challenge to the IS organization with a mature application portfolio is the integration of maintenance into the careers of its staff. Both internal and external careers, as described by Van Maanen and Schein (1977), are relevant here. Internal careers consist of the steps and stages seen by individual staff as marking personal progress. External ones have the organizationally recognized steps and stages as represented by job titles, salary structure, etc. Both provide the 'anchors' which shape career aspirations and choices (Schein, 1977). Congruence between internal and external careers within an organization is a prerequisite to job satisfaction and motivation (Van Maanen and Schein, 1977; Ginzberg and Baroudi, 1988).

As discussed above, a current problem is the perception of maintenance as low-level, demotivating work (Couger and Colter, 1985; Goldstein, 1985). Some see this issue as rooted in the core job dimensions of skill variety, task identity, task significance, autonomy, and feedback. Remedies in terms of job design and assignment, such as those suggested above, are therefore recommended. Our own view, however, is that the low status of maintenance is due in significant part to managerial inattention to maintenance and to the career path implications of maintenance assignments.

Too many careers begin and end in maintenance, while the years in between are spent in new system development. Newcomers are too often initiated in maintenance before 'advancing' to system development (Ball, 1988). Similarly, oldtimers skilled in earlier technologies too frequently find themselves retired to the maintenance pastures. More innovative career paths, in which, for example, responsibility for a major installed system is a significant mid-career achievement presenting further opportunities for advancement, might do much to alleviate the current motivational issue.

Advancement opportunities both within IS and within the business of the parent organization may be important here. Significant maintenance responsibility might well be employed to prepare an individual for promotion to, for example, a staff or management position within the user organization served by the system.

SUMMARY

Building the maintenance staff requires a strategy as well as supporting policies. One useful strategy may be to establish responsibility for maintenance of a strategic system as a major career stepping stone both within IS and within the business of the parent organization. Supporting policies in staff selection include hiring on the basis of a broad, business-oriented, rather than a narrow, computer-oriented, educational background, as well as employing internal transfers on the basis of their experience in system use and operation.

In first assignments, maintenance should not be used as a training ground. Rather, the policy should be to assign new people to systems of lesser strategic importance, whether these are new or installed. Ongoing classroom training in the application system portfolio should also be a helpful practice. Job rotation may be similarly employed to broaden the base of system familiarity. Finally, staff demographics should be monitored for purposes of diagnosing problems of organizational fit.

Building an effective maintenance staff requires, in the end, a new view of maintenance. In this and the preceding chapters we have laid some groundwork for this view. In the next and last chapter we sum up and consider the future for maintenance.

REFERENCES

Allen, T. J., and Katz, R. (1986) 'The dual ladder: motivational solution or management delusion?' *R & D Management* **16**, 185–197.

Ball, M. (1988) 'Creating careers out of maintenance', *Computerworld*, **22**, 14, April, 60–61.

Baroudi, J. J., and Ginzberg, M. J. (1986) 'Impact of the technological environment on programmer/analyst outcomes', *Communications of the ACM*, **29**, 6, 546–55.

Bartol, K. M., and Martin, D. C. (1982) 'Managing information systems personnel: a review and conceptual framework', *MIS Quarterly*, Special Issue, December, 49–70.

Canning, R. G. (Ed.) (1980) 'Finding qualified EDP personnel', *EDP Analyzer*, **18**, 8.

Couger, J. D. (1988) 'Motivating IS personnel', *Datamation*, **34**, 18, 15 September, 59–64.

Couger, J. D., and Colter, M. A. (1985) *Maintenance Programming: Improving Productivity Through Motivation*, Prentice-Hall, Englewood Cliffs, NJ.

Couger, J. D., and Zawacki, R. A. (1980) *Motivating and Managing Computer Personnel*, John Wiley, New York.

Ginzberg, M. J., and Baroudi, J. J. (1988) 'MIS careers—a theoretical perspective', *Communications of the ACM*, **31**, 5, 586–94.

Goldstein, D. K. (1985) 'Work-related correlates of job satisfaction in programmer analysts: an examination of task differences', *Proceedings of the Sixth International Conference on Information Systems*, Indianapolis, Indiana, 16–18 December, pp. 158–77.

Hackman, J. R., and Lawler, E. E. (1971) 'Employee reactions to job characteristics', *Journal of Applied Psychology Monograph*, 259–86.

Hackman, J. R., and Oldham, G. R. (1975) 'Development of the job diagnostic survey', *Journal of Applied Psychology*, **60**, 2, 159–70.

Hartog, C., and Rouse, R. A. (1987) 'A blueprint for the new IS professional', *Datamation*, **33**, 20, 15 October, 64ff.

Kerr, S., Von Glinow, M. A., and Schriesheim, J. (1977) 'Issues in the study of "professionals" in organizations: the case of scientists and engineers', *Organizational Behavior and Human Performance*, **18**, 329–45.

McLaughlin, R. A. (1979) 'That old bugaboo, turnover', *Datamation*, October, 97–101.

Pelz, D. C. (1967) 'Creative tensions in the research and development climate', *Science*, **157**, 157, July, 160–65.

Pfeffer, J. (1983) 'Organizational demography', in *Research in Organizational Behavior* (Eds L. L. Cummings and B. M. Staw), **5**, JAI Press, Greenwich, Conn., pp. 299–357.

Pfeffer, J. (1985) 'Organizational demography: implications for management', *California Management Review*, **28**, 1, 67–81.

Schein, E. H. (1977) 'How "Career anchors" hold executives to their career paths', *Personnel*, May–June, reprinted in *Managing Professionals in Innovative Organizations* (Ed. R. Katz), Ballinger, Cambridge, Mass., 1988.

Swanson, E. B., and Beath, C. M. (1986) 'The demographics of software maintenance management', *Proceedings of the Seventh International Conference on Information Systems*, San Diego, California, 15–17 December, pp. 313–26.

Van Maanen, J., and Schein, E. H. (1977) 'Career development', in *Improving Life at Work* (Eds J. R. Hackman and J. L. Suttle), Goodyear, Santa Monica, Ca., pp. 30–95.

Withington, F. G. (1987) 'Managing your IS pros', *Datamation*, **33**, 20, 15 October, 77ff.

CASES

Introduction

We present the last group of three cases. Case 7.1, Integrated Information Technologies, describes the largest of the twelve IS organizations among the cases. Its maintenance problems are assessed as normal by its management. However, issues of staff professionalism, among others, may be readily identified. 'I would like to see my programmers being more professional,' the IS head manager asserts.

Case 7.2, Metropolitan Gas Company, describes maintenance in an IS department where systems analysts are organized separately from programmers. While the former policy was to hire inexperienced people, train them in IS, and encourage them to make their career with the company, a new recruiting emphasis is to hire experienced people with certain needed technical skills.

Case 7.3, Big City State University, describes maintenance in an IS department where a significant number of the staff have graduate-level educational backgrounds. The department is also relatively new, having been organized only $6\frac{1}{2}$ years ago.

Case 7.1. Integrated Information Technologies, Inc.

The organizational environment

Integrated Information Technologies, Inc. (InfoTech) is one of the world's leading high-technology companies, providing a diversified set of information products which are internationally developed, manufactured, and marketed. Its management emphasizes a set of four goals: growth consistent with that of the industry; technological leadership; low-cost production; and profitability.

InfoTech's Large Systems Division (LSD) is responsible for the development and manufacture of the most powerful and advanced products in the InfoTech line. It operates at three principal US locations, including the Eastcoast Manufacturing Location, situated in a mid-size town about two hours away by car from a major metropolitan area.

The current principal LSD product line, introduced in 1980, is among the most successful in InfoTech history. Shipments in 1983 increased by 70 per cent over those of 1982, and production capacity at the East Coast Location is presently being significantly increased, though the number of plant employees is expected to remain at about the current level. New plant additions in 1983 approximated 700 000 square feet, and continued construction work remains everywhere evident at the main plant site.

LSD management is, however, by no means complacent in the face of this success. Emphasis on continued improvement in product quality and lowered unit costs of production characterize the work life at the Eastcoast Manufacturing Location. Recognition of the longer-term competitive challenge from Japan clearly underlies much of this emphasis.

Zero-defect shipment of the LSD product line provides an illustrative division objective. Recently, 70 per cent of shipments of the leading product in the line were reported to have met this standard, considered an excellent achievement, given the product size and complexity.

Manufacturing is also becoming significantly more automated at the Eastcoast Manufacturing Location. Computer-Aided Design (CAD), which has been increasingly employed in product development, has given substantial impetus to Computer-Aided Manufacturing (CAM) in support of process automation, operational logistics, and product testing. The use of robotics has also been initiated.

Thus with innovation in manufacturing a necessity, the Eastcoast Manufacturing Location is characterized by the steady introduction of significant changes in its processes. The Information Systems department, which reports directly to the Plant Manager, finds itself under continuing pressure to provide information support services responsive to these changes and developments.

The Information Systems organization

Information Systems at InfoTech's Eastcoast Manufacturing Location is organized as shown in Figures 7.3 and 7.4. Three departments report to C.H., Manager of IS. Systems Development is responsible for development and maintenance of the application system portfolio. Systems Operations is responsible for the operation of the data-processing installation. Systems Architecture is

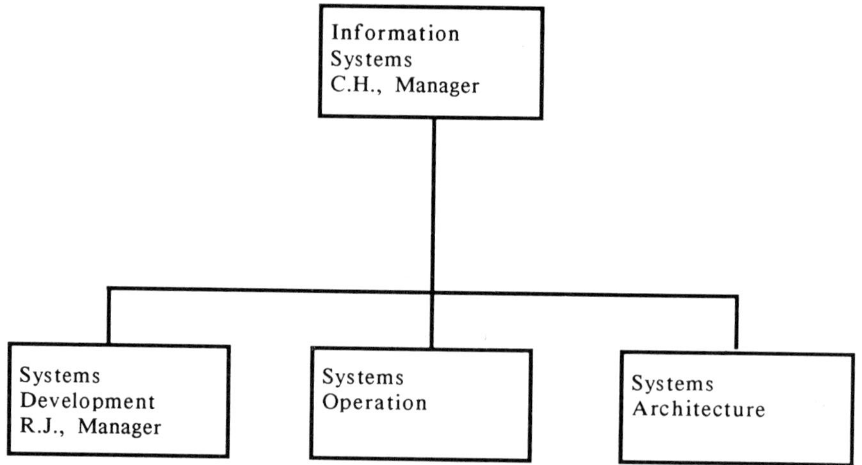

FIGURE 7.3 The Information Systems Department

charged with the formulation of strategies and plans and with the establishment of controls over both development and operations.

C.H. is in his third year as IS Manager. He has been with InfoTech Eastcoast Manufacturing for 21 years and was formerly manager of Systems Operations. His predecessor, who had come to IS from InfoTech Marketing, departed to assume the IS directorship of another InfoTech business unit.

R.J., Manager of Systems Development, has been in his present position since 1982. Previously, he served as Manager of Systems Architecture. As with his boss, he has moved up the management ranks within the IS Department at the Eastcoast Manufacturing Location.

The Systems Development staff numbers 266 individuals, down from 279 the previous year. The staff is organized at the first level into 18 units, which are grouped in turn into five departments whose managers report directly to R.J. (as shown in Figure 7.4).

The five departments are seen to be organized according to area of application. Technical Systems and Process Automation provide direct support of specific manufacturing operations. Material Logistics and Data Logistics serve manufacturing scheduling, supply, co-ordination, and control functions. Planning and Control Systems support the management of personnel and financial resources.

Median length of service in the IS organization is roughly 3 years. Thirty-five individuals have been with IS less than 1 year. More than 100 (106) have been with IS between 1 and 3 years. The balance (125) has been with IS more than 3 years, and of this number, 44 have 10 or more years of IS experience.

The majority of the IS staff (162 individuals, 61 per cent of the total) joined IS directly out of school. Another 94 (35 per cent) came to IS from other positions

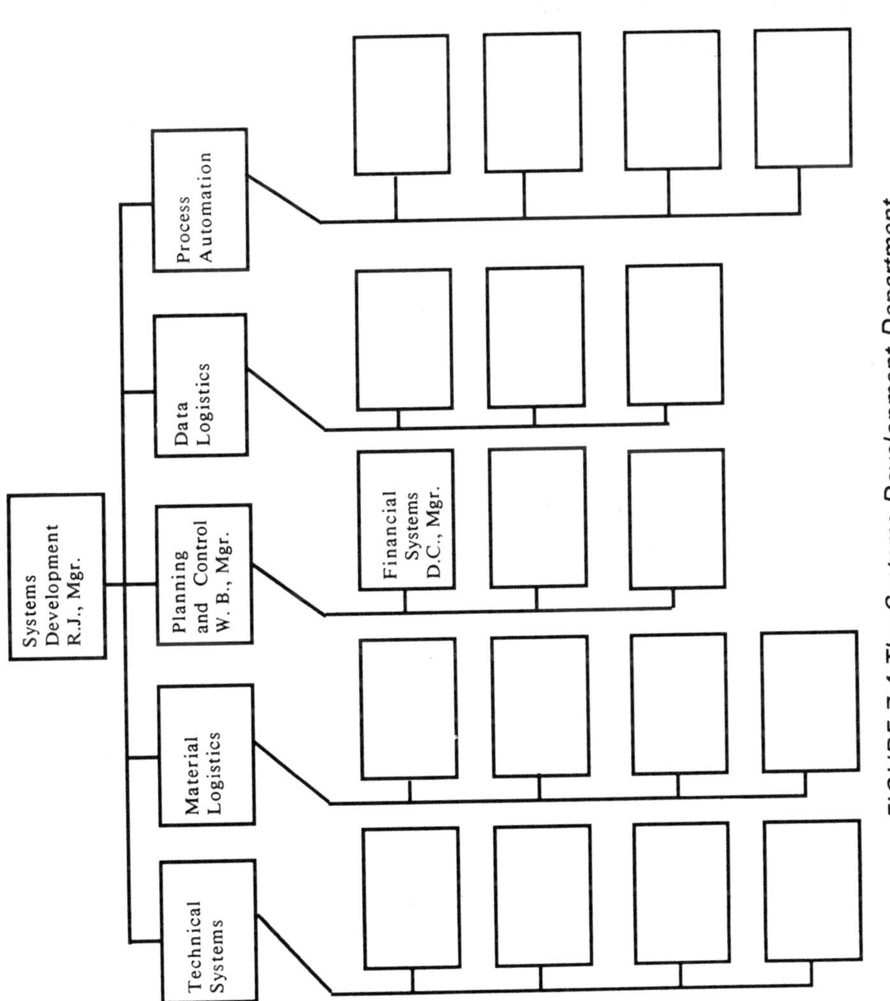

FIGURE 7.4 The Systems Development Department

within InfoTech. Only 10 (4 per cent) were recruited from positions with other organizations.

W.B., manager of Planning and Control Systems, and D.C., who reports to him as manager of Financial Systems Support, provide illustrative examples of those who have joined IS from other positions rather than coming directly out of school. W.B., who has been with InfoTech at its Eastcoast Manufacturing Location for 6 years, joined the company as a production control analyst upon graduating from a local college and moved subsequently to IS as manager of a technical systems department. He was promoted to his current position within the last year. D.C., also with InfoTech for 6 years, worked previously with another company before joining InfoTech locally in its IS Systems Operations unit, where she subsequently assumed her first management position. She moved to her current position in Systems Development eighteen months ago.

A good number of those who join IS from other positions within InfoTech come with a technician level of education and training. These individuals are sometimes placed in IS in lieu of those who might be recruited externally, when IS has open positions in its headcount but is not given permission to hire.

Those who leave IS typically move to other systems and programming positions within InfoTech, at other manufacturing locations, or elsewhere within the company. Some leave. Reflecting upon the reasons for a relatively high attrition rate, R.J. notes: 'What a lot of them get into [here] is maintenance, which means they're on call for stuff, [and therefore find themselves working unpredictable hours, on overtime and weekends]'. Among those who leave the company altogether, 'A lot of them are single women who go off to get married,' R.J. adds.

Approximately 65 per cent of the staff possess a college degree at some level. Forty-seven members (18 per cent) hold a two-year college degree as their highest qualification. Nearly half (122, 46 per cent) hold a bachelor's college degree and five (about 2 per cent) possess a graduate one.

All staff members are formally classified as programmers, and are assumed accordingly to have programming skills, though the work of some is perhaps more accurately described as systems analysis. Formally, however, systems analysts positions exist in the user departments rather than in IS.

Twenty-seven IS staff members (10 per cent) are members of professional associations. The majority of these memberships (15) are with ACM (Association for Computing Machinery). No one holds the Certificate in Data Processing (CDP).

The average IS staff member received about two weeks of working-hour classroom education and training during the past year. Fifty-one per cent (135 individuals) received two weeks or more and 47 per cent (126) received less than two weeks but at least one. The balance (five individuals) received less than one week.

The maintenance and enhancement of installed systems consumes a high percentage of staff time. One hundred and twelve staff members (42 per cent) spend more than two-thirds of their effort on maintenance and enhancement of existing systems. A smaller number, 82 members (31 per cent), spend more than two-thirds of their time on new system development. Seventy-two members (27 per cent) balance their effort relatively evenly between maintenance and enhancement of existing systems, and new system development.

Major enhancement of existing systems occupies a substantial portion of staff time, on the whole. When this activity is grouped with new system development work the relative staff effort on maintenance is estimated to be only 21 per cent of the total (with major enhancements and new system development estimated at 63 per cent and overhead at 16 per cent).

There exists no formal distinction between maintenance and new system development staff. With departments organized by area of application, the allocation of effort to maintenance and new system development varies across units according to the currency of the unit's application mix.

Financial Services Support provides an example of a department that works principally on maintenance and enhancement of existing systems. Its applications, which include Cost Accounting and Accounts Payable, are among the most traditional and well established of those in the IS portfolio.

Direct contact with users of the applications is frequent. One hundred staff members (38 per cent) are estimated to meet daily with users and another 120 (45 per cent) meet at least weekly. Thirty-five members (13 per cent) meet at least monthly and only 11 individuals (4 per cent) less frequently or not at all.

Organizational techniques that have been established to support application system maintenance include: a user change request procedure, a change request review board, an operation and maintenance cost charge-back system, a formal retest procedure for change implementation, and scheduled maintenance (the batching of changes). However, periodic maintenance audits and acceptance reviews (in transferring software from development to maintenance) are not used.

It is worth noting that user organizations are understood to 'own' the application systems that serve them, under the prevailing philosophy. Users are accordingly responsible for the 'business case' underlying all application development work, including enhancements to existing systems. This development work is organized on a project basis and is guided by a phase-review procedure. Five phases of development are subject to review on each project on a mandatory or optional basis according to the magnitude and nature of the task. They are: feasibility; general design; detail design; pre-installation; and post-installation. Management authorization for a project to proceed from one phase to the next is required and concludes each review.

System ownership is reflected in particular by the charge-back system, in which the costs of operation are apportioned to systems according to resources used, with the resulting charges appearing in the budgets of the systems' owners. In the case of Systems Development personnel, time is apportioned to manufacturing products on both direct and indirect bases for cost accounting purposes.

Work methods in use include structured programming, structured walk-throughs, and top-design designs. Documentation tools employed include: data dictionary, data-flow diagrams, system development and maintenance journal, operations-error history, and user manuals.

The application system portfolio

The current application system portfolio comprises 89 major installed systems, an increase of seven over last year. These systems serve an estimated 1300 'serious users'.

The portfolio may be described by the classes of application systems maintained by each of the five units comprising Systems Development. Technical Systems is responsible for 23 systems providing direct support of manufacturing and test operations. Process Automation supports 13 systems involved in direct tool control and automatic testing. Material Logistics Control, with 13 systems, and Data Logistics Control, with 15, support all aspects of manufacturing logistics, from manufacturing planning, and order entry and release, to tracking and floor control, and purchasing and warehousing. Planning and Control Systems maintains 25 systems supporting financial and personnel functions.

Application systems vary widely in age. Twelve (13 per cent) are new within the last year and 15 (17 per cent) are 1 to 3 years old. Another 18 systems (20 per cent) are 3 to 6 years old and 20 (22 per cent) are 6 to 10 years of age. Twenty-four systems (27 per cent) are over 10 years old. The age of the average application system is thus about 6 years.

A substantial variance in application system size also exists. The median system size is estimated at 30 000 executable source statements. The quartiles of the size distribution are estimated at 15 000 and 100 000 statements.

The majority of the application systems (54, 61 per cent) employ PL/1 as the programming language. Another 19 systems (21 per cent) make use of PLS, a subset of PL/1. A substantial number (33, 37 per cent) use Assembler. (Ten of these, 11 per cent, are written entirely in Assembler.) Other languages used include EDX (in System/1 applications) and COBOL, RPG, and FORTRAN (in two applications each).

The hardware and system software environment is IBM and IBM-compatible. Sixty-seven application systems, including all those supporting the manufacturing logistics, and planning and control functions, are processed on the equivalent of five IBM 3081s operating under MVS/JES3 IMS. The balance of the application systems (22) are supported in a variety of environments. Fifteen of these are supported by the equivalent of seven 4341s operating under MVS JES2. One application is supported by a configuration of five 4331s operating under DOS/CICS. Two are processed by the equivalent of four 3081s operating under MVS/JES3. One is processed by two devoted 3081s in a VM environment. Three are supported by a system of 50 System/1s operating under EDX.

Twenty-one systems employ a data dictionary and a user query language is used by 10 systems. Fifteen incorporate an off-line report generator and 15 allow interactive report generation. APL, GIS, and Select/360 are among the tools employed for these purposes. Eight systems use ADF, as an off-line application generator, and three incorporate a tutorial function. The majority of the application systems (65, 73 per cent) employ structured program code.

All applications are InfoTech-developed. About half (43, 48 percent) of these were locally IS-developed. A comparable number (44, 49 per cent) were originally developed in other InfoTech locations and have been locally adapted. Two were originally developed by a user organization.

A relatively high proportion of the application system portfolio (25 systems, 28 per cent) is considered to be leading edge in terms of user functions provided. This reflects InfoTech's manufacturing innovations, in substantial part. The portfolio is also highly integrated. Seventy-eight systems rely on others for their input data and 65 are relied upon for input data by others.

Approximately 750 user work requests comprise the current 'application backlog'. Included is work in process as well as work queued and on-hold. Work queued includes low-priority work yet to be 'sized' (in terms of estimated effort to complete). The total formally estimated effort associated with the backlog is about 6 man-years.

Twenty-one major new systems are currently under IS development and 17 of these are scheduled for installation within the next year. Eleven of the systems under development will replace 16 in the current installed portfolio. Six of the systems to be replaced are more than 10 years old, four are 6 to 10 years old, and six are less than 6 years of age.

Technical necessity is perhaps the most important reason for system replacement. Illustrative of this type of necessity are changes in manufacturing procedures and the obsolescence of data-processing equipment. The burden to maintain, use, and operate installed systems also motivates the replacement decision process.

The management problem set

To provide an assessment of the problems of maintaining the current installed application system portfolio a number of IS department managers completed the Problem Assessment Questionnaire. Average responses were computed for 26 candidate problem items.

On average, two problems were evaluated as 'somewhat major' for IS: quality of application system documentation and user demands for enhancements and extensions. Competing demands for maintenance programmer personnel time was considered more than a 'minor' problem, on average, ranking third in order of importance. A number of problems were considered 'minor': turnover of maintenance personnel; unrealistic user expectations; adequacy of system design specifications; meeting scheduled commitments; inadequate training of user personnel; and turnover in the user organization.

Statistical analysis of the problem item responses, and comparison of the results with a reference survey population, produced the following problem factor profile:

User knowledge	0.16 Normal
Programmer effectiveness	0.00 Normal
Product quality	0.25 Normal
Programmer time availability	0.57 Normal
Machine requirements	−0.20 Normal
System reliability	−0.11 Normal

The problems of maintenance in IS, as assessed by its management on the questionnaire, are thus normal when compared to those of other organizations surveyed. These 'normal' problems may be further understood in the context of the more specific views of individual managers.

W.B. stresses the need to understand the 'why's' of maintenance work in order to better manage it. 'If I don't understand what's causing it, I can't reduce it,' he says, adding that the current work-reporting system is not adequate for this purpose. The application backlog is also a current concern. A recent survey of users produced a number of complaints on this score, and Information Systems has now been instructed by top management to provide a measurement system by which progress in dealing with the problem can be addressed.

Measuring the real demand for work is seen as 'very difficult' by R.J., who estimates that more work requests would be submitted should the users perceive that lower-priority work might get done rather than queued indefinitely. The current effort to relieve the backlog by means of an Information Center is also viewed by R.J. with some skepticism. Once users experience the ease with which they can provide themselves with reports they may conclude 'If I can do this, you guys can probably do more,' R.J. suspects.

As viewed by C.H., the problem of maintenance of existing systems is tied closely to that of new system development. The development staff, responsible for both, may simply have 'more work than they can do', C.H. admits. Pressure for new development is continuous; it provides additional systems to be maintained, which in turn makes allocation of resources the more difficult.

With regard to maintenance itself 'We have some very old stuff,' C.H. acknowledges, adding, 'No one here knows how it works anymore'. Nevertheless, with little slack in personnel resources the tendency is to replace older systems later, 'when they have screamingly reached end of life', rather than earlier.

An example of the type of problem that characterizes an older system was provided by D.C. in the case of the Cost Accounting system maintained by her department. Cost figures of negative amounts had suddenly begun to appear in output from the system. Eventually, these errors were traced to the assumption by the system that unit costs of parts could not equal or exceed $10 million. This assumption, which had been acceptable for many years, was now invalid. Searching for this bug and making the necessary system repairs ultimately required 2000 hours of effort (about a man-year).

Though D.C.'s Financial Systems Support department is substantially a maintenance unit, its morale was found to be relatively good in a recent internal opinion survey. D.C. attributes this to the high level of system responsibility developed through assigning individuals to systems on a one-to-one basis to the extent possible, the ability to innovate by 'pushing the front ends' of old systems, and the significant amount of interaction with users that takes place. At the same time, with a department of 17 programmers reporting directly to her, D.C. admits that her span of control is perhaps rather stretched.

With a median length of department service of 3 years, is there a personnel turnover problem in Information Systems? C.H. thinks not. Turnover is significant, he admits, but it is a managed (planned-for) process. Given the turnover, however, and the fact that new hires are typically fresh out of school (typically with computer science preparations), one admitted weakness is a shortage of project management skills in the organization.

With regard to future problems on the horizon, C.H. cites end-user computing as a concern. Where such computing is 'legitimate' how do we facilitate it, he asks. Further, who should do what? 'We're the professionals,' says C.H., but we have to contend with 'the engineer who would do it all'.

The emergence of fourth-generation languages poses a challenge, C.H. feels, asking 'How do I get that into my own programming shop?' The problem is that Information Systems has grown up around large-scale IBM technology, and its people continue to think in these terms. 'I've been trying to change that [though],' C.H. adds, pointing out that he recently obtained 100 tickets to Info '84 and encouraged his staff to attend and shop. 'I'm saying, buy it, if you think you like it, buy it,' C.H. emphasizes, underscoring his commitment to experimenting with non-traditional, emerging software and hardware technology.

Historically, Information Systems has looked to its own resources for innovation. Increasingly, C.H. is convinced, it must turn to the outside world. 'I would like to see my programmers being more professional,' he concludes.

Questions

(1) Does system maintenance pose significant problems for IS at Integrated Information Technologies (IIT)? If so, what is the nature of these problems? If not, why not?

(2) Formally, all IS staff at IIT are classified as programmers. System analyst positions exist only in the user departments. How is this consequential or not for IS's view of its overall task? How is it consequential or not for IS staff careers?

(3) 'We're the professionals,' asserts C.H., the manager of IS, '[but we have to contend with] the engineer who would do it all.' Would IS's user departments see things the same way? How does IS professionalism at IIT compare with that at other organizations?

Case 7.2. Metropolitan Gas Company

The organizational environment

Metropolitan Gas Company (MetroGas) is the nation's largest gas distribution company, serving over 4 million customers, more than a million more than the next largest gas distribution utility in the United States. MetroGas is the principal subsidiary of Western Energy Corporation. The parent company also owns Western Gas Supply Company, which buys, transports, and stores gas within California for resale to MetroGas. Together, MetroGas and the Gas Supply Company comprise Western Energy's utility sector, of which MetroGas is by far the larger part.

In 1983 the parent company's utility sector represented 67 per cent of consolidated assets ($2.7 of $4 billion), 90 per cent of consolidated revenues ($4.5 of $5 billion), and 89 per cent of consolidated operating income ($405 of $455 million). Other lines of business include exploration and production of oil and gas, interstate and offshore natural gas transmission, and land development.

Overall, the financial health of Western Energy is quite good. In 1984 its common stock was valued at its record high, operating income was a record $555 million, and dividends were increased for the eighth straight year. Over the last 10 years, counting both dividends and stock price appreciation, MetroGas's shareholders have enjoyed an average annual return of 25 per cent. That compares to a 15 per cent average annual return for the Standard and Poor's 500.

Utility companies are regulated by a Public Utilities Commission (PUC) to 'maintain a financially strong, viable utility structure which assures safe, reliable and efficient gas service to customers' (Western Energy 1984 annual report). In general, the PUC authorizes a 'gas margin' (gas sales revenues less cost of gas sold) to recover operating expenses, interest on debt, and return on equity. However, the utility's income and earned rate of return can differ from that authorized by the PUC to the extent that operating expenses or the rate base vary from authorized levels. For example, effective 1 January, 1984, the utility was authorized by the PUC to increase rates to produce a rate of return of 12.92 per cent; during 1984 a rate of return of 13.4 per cent was actually earned.

Figure 7.5 approximates the MetroGas management organization. The company is headed by a Chairman/CEO and a President. An Executive Vice-President, who reports primarily to the Chairman/CEO, heads the operating wing of MetroGas and is responsible for gas transmission and storage, consumer services, engineering and research, 13 gas distribution divisions, distribution and

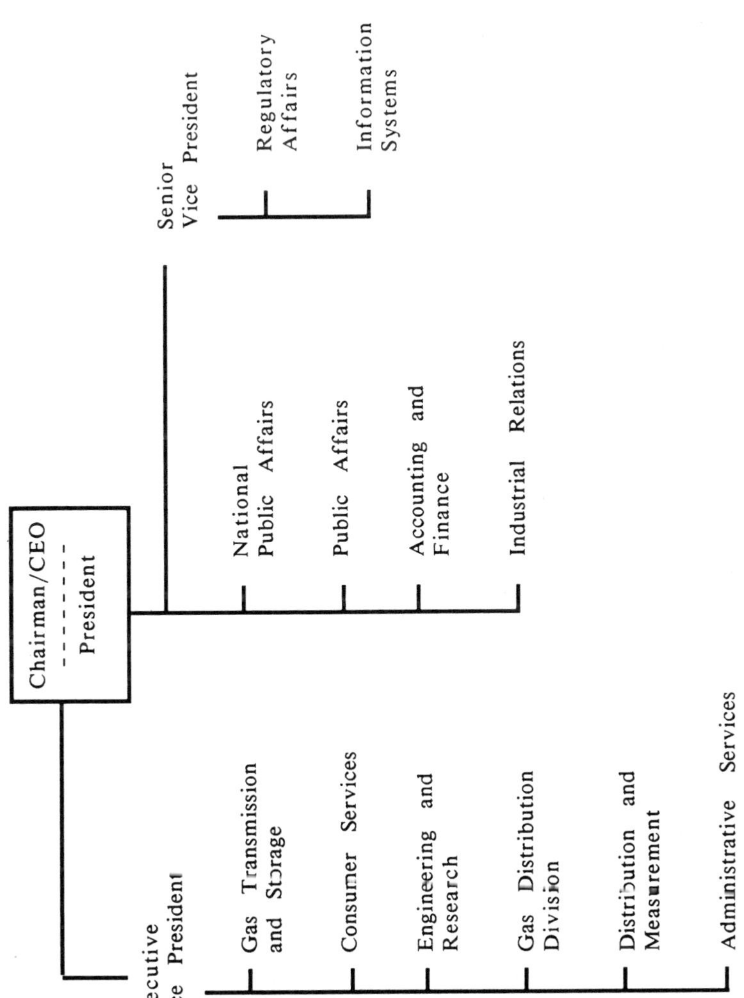

FIGURE 7.5 MetroGas organization structure

measurement, and administrative services. In the staff wing of the company, reporting to the President, are Vice-Presidents of National Public Affairs, Public Affairs, Industrial Relations, and Accounting and Finance, and a Senior Vice-President responsible for Regulatory Affairs and Information Systems.

The Information Systems organization

The mission of MetroGas's Information Systems department is to provide computer-related service to its user community at MetroGas. The major users of IS's services are, in MetroGas's staff wing, the Accounting and Finance and Industrial Relations groups, and in MetroGas's operations wing, the Administrative Services, Distribution and Measurement, and Consumer Services organizations.

Figure 7.6 approximates the organization of the IS department. Reporting to the Vice-President of IS are Managers of Data Security, Information Systems, and Information Services. The Manager of Information Systems, C.R., is responsible for Computer Operations, Distributed Computing (operators of a group of distributed minicomputers in 13 gas division offices, which primarily support requests for information on customer accounts) and Computer Systems and Programming, headed by A.P. The Information Services department includes a staff support group (which prepares budgets, workforce projections, etc.), the clerical pool, and Computer Systems Services (CSS), which prioritizes requests for IS services and does feasibility studies such as a current study on office automation.

The Information Systems 1985 annual budget is around $52.5 million for all categories of expense, a 21 per cent increase over the $43.2 million budget for 1984. Application system and programming wages for 1985 were budgeted at $7.9 million, a 20 per cent increase over 1984.

Five supervisors report to A.P., the Manager of Computer Systems and Programming (CS & P). One heads a group responsible for training, quality assurance, and project control reporting and the other four supervisors divide responsibility for sections of the applications portfolio. The allocation of systems to supervisors is by client area, for the most part, as indicated in Figure 7.6. A corollary of this allocation scheme is that supervisors tend to have responsibility for a set of applications of similar age and technology. For example, B.E.'s payroll and materials management applications, the oldest in MetroGas's portfolio, are batch systems written in 'unstructured' COBOL. In contrast, MetroGas's market services (gas conservation) systems, some of its newest, use some purchased software and are on-line six days a week.

The total applications staff in CS & P (those programmers and analysts working directly on application systems) is budgeted at 118 full-time employees, of which 12 are first-level managers or supervisors. This staffing level represents a 5 per cent increase over the previous year. At present 113 of the 118 positions are filled.

The staff under each supervisor is usually organized around major applications

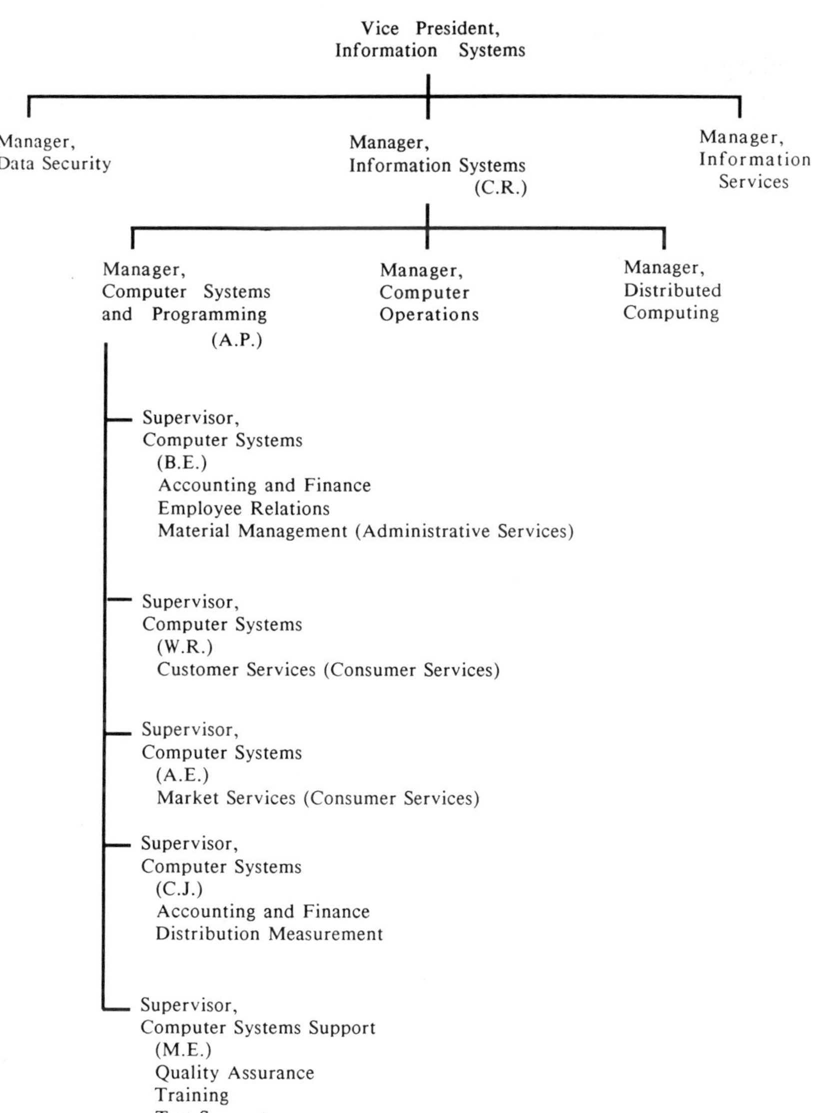

FIGURE 7.6 Information Systems organization

or application groups. For the most part, staff members have job titles and responsibilities as analysts or programmers rather than as programmer/analysts. Within the application groups work assignments are primarily for either maintenance or new system development. Sixty-nine (44 per cent) of the current 113 applications staff members allocate more than two-thirds of their effort to maintaining and enhancing applications. Thirty-two people (28 per cent) more nearly balance their effort between maintenance and development and 31 (28 per cent) devote more than two-thirds of their time to new system development.

In general, current practice is for all members of the applications staff to have both maintenance and development responsibilities. Recently, however, A.P., the CS & P Manager, made maintenance of the Customer Information System (CS & P's largest system) the primary responsibility of a few individuals, leaving others to concentrate full-time on development. Those having primarily a maintenance assignment were selected because of their excellent maintenance skills with respect to this very critical application and because they viewed the assignment as an opportunity rather than as a dead end.

Overall, contact between the CS & P staff and its user community is not widespread, as might be expected where analysis and programming tasks are separated. At MetroGas, analysts frequently act as liaison between users and programmers. In addition, service requests initiated by users are routed to the Computer Systems Services group, where such requests are evaluated and prioritized. Only 20 per cent (22 people) of the applications staff work face-to-face with users daily. Thirty-nine (35 per cent) work directly with users at least weekly but not daily. Another 39 work directly with users less frequently but at least once a quarter.

More than half of the current application staff (67 of 113 individuals, or 59 per cent) came to CS & P from other positions within MetroGas. Among these, seven came from other MetroGas information systems organizations and 60 (53 per cent) came to CS & P from MetroGas business units. C.R. estimates that about half the analysts in CS & P came from user groups. Of those who came to CS & P with no MetroGas work experience, 30 were students, seven held positions in outside information systems organizations, and nine were working for other companies in non-IS jobs.

MetroGas has a formal program, called the 'Readiness for Management Program', that permits supervisors to nominate non-management employees for management-graded positions in the company. Almost all CS & P's positions are management graded. Employees with an interest in data processing who are ready for management positions (or who already hold management-level ones) are subsequently tested for an aptitude for data processing. According to C.R. this program brings skills and knowledge of the company to IS and it allows IS to hire staff with whom the company is familiar.

Until recently, the pattern at CS & P was to hire inexperienced people, train them, and encourage them to make their careers at MetroGas. While long-term employment is still the goal, the current recruitment emphasis is on people with five or more years of experience, particularly in certain skill areas, such as database and telecommunications, that CS & P considers vital to its future. This trend has been partly facilitated by cutbacks at some major employers in the metropolitan area which has temporarily increased the number of qualified, skilled programmers and analysts in the market.

C.R. points out that in CS & P there is an obvious career ladder from associate programmer to supervisor of computer systems for those interested in a management career. For those who prefer a technical career, the ladder leads to systems programming work. Developmental rotations into and from user departments are also possible. A.P., in fact, is in his assignment as Manager of CS & P on a rotation from a user organization.

Reflecting their expressed interest in hiring people who will make their careers at MetroGas and their efforts to keep people they hire, length of service with the company among the application staff is relatively high. Nearly half (47 people, 48 per cent) of the staff have been in IS for more than 3 years, seven of them have been on the IS application staff for more than 10, 44 (38 per cent) have been in IS for 1 to 3, and 15 (13 per cent) were hired during the last year.

In all, 78 applications staff members (69 per cent) hold four-year college degrees and nine of these (8 per cent of the 113 current staff) have an advanced one. Eighteen people (16 per cent) have a two-year college degree. Relatively few of the people with college degrees majored in computer science; many of them have liberal arts or business degrees. One supervisor expressed a preference for people who had worked their way through school.

CS & P has an elaborate self-paced entry training program that all inexperienced people complete, irrespective of whether they are coming from other MetroGas units or have just graduated from college. Independent study courses are also available, as are those taught by vendors of products used (such as RAMIS). The majority (65 per cent or 76 of 118 individuals) of the applications staff received more than two weeks of working-hour classroom education and training during the previous year. Thirty-six of these (31 per cent of the total) had more than four weeks of training, 40 (34 per cent) had two to four weeks, and 29 (24 per cent) had one to two weeks. Nine people had less than one week of training and only four had no training at all.

Professional association memberships among the applications staff are not extensive. Two individuals are members of the Association for Systems Management; none are members of the Association for Computing Machinery or the Data Processing Management Association. Three individuals hold the Certificate in Data Processing (CDP) and one is a Certified Systems Professional (CSP).

Organizational techniques established by the Computer Systems and Programming group include a formal user change request procedure and application reviews by the internal audit group whenever there is a major system change (or annually, if there are no changes).

The only part of the applications portfolio for which operating and maintenance costs are charged back to the user is in the area of Conservation Systems. These systems support a Market Services program to encourage consumer conservation of gas. This special conservation program was approved by the PUC as an area of expense separate from the normal business expenses of the company. As a result, all costs of the program, including those of systems development and maintenance, are accumulated and accounted for separately.

Control of other CS & P expenditures is accomplished mostly by associating applications staff with user areas being supported. 'Defining our groups like the user groups helps,' says A.P. 'Then you can tell the user, "Here are five people who are supporting you. If you have a lot of enhancements, your development will be slow." They understand that easily.' Assigning development and maintenance tasks to different individuals, where that is feasible, is partly motivated by a desire to clarify the amount of support a particular user is receiving.

Among work methods established by CS & P for application system development and maintenance are: structured programming, structured walk-through, top-down design, program development library, and checkpoint review. In the opinion of B.E., a supervisor, walk-throughs have the largest positive impact on maintenance of all these techniques. 'Newer people get a lot of their experience this way. They get a lot of good free advice. It saves a lot of headaches down the line.' A.E. agrees. He believes that design walk-throughs, in particular, help put up error-free code.

Tools currently used for documentation during application development and maintenance are: data dictionary, user manual, pseudo-code, data-flow diagram, and system development journal. Pseudo-code and data-flow diagrams are considered working, not permanent, documents, so they are not maintained. A.E. is lukewarm on the utility of the data dictionary for the on-line CICS programs his group maintains. He believes it is more useful in the IDMS environment.

The application system portfolio

MetroGas's current application system portfolio includes 25 major installed systems, serving a user population of over 9000 throughout the company. Principal users of systems in its portfolio are:

Accounting and Finance	Seven systems
Administrative Services	Five systems
Distribution and Measurement	Three systems
Consumer Services	Seven systems
Gas Transmission	One system
Information Systems	Two systems

Three major systems were installed last year and 10 major new ones are currently under development, five of which are scheduled for installation within the next year. Of the 10 systems currently under development, six will replace those currently in the application portfolio. On average, the systems being replaced are about 10 years old; the average age of the 25 currently installed systems is around 6 years. Replacement is most frequently due to an excessive burden to maintain and use.

One of the systems being replaced is the Residential Conservation Services (RCS) system. The specific reason for replacing this system is that the company, in response to a perceived change in the marginal utility of energy audits, has changed its policy on offering energy audits from a proactive to a passive stance. Hence the volume of audits has been considerably reduced. In addition, the prevalence and ease of use of microcomputers makes it feasible to move the system from a mini-based east coast service bureau processing mode to a PC-based system in Los Angeles. 'It will save a few million bucks,' says the supervisor of the development team.

The Materials Management system is also being replaced. The current system is 10 years old and suffers from the usual ills of systems of its generation. 'The design is poor, the programming is poor, the unit testing was poor. There were no walk-throughs, of course,' says B.E.. 'It has a terrible reputation, even though it runs OK now. It's very difficult to enhance.' The replacement system will have several new features, including some that provide functionality to purchasing and others that consolidate several vendor files.

All the application systems operate in an IBM environment using either IBM 3081K or IBM 3081KX systems. COBOL is the application system language employed by all 25 major systems. Four applications also use some Assembler code, three have some reports in RAMIS, and one also uses a general retrieval system, 'Dyl-280'. According to B.E., RAMIS is more self-documenting than Dyl-280. Both these languages are used primarily for report writing, particularly for one-time, non-production retrievals.

All but one major application system (the current RCS system) were developed by CS & P. B.E. notes that their experience with purchased systems has been 'fairly miserable', Once, in the past, vendor salesmen sold a user a system that did not do the job. Another was developed outside at, they estimate, three times what it would have cost in-house. One major application system, RCS, produces direct services to customers in the form of an energy audit. No systems were considered by CS & P supervisors to be leading-edge applications in the sense of providing users with functions beyond those typically available to their counterparts in other gas companies.

Interdependence among the 25 major systems is relatively low. Twelve systems rely on others for data input, and 17 pass data to other systems. The major areas of interdependence are among the accounting applications and in systems that access customer files.

Eighteen (72 per cent) of the 25 major application system use structured program code. Ten systems (40 per cent) use a data dictionary and report generator (either RAMIS or Dyl-280) and five (20 per cent) have re-usable program code. A user-query language, interactive report generator, off-line application generator, and tutorial function are each employed by one major application system.

The management problem set

To provide an overall perspective on the extent of various problems experienced at CS & P in managing the application portfolio, C.R., the Manager of IS, completed a Problem Assessment Questionnaire. Of 26 possible problem items, two were considered to be major problems: user demand for enhancements and extensions to application systems and competing demands for maintenance programming personnel time. To the predefined list of 26 problem items C.R. added two others he considers major problem areas: integrating DBMSs and support and integration of micros. Demand for integration drives maintenance requests of a particularly difficult type, he notes.

Statistical analysis of the problem item responses and comparison of the results with a reference survey population produces the following problem profile:

User knowledge	0.16	Normal
Programmer effectiveness	0.85	Normal
Product quality	0.49	Normal
Programmer time availability	0.57	Normal
Machine requirement	−0.20	Normal
System reliability	0.10	Normal

That is, all the problems are equivalent to those experienced among the reference survey population.

In the opinion of C.R., user knowledge has been more of a problem in the past than it will be in the future. It is being mitigated by an evolution from a batch to an on-line environment. 'We acted as their crutch with the batch systems,' adds C.J., 'resolving data entry problems, reconciling edit errors. With on-line systems users have a better understanding of how their systems work, how the data flows through the systems.' On-line systems, he notes, are more self-training.

With respect to the problem of programmer time availability, C.R. discussed his reservations about the viability of completely separating maintenance and development assignments. 'It depends on how it's managed,' he said. 'But it's difficult to avoid the myth that "development" means doing "creative work", and "maintenance" is somehow second class, even though maintenance programmers are generally very skilled.' In a similar vein, A.E. noted that developers have more current, more 'saleable' skills, while maintainers, on the other hand, pursue the thankless task of 'trying to understand someone else's logic, and digging through cobwebby code'.

To avoid the 'second-class citizen' syndrome, CS & P supervisors generally spread the maintenance tasks around and rotate people from association with one system to another, for variety. 'But,' says C.R., 'then we sacrifice in-depth familiarity with the system being maintained.' When they can find someone who is interested and willing to be assigned permanently to maintenance of a system, they get the 'best of both worlds—contented staff and maintenance done efficiently by people familiar with the system'.

Programmer productivity, an issue that gets a lot of C.R.'s attention at this time, may eventually solve part of the problem of programmer availability both for maintenance and for development. CS & P has experienced productivity gains in the past from better documentation, better audit trails, and a workstation for every programmer. C.R. sees the problem of programmer productivity as having two sides, a motivational side and an instrumentation one. With respect to instrumentation, CS & P is now considering adding more tools for the programmer, perhaps along the line of the programmer's workbench concept. 'Without a measure of programmer productivity,' says C.R., 'it is difficult to know how much to invest.'

Overall, C.R. is satisfied with the effectiveness of the maintenance activities at CS & P. Beyond the unceasing search for improvements in productivity he has no major changes in mind for the maintenance area. 'It's just a necessary evil,' he concludes.

Questions

(1) As C.R., manager of IS at Metropolitan Gas Company, views maintenance in his organization, 'It's just a necessary evil'. Would you agree, under the circumstances? If so, why? If not, why not?

(2) Is the Computer Systems and Programming (CS & P) staff at Metropolitan Gas Company oriented toward careers in IS or toward careers in the company business? What policies account for this orientation?

Case 7.3. Big City State University

The organizational environment

Big City State University (BCSU) is one of the nine campuses of a statewide public university system. All the campuses adhere to the same admission guidelines and academic standards, yet each has its own distinct character, atmosphere, and academic individuality. The combined enrollment is 140 000 students, 90 per cent of them state residents. Nearly one-third study at the graduate level.

The statewide system is governed by a Board of Regents whose regular members are appointed by the Governor. In addition to setting broad general policy and making budgetary decisions for the system, the Regents appoint the president of the University, the nine chancellors, and the directors, provosts, and deans who administer the affairs of the individual campuses and divisions of the University.

The Regents delegate authority in academic matters to the Academic Senate, which determines academic policy for the University as a whole. The Senate, composed of faculty and certain administrative officers, determines the conditions for admission and granting of degrees, authorizes and supervises courses and curricula, and advises University administrators on budgets and faculty appointments and promotions. Students participate in policymaking at both campus- and statewide levels.

Big City State University is a large and complex institution devoted to scholarship, research, and public service. More than 140 buildings house two colleges and eleven professional schools and serve 33 000 students.

Undergraduates may earn a Bachelor of Arts or Bachelor of Science degree in one of 94 different disciplines; graduate students may earn one of 69 master's and 89 doctoral and professional degrees. As one of the outstanding research universities in the nation, BCSU receives approximately $135 million a year in extramural grants and contracts to support its research activities. Library facilities at BCSU, rated third in the nation last year by the Association of Research Libraries, consists of the University Research Library, the College Library, 17 specialized subject libraries, and several reading rooms.

BCSU's top administrative officer is Chancellor Y.C., who has provided dynamic leadership for the campus since he took office in the fall of 1968. Recently, he was elected to serve as chair of the Association of American Universities. A detailed administration organization chart is shown in Figure 7.7.

The focus of this study is the Administrative Information Services (AIS) group, which reports to the Vice-Chancellor of Academic Administration, along with personnel. AIS provides computing services for various administrative and staff departments at BCSU, including the Administrative Vice-Chancellor (responsible for Finance, Staff Personnel, and Business) and the Vice-Chancellor of Student Affairs (responsible for the Registrar's office, Financial Aid, and Undergraduate Admissions), who are AIS's principal users. The Vice-Chancellors of Public Affairs and Planning are also major users of AIS services.

Administrative Information Services

The Administrative Information Services (AIS) 1984 annual budget was approximately $7.9 million for all categories of expense, an 8 per cent increase over the $7.3 million budget of 1983. Application Systems and Programming wages for 1984 were budgeted at $2.1 million, a 12 per cent increase over 1983. The AIS budget is less than 1 per cent of the total BCSU operating budget, relatively low compared with the general Information Systems budget in a university (about 1–1.5 per cent, according to informal surveys conducted by BCSU staff). The budget is appropriated by the Chancellor from the University general funds and is based upon AIS management's estimate of amounts needed.

The Assistant Director of AIS reports to the Director of AIS, who in turn reports directly to the Vice-Chancellor of Academic Administration. As shown in Figure 7.8, AIS is composed of four major divisions, all reporting to the Director and Assistant Director. Applications Control and Support is responsible for end-user computer support and systems support for AIS functions that cross applications, such as data administration, EDP control and audit, project management, and standards. Applications Services performs all the programming and analysis for both new and existing application systems. Operating systems and teleprocessing are the responsibilities of the Systems Programming and Network Services division. The fourth division, Data Processing Services, is primarily in charge of daily operations and user relations, which includes production services and technical support.

The division of responsibilities between the Director and Assistant Director of AIS is fluid, depending more on individual skills and preferences than on formality. Broadly speaking, the Assistant Director's responsibilities focus on the management of day-to-day operations, while policy decisions, especially those related to the technical environment, are more often made by the Director.

Currently, there are 45 application systems analysts and programmers in AIS, a 12 per cent increase over last year. Twelve of the 45 are first-level managers (supervisors). Median length of service of the applications staff is approximately 3 years. About 25 per cent staff members (11) have been with the organization for less than 1 year. AIS itself is only $6\frac{1}{2}$ years old, having been formed when Statewide decided to decentralize some information processing to the various campuses.

More than half (69 per cent) of the applications staff has no job experience at BCSU, apart from their current positions. Twelve individuals (27 per cent) came from BCSU's graduate school of management and other schools as students, but all have prior work experience in other organizations. Sixteen staff members (36 per cent) previously held positions in information systems organizations outside BCSU. Of those with prior BCSU experience (14 individuals or 31 per cent of total applications staff), 11 held positions in other BCSU computing organizations and three came from other BCSU operating groups. Only one of the original handful of people who came from other BCSU organizations to form AIS remains in the applications staff.

The applications staff is highly educated and has a strong professional orientation. A total of 39 individuals (87 per cent) possess a four-year college degree and 16 of these (35 per cent of the 45 total) have an advanced one. Seven are currently enrolled in a BCSU doctoral program in management and one other in an MBA program for the fully employed. In addition, several people have a University Extension (UNEX) certificate of professional designation in application programming and two (4 per cent) hold the Certificate of Data Processing (CDP). None of the application staff have personal memberships in ACM, DPMA, or ASM, but AIS has an organizational membership that is used by the staff.

The amount of formal working-hour classroom education and training received

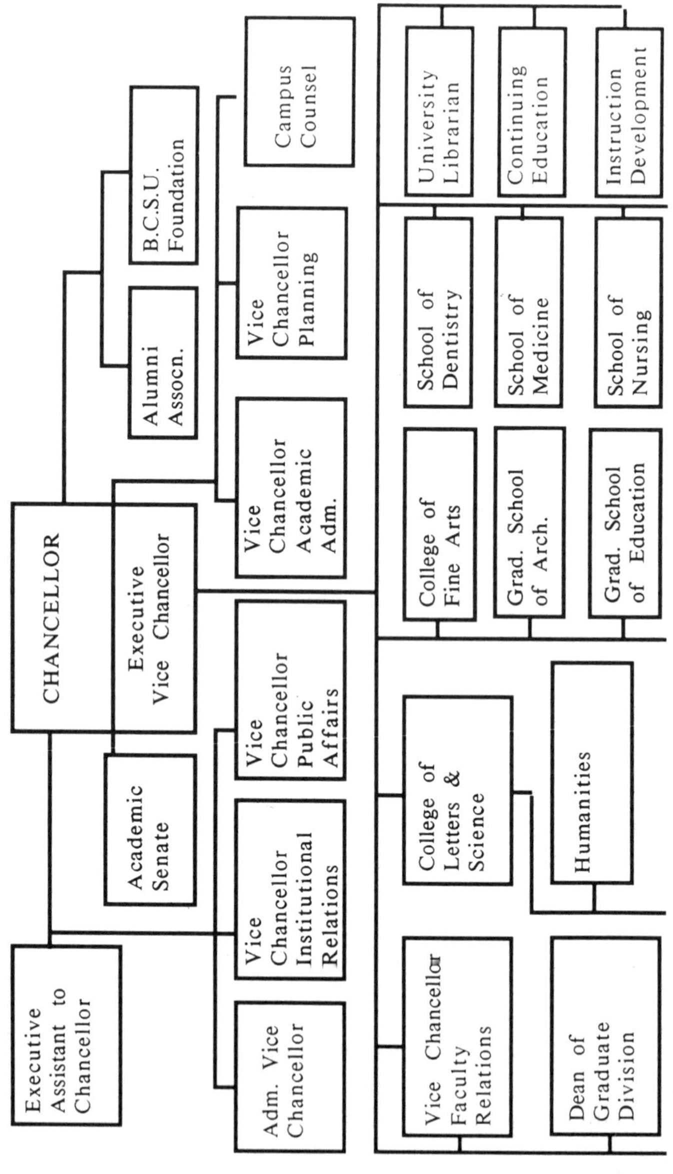
CHANCELLOR
Executive Assistant to Chancellor
Executive Vice Chancellor
Academic Senate
Alumni Assocn.
B.C.S.U. Foundation
Adm. Vice Chancellor
Vice Chancellor Institutional Relations
Vice Chancellor Public Affairs
Vice Chancellor Academic Adm.
Vice Chancellor Planning
Campus Counsel
Vice Chancellor Faculty Relations
College of Letters & Science
College of Fine Arts
School of Dentistry
University Librarian
Dean of Graduate Division
Humanities
Grad. School of Arch.
School of Medicine
Continuing Education
Grad. School of Education
School of Nursing
Instruction Development

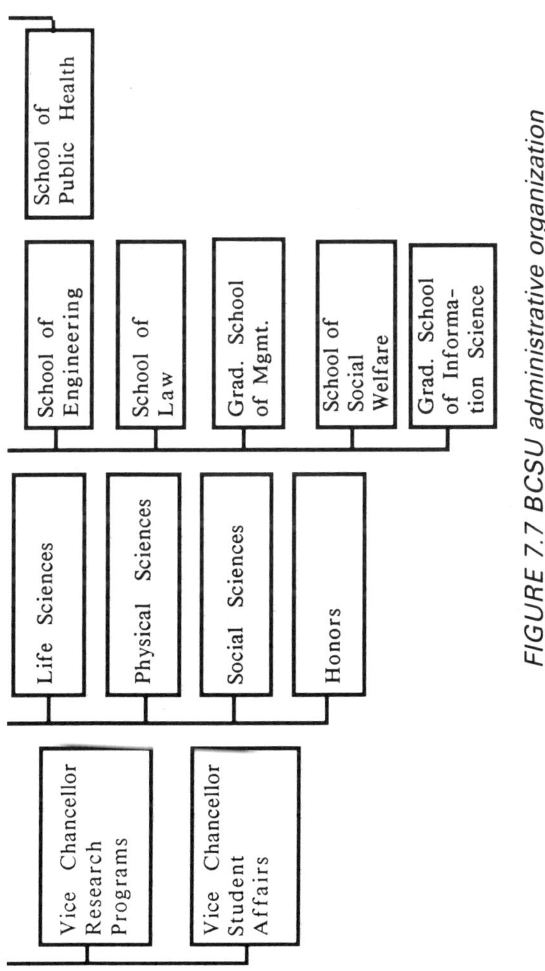

FIGURE 7.7 BCSU administrative organization

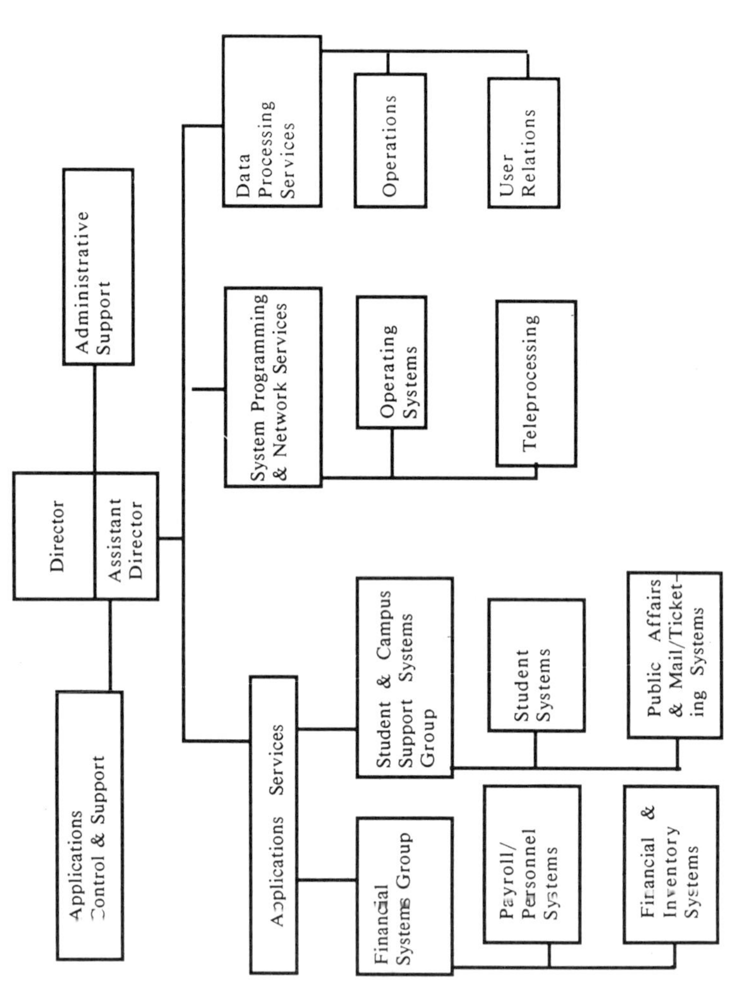

FIGURE 7.8 BCSU Office of Administrative Information Services organization chart

by the applications staff is lower than average, but AIS encourages enrollment in the UNEX certificate program and many staff members take computer-related courses on campus as part of their degree programs. During the past year, no one had more than four weeks of training; 13 people (29 per cent) received between one and four weeks of training; 21 (47 per cent) received less than one week of training; and 11 (24 per cent) had no formal individualized training at all.

All applications staff work face to face with users, on occasion. About two-thirds (32 individuals) work with users on a daily or weekly basis; others work with users less frequently but at least quarterly.

Throughout the application staff, work assignments are primarily for either maintenance or new system development. Fourteen people (31 per cent of the 45 total) currently allocate more than two-thirds of their effort to maintaining and enhancing applications. Another 14 (31 per cent) more nearly balance their time between maintenance and development, and 17 (38 per cent) devote more than two-thirds of their effort to new system development.

The maintenance and the new system staffs are not organized as separate departments in AIS. In fact, the distinction between maintenance and development in AIS is not emphasized; rather, the distinction which AIS prefers is between systems that are 'in production' and those 'not yet in production'. As described by S.G., the 'production' work (including, but not limited to, system maintenance) is defined as the 'basic level system work required to ensure the systems will run reliably, both short term and long term'.

The concept of the 'Stable Base System' is given the highest priority in AIS's annual plans. This is a system which is reliable, well controlled, maintainable, and meets basic BCSU and statewide requirements. System enhancement and new system development are ranked second and third, respectively, in AIS's maintenance work priority, behind meeting the Stable Base System requirements. The Stable Base System is a local, rather than statewide, concept.

Eleven Stable Base System criteria are stated in the AIS user's guide standards manual. These include: consideration of the user's guide standards, control and security, data administration, technical documentation, data-processing design, user/production services interface documentation, functional office 'base' operating requirements, statewide and external agency requirements, BCSU interface requirements, user documentation, and applications planning/tracking. As might be expected, some Stable Base System criteria are more specific than others.

For example, data administration, BCSU interface, and user/production services interface documentation requirements are well defined, but there are no guidelines as to what is a 'sound data-processing design'. However, a document outlining design guidelines is being developed as is a specification for the content of a technical document for AIS-developed systems.

Much of the effort for Stable Base Systems at AIS is devoted to sustaining 'current-level' hardware/software to ensure a 'highly productive, reliable, secure, auditable, and maintainable environment'. Such an environment is considered essential in order to meet their service objectives of subsecond response times for on-line production systems and adequate turnaround ones for production schedules, programming, and end-user queries. In addition, state-of-the-art systems and technology serve as an attraction at AIS that helps recruit and keep good people.

On the whole, the AIS organization is geared by management toward 'production' in terms of promotions and staff status. Staff members must assume full responsibility for production systems in order to become full project managers. As a result, individuals who work exclusively on new system development projects have less opportunities for advancement. Currently, 10 people are working solely on new systems development.

System development for in-house developed software begins with a 'shell', code written as a standard structure for all the programming work. This basic 'shell' is considered by AIS managers to be very helpful for system maintenance, since it keeps all the programs structurally consistent, avoids programming redesign, and also enables lower-level people to do more sophisticated work.

Organizational techniques established by AIS for application maintenance include: user change request procedure, change request review board, operation and maintenance cost charge-back system, maintenance escort (participation of maintainers in system development), acceptance review (in transferring software from development to maintenance), scheduled maintenance (changes batched and implemented according to predetermined schedule), automated tools (DOCUTEXT, a system from Diversified Software Systems, Inc., which produces production and cross-reference documentation from the programs' job control statements and a data dictionary), and annual maintenance planning.

Annual maintenance planning consists of three levels of planning procedures: the AIS plan, Individual Application Plans, and the Project Management System for tracking projects. The AIS plan is prepared by the Assistant Director at the beginning of each fiscal year. It contains the strategy for that year and estimated allocation of resources and also provides the framework for the individual applications plans as well as a means of communicating AIS applications direction to the University. An Individual Application Plan may be done for a single application or, if appropriate, for a number of closely related ones. Included in this plan are the objectives and general description of the application(s), project organization and responsibilities, project schedule, long-range outlook, and all the major tasks and/or issues relevant to the application(s). The Project Management System is used as a tool to track and monitor all active tasks and is intended to accurately reflect work in process.

Among work methods established by AIS for applications system development and maintenance are: structured programming, structured walk-through, top-down design, program development library, checkpoint review, programmer workbench (combination of TSO/ISPF, FOCUS, utilities, SDF screen generator), and prototyping with FOCUS. AIS's programmer workbench facility is not just for system development. 'It is used extensively,' says S.G., 'in troubleshooting and analyzing problems for production systems.' AIS's use of FOCUS is governed by a set of guidelines for appropriate use developed by AIS. For example, AIS avoids using FOCUS programs for critical processes, such as paycheck generation or admissions letter production. It is considered too unreliable for situations where programs 'must run'. Maintainability of FOCUS programs like maintainability of COBOL programs, says S.G., is dependent on using FOCUS properly and appropriately. FOCUS code can easily become convoluted when, for example, complicated breaks or matching are necessary. AIS will sometimes rewrite such a program into COBOL to enhance its maintainability or performance. Straightforward FOCUS programs, on the other hand, 'have proven easy to maintain', says S.G.

Tools currently used for documentation are: data dictionary, user manual, system-maintenance journal (for Payroll only), operations error history, program specifications standards, maintenance request forms, text plan standards, flow charts, and DOCUTEXT reports.

The application system portfolio

The current application system portfolio consists of 28 major installed systems, serving over a dozen departments at BCSU as follows (number of systems in parentheses; some systems serve multiple users):

- Administration
  - Finance (five)
  - Accounting (four)
  - Business (five)
  - Community Safety (one)
  - Facilities (one)
- Student Affairs
  - Registrar (six)
  - Student Relations (one)
- Academic Administration
  - Personnel (one)
  - Administrative Information Services (two)
- Public Affairs (one)
- Planning (two)
- Law School (one)
- Central Ticket Office (one)

AIS's principal users are the Administrative Vice-Chancellor, responsible for BCSU's financial departments, and Student Affairs, including the Office of the Registrar, Financial Aids Office, and Undergraduate Admissions. Within these areas, systems tend to be interwoven but not linked with other users' systems in the AIS application system portfolio. Other users of AIS services include Public Affairs, Planning, the Law School, the Panhellenic Society, Student Parking, and Central Ticket Office. Systems for these users tend to be independent from others in the application system portfolio.

Overall, 10 of the systems in the application portfolio (36 per cent) are relatively independent in that they rely on no other major systems. Seventeen (40 per cent) constitute the focal points in the portfolio in that they are relied upon for input data by other major systems.

The average age of the installed systems is about 5 years. Two of the 28 systems were installed last year and five major new ones are currently under development, with three of these scheduled to be installed within the next year. Three of the five new systems under development are replacement ones. Two of the three systems being replaced are relatively new (1–3 years old) but have become an excessive burden to maintain. Both were converted automatically from Autocoder to COBOL by the statewide computing facility two years ago and are considered to be virtually unmaintainable. The third system being replaced is Cashiering/Registration. This replacement was triggered by a need to replace obsolete equipment. The Registrar's cash registers and the punched-card equipment used to process registration cards will not be supported by their manufacturers in the near future.

About a third of all the major application systems (16 in all) were developed for all campuses by Statewide Computing Services (SCS). All these systems have been modified by AIS to take into account the uniqueness of the BCSU context. These systems are enhanced by both SCS and AIS. Modifications are installed and tested exclusively by AIS and seven systems in the application system portfolio (25 per cent) were developed exclusively by AIS. Four systems (14 per cent) were purchased off the shelf and modified for AIS, two quite extensively. These systems are maintained by AIS, not by their developers.

Two of the installed systems were considered by AIS management to be leading-edge applications in terms of user functions provided. The Data Dictionary system, a FOCUS system, is input/output rather than processing oriented, enhancing its ease of use. The Public Affairs Information System provides a comprehensive database in support of solicitation for BCSU and has generated interest at a number of major universities. Ten systems provide direct services to students, alumni, and their organizations.

COBOL is the predominant applications system language, employed by 17 (60 per cent) of the major systems. As part of the Stable Base System policy, all COBOL programs will be converted to COBOL II in the near future. Eleven systems use FOCUS, eight run PL/1, and Assembler and SAS are each employed very minimally by one major system. Over the long term, AIS plans to replace the PL/1 systems. In order to minimize the number of languages supported, they have standardized on COBOL, FOCUS, and SAS.

The operating environment at AIS is currently IBM-compatible (Amdahl

470/MVS-SP), but will change to an IBM 3081K, running MVS-XA, at the end of 1984. No other operating systems are employed by the application system portfolio, probably due to the Stable Base System policy, which requires that all systems operate under the most current version of AIS's system software.

All the systems in the application portfolio use FOCUS as a standard report generator, both interactively and off-line and all operate some structured program code but to varying degrees. All also use reusable program code (COPYLIB's, FOCUS Masters, etc.). Eight systems (28 per cent) use AIS's data dictionary. Two major systems (Student Records and Admissions) are included in the Statewide data dictionary. Three systems use a database management system.

The management problem set

To provide an overall perspective on the extent of various problems experienced at AIS in managing the application portfolio, S.G., the Assistant Director of AIS, completed the Problem Assessment Questionnaire. Among 26 possible problem items, four were considered by S.G. to be 'major problems': user demand for enhancements and extensions to application systems; quality of original programming of systems; competing demands for maintenance programming personnel time; and data integrity.

Statistical analysis of the problem item responses and comparison of the results with a reference survey population produced the following problem profile:

User knowledge	0.64	Above normal
Programmer effectiveness	0.34	Normal
Product quality	0.65	Normal
Programmer time availability	1.15	Above normal
Machine requirements	−0.59	Normal
System reliability	0.09	Normal

Maintenance problems at AIS, as assessed by S.G., are thus interpreted as normal in the four factors relating to programmer effectiveness, product quality, machine requirements, and system reliability. User knowledge and time availability are judged as being somewhat more problematic in comparison to the reference survey population.

This may reflect a greater sensitivity on S.G.'s part to issues of user knowledge and programmer time availability. Alternatively, it may be related to AIS's unique emphasis on preventive maintenance. Compared to organizations making only corrections and enhancements, AIS can be seen as having a larger maintenance burden, increasing the pressure on programmer time availability. In addition, convincing users that preventive maintenance will pay off in long run is no simple task, perhaps contributing to problems of user knowledge.

In summary, the overwhelming emphasis at AIS is on providing reliable, stable systems for its user community. The high priority given to Stable Base Systems in the annual plans and AIS standards speaks to the organization's dedication to this goal. This attitude is further supported by personnel policies that focus attention on the management of production systems. High levels of academic and professional training among the AIS staff combine to help AIS meet its reliability and stability goals.

In the future, the Stable Base System concept will remain important, according to S.G. Emphasis will be on establishing clear standards for some of the Stable Base System criteria and developing ways to insure that these are met over the life of the system.

One of the results of the emphasis on system quality has been that the data in AIS's application portfolio are becoming more well defined, more meaningful, and potentially more useful. In addition, a recent grant for academic computing is expected to accelerate the implementation of campus networks and therefore data access and computing in general. AIS's annual plan notes that 'AIS will face both an organizational environment increasingly anxious to do computing, and a campus technological structure that will support such computing'. AIS's ability to rise to this challenge is viewed by S.G. as fulfilling the promise of the Stable Base Systems concept.

Questions

(1) How is the distinction between system development and maintenance blurred by Administrative Information Sercices (AIS) at Big City State University? What purpose, if any, is served by this blurring?
(2) How does the concept of the Stable Base System facilitate the definition of the overall AIS task?
(3) How do AIS career paths support departmental strategy?

Postscript

Other cases from earlier chapters provide further illustrations of staffing the maintenance function. United Food Stores (Case 4.3) hires on the basis of prior work experience. Turnover is high but management is proud of its staff skills. Advance Technologies Manufacturing (Case 5.1) is located in a relatively small company town. Its IS staff has little experience elsewhere. Their careers tend to be with the company. At Nationwide Soft Drink (Case 6.1) maintenance personnel seek to 'move up' to development. Turnover in IS as a whole is low, but over the last four years turnover in maintenance has been 100 per cent.

Chapter 8

THE FUTURE FOR MAINTENANCE

INTRODUCTION

In this chapter we sum up, with an eye toward the future for maintenance. We begin by discussing the nature of the problem factors identified by the IS managers in each case and examine how the cases differed with respect to these problems. The connection between the Relational Foundations Model and problems in maintenance is accentuated in this discussion. We conclude with some suggestions for future research, followed by some recommendations for IS management. These are based both on the material presented in this book and on our experience as practitioners and researchers in the area of software maintenance. We venture out on a limb in making our recommendations, and hope that future researchers and practitioners will question, challenge, and improve upon our ideas.

THE PROBLEMS OF MAINTENANCE

As described in Chapter 2, the hypothesis guiding the research documented in this book was: Problems in the maintenance of application systems occur in substantial part because of lack of fit among and between the portfolio of application systems and those responsible for the maintenance task, both in the IS and in the appropriate user departments. That is, the problems of maintenance are viewed as being shaped by the characteristics of the application systems, the IS staff, and the users of the applications, and by the nature of the relationships between these three entities, including systems–staff, staff-users, and systems–users relationships.

We also mentioned in Chapter 2 that, in completing the questionnaires at each case-study site, an IS manager described the degree to which 26 potential problem items contributed to the problems of maintaining systems in his or her firm. This part of our survey instrument was adopted from a prior study by Lientz and Swanson (1980), as described in Chapter 3. Thirteen of the 26 items were combined into six problem factors indices (see Table 3.5 in Chapter 3). Strictly speaking, these indices explain the variance in problem identification among previous respondents. More loosely interpreted, they summarize six points of managerial attention with respect to maintenance, i.e. user knowledge, programmer effectiveness, product quality, programmer time availability, machine requirements, and system reliability. It is apparent that, as the Relational Foundations Model suggests, user characteristics (e.g. user knowledge), programmer characteristics (e.g. programmer effectiveness), and application

TABLE 8.1 Problem factors by case

	Below normal	Normal	Above normal
(1) User knowledge		All other cases	HighTech Diablo BCSU AdvTech
(2) Programmer effectiveness		All other cases	SofDrink
(3) Product quality		All other cases	HighTech AdvTech
(4) Programmer time availability	SmallMan	All other cases	SofDrink HighTech BCSU WestAero
(5) Machine requirements		All cases	
(6) System reliability		All other cases	Diablo NatFoods AdvTech WestAero

'Normal' indicates that the respondent's scoring of items contributing to the problem factor were not significantly different from those of the reference population.

characteristics (e.g. product quality) were all seen by the original set of IS managers to be important problem factors.

Of course, IS managers may or may not perceive correctly the sources of their difficulties in maintenance. Individual managers have relatively limited comparative data with which to evaluate maintenance situations. However, when managers judge a problem item to be a 'major problem in maintaining the application system portfolio' we believe they are revealing their theories of maintenance. Their theories are context dependent, to be sure, but they are richly informed from daily contact with maintenance issues. We believe that IS managers' theories of maintenance deserve our attention. Table 8.1 summarizes how the IS managers in the dozen cases saw the six problem factors.

On average, the IS managers in the twelve cases in this study found the 26 items and the six problem factors to have more pronounced effect on their maintenance difficulties than did the much larger and more diverse Lientz and Swanson sample, as described in Chapter 3. However, like the earlier group of IS managers, these managers identified three particular items to be the major contributors to problems in maintaining the application system portfolio (see Table 8.2):

Ranked #1, 'User demands for enhancements and extensions to application systems';
Ranked #2, 'Competing demands for maintenance programming personnel time'; and
Ranked #3, 'Quality of application system documentation'.

TABLE 8.2 Rank order of problem items

Rank		Problem item	Mean	Range
1	d	User demands for enhancements and extensions to application systems	4.250	3–5
2	h	Competing demands for maintenance programming personnel time	3.917	1–5
3	b	Quality of application system documentation	3.833	3–5
4	s	Unrealistic user expectations	3.500	2–5
5	f	Quality of original programming of application system	3.500	2–5
6	x	Meeting scheduled commitments	3.417	2–5
7	u	Inadequate training of user personnel	3.167	2–5
8	k	Lack of user understanding of application system	3.167	2–5
9	a	Turnover of maintenance personnel	3.000	2–4
10	v	Adequacy of application system design specifications	2.917	2–5
11	z	Turnover in user organization	2.917	1–4
12	g	Number of maintenance programming personnel available	2.833	1–5
13	c	Changes made to system hardware and software	2.750	1–5
14	m	Processing time requirements of application system programs	2.667	2–4
15	w	Budgetary pressures	2.667	1–4
16	t	Adherence to programming standards in maintenance	2.583	1–5
17	p	Maintenance programming productivity	2.500	1–4
18	r	Data integrity in application system	2.500	1–5
19	e	Skills of maintenance programming personnel	2.417	1–4
20	n	Motivation of maintenance programming personnel	2.417	1–4
21	o	Forecasting of maintenance programming personnel requirements	2.250	1–5
22	i	Lack of user interest in application system	2.250	1–4
23	q	System hardware and software reliability	2.250	1–4
24	j	Application system run failures	2.000	1–3
25	l	Storage requirements of application system programs	1.667	1–3
26	u	Management support of application system	1.667	1–3

Question: 'Overall, in your judgement, to what extent are (or have been) the following a problem in maintaining the current installed application portfolio?'
Scoring: Major problem = 5, minor problem = 3, no problem at all = 1.

The appeal of the first ranked item, 'User demands for enhancements and extensions...' is so universal that this item accounts for little variance among respondents (Lientz and Swanson, 1980). As a result, it does not appear in the user-knowledge problem factor index. However, its prominence among the 26 items speaks to the importance of user characteristics in contributing to the problems of maintaining systems.

We turn now to consideration of the six problem factors and related problem items. Our interest here is to understand how these factors become problematic with respect to maintenance.

1. User knowledge

Difficulties in the IS–user relationship that bear upon maintenance beyond demands for enhancements and extensions are highlighted by three other high-ranking items: #4, 'Unrealistic user expectations'; #7, 'Inadequate training of user personnel'; and #8, 'Lack of user understanding of application system'. The ubiquity of the users as sources of maintenance headaches speaks to both the fact that user requests for service seem uncontrollable and unpredictable on the part of IS and to a difficulty many professional service providers encounter—the communication barrier that exists between the skilled and the unskilled.

Among the 12 organizations, four found user knowledge to be more problematic (more than one standard deviation above the mean) than did the average among the reference population (that is, Lientz and Swanson's survey sample, 1980): West Coast High Tech Manufacturing, Diablo National Laboratories, Big City State University, and Advanced Technology Manufacturing (see Table 8.1). Why might that be the case? We speculate on each situation.

At West Coast High Tech Manufacturing the principal mission of the IS group is to support a manufacturing operation. A new Manufacturing Resource Planning system is currently under development to replace a major portion of the application portfolio. Meanwhile, users are limping along with a set of systems that are difficult to operate and maintain. Because of poor documentation, some of the capabilities of the current systems have been 'lost' because users are unaware of them, which may have a bearing on the manager's view of user knowledge contributing to maintenance problems at that firm.

At Advanced Technology Manufacturing many user groups are physically distant from the maintainers, at separate manufacturing sites, some outside the United States, owned by the same parent company. This physical separation may intensify problems of communication between maintainers and users, particularly when the former are answering user questions, which, as one manager pointed out, is 'the biggest chunk of maintenance'.

At Diablo National Laboratories the 'user knowledge problem' is currently the focus of substantial management attention. A major new strategy being pursued at Diablo is a transition to a distributed processing environment. End-user computing, on both a IBM 4341-based network and personal computers, will require the development of more sophisticated user information technology skills, which are being developed in part by rotation of job assignments between IS and the user departments.

At Big City State University, we were told, there is a fairly wide gap between an extremely well-educated and professional IS staff and a relatively computer-illiterate user community, comprising mostly clerical public servants.

These are all good examples, we believe, of how users and 'user knowledge' come to be problematic for maintenance units.

2. Programmer time availability

Besides the item ranked #2, 'Competing demands for maintenance programming personnel time', other items that are probably related to the scarcity and allocation of staff resources to maintenance and development are those ranked #6, 'Meeting scheduled commitments', and #9, 'Turnover of maintenance personnel'. These items relate to difficulties concerning the availability of programmers.

Among the 12 organizations, only one, Small City Manufacturing, was significantly below normal on the factor of programmer time availability (that is, finding it less problematic), while four were significantly above normal (finding it more problematic): Nationwide Soft Drink, West Coast High Tech Manufacturing, Big City State University, and Western Aeronautics. We explore these differences.

Small City Manufacturing and Western Aeronautics provide an interesting contrast on this issue. The IS department at Small City Manufacturing has been relatively recently formed as part of a new emphasis on decentralized profit responsibility. The new manufacturing IS group includes programmers from the 'Mother IS unit' and analysts transferred in from user areas. Eventually, the new unit will be responsible for development and maintenance of systems for the manufacturing function, but currently its slate includes only maintenance responsibilities. In our opinion, the new IS group at Small City Manufacturing has some slack in its staff resources and hence does not experience a programmer time availability problem.

Western Aeronautics' IS staff does, however, have a programmer time availability problem. It is currently also doing only maintenance, but for a very different reason. At this firm the objective is to conserve resources until the next big contract is signed, and the formal strategy for conservation is to do only maintenance. However, as any IS manager can appreciate, it is very difficult to stem the tide of requests for applications just because staff resources are scarce. More than likely, it seems, Western Aeronautics has fewer staff resources than it needs to do the work desired and thus experiences a programmer time availability problem. Nationwide Soft Drink, similarly, has a comparatively small maintenance group, and so may also be maintaining their application portfolio with few or no slack resources.

West Coast High Tech Manufacturing has staffing limitations of a different type. With a very small staff, IS management has far fewer degrees of freedom in making assignments, which undoubtedly puts a squeeze on programmer resources.

Big City State University may find programmer time availability to be a problem because its IS agenda includes bringing systems up to 'stable base criteria', a 'hygiene' activity that is relatively rare in IS organizations. We suspect it is this activity that competes for programmer time at Big City State University.

From examples such as these the problem of programmer availability can be understood to be partly rooted in the systems–staff relationship, involving, on the systems side, the nature and quality of the application systems and, on the staff side, demands for staff attention.

3. Product quality

Problems with the original system, such as the item ranked #3, 'Quality of application system documentation', are echoed in other high-ranking items describing problems with the quality of the developer's product: #5, 'Quality of original programming of application system', and #10, 'Adequacy of application system design specifications'.

Two IS managers among our cases, at West Coast High Tech Manufacturing and Advanced Technology Manufacturing, found product quality to be significantly more problematic than did others. At both these sites the portfolio is highly integrated, offering leading-edge functionality to a high-technology manufacturing department. Also, at both sites important applications in the portfolio are developed in one organization and used in another. Thus in these two sites we see two sides of the external development issue.

At West Coast High Tech Manufacturing much of the application software is developed by a corporate IS group at the parent company headquarters and then used at the manufacturing site and maintained by the local IS staff. Maintainers, that is, are separated from developers but co-located with users. The maintainers, with no development experience, are dependent on good documentation. Inevitably, as the systems age, as they have at West Coast High Tech, the maintainers face an increasingly difficult task. Therefore at this firm, product quality and its effect on maintenance is a major focus of managerial attention.

The IS group at Advanced Technology Manufacturing, in contrast, develops and maintains some systems that are used not only in their host organization but also at other manufacturing sites belonging to their parent company. That is, at this firm the developers and maintainers are co-located but they are separated, in some cases, from the users of the systems. For this IS staff, product quality is also of paramount importance, as the systems will be used in environments with which the maintainers are less familiar, by people whom they may not have seen. An extra burden is thus placed on the developers to deliver robust systems. As one manager states, 'We should be doing things right the first time, and doing them in ways so the user doesn't get confused.'

Product quality is thus a problem that can be understood sometimes as one between IS staff and systems and on other occasions as one between systems and users. That is, if programmers develop systems of poor quality, which are hard to enhance, a maintenance problem arises. In other cases, problems of product quality stem from a user environment that is particularly demanding, perhaps because it is quite varied or because users are not knowledgeable about computing.

4. Programmer effectiveness

Among items that were actually considered more minor we find a group related to the abilities and skills of the maintenance staff itself: #17, 'Maintenance programming productivity', #19, 'Skills of maintenance programming personnel', and #20, 'Motivation of maintenance programming personnel'. One interpretation of this result would be that maintenance personnel are a relatively minor part of the overall maintenance problem. However, another, and one which seems more likely, is that, for the most part, the maintenance staffs in these cases are not clearly distinguished from the development staffs and thus cannot be independently evaluated by the respondents to our questionnaire.

Among the 12 cases, only one, Nationwide Soft Drink, claims significant problems related to programmer effectiveness. It is worth noting that at this firm the maintenance staff is separated from the development staff, and thus an independent evaluation of the maintenance staff is, in fact, feasible. We believe that programmer effectiveness is an issue in this organization primarily due to the maintenance manager's sensitivity to possible motivation problems among the maintenance staff, or, as he calls it, 'the stigma of maintenance'. He has adopted several policies, such as rapid promotions, an informal 'team leader' title, and opportunities to 'move up to development' in an effort to counteract low morale.

The problem of programmer effectiveness, apparently, is primarily one related to the staff and its organization.

5. Machine requirements and system reliability

Items that are viewed as contributing little or not at all to problems of maintenance include #25, 'Storage requirements of application system programs', #24, 'Application system run failures', and #23, 'System hardware and software reliability'. These more technical problems may be perceived by IS managers as either more controllable or less prevalent than those related to developers, maintainers, and users.

None of the twelve cases scored outside the normal range on the machine requirements problem factor. Four found system reliability problems that were above normal: Diablo National Laboratories, Western Aeronautics, National Foods, and Advanced Technology Manufacturing. At Diablo National Laboratories and Western Aeronautics the difficulty seems to have stemmed from reliability problems following system upgrades. At National Foods, on the other hand, the reliability problems may have been more related to data integrity. Advanced Technology Manufacturing is particularly sensitive to system reliability because they are offering maintenance services affecting customers of their host organization and other manufacturing sites of the parent organization, as mentioned earlier. In none of these cases, however, did system reliability seem to be a significant point of attention for IS managers during our conversations.

6. Summary

By far the most significant problems regarding maintenance, according to IS managers in our cases and elsewhere, are to be found in the IS–user relationship. The universal appeal of the first-ranked problem item, 'User demands for enhancements and extensions to application systems', and the first problem factor index, 'User knowledge', speak to the importance of further study of this relationship. We discuss this in more detail below.

DIRECTIONS FOR FUTURE RESEARCH

A significant tradition of research on the technical aspects of maintenance exists, such as that on complexity metrics, software structure, and automated verification of specifications (see Chapters 5 and 6). From this research a new generation of tools for maintainers is likely to appear. With increasing frequency, we also see research on management issues in maintenance. However, substantive research on managerial issues is very expensive and time consuming, and the scope of most research studies in this domain is fairly limited, but it is, as the current research shows, extremely important.

Research in the management of maintenance should include analysis at the organizational level. Studies of the work of the individual IS staff member are too narrow to address the managerial and organizational issues in maintenance. We have argued here that a focus on the portfolio as a whole and on individual systems as related parts of this whole is necessary to make sense of maintenance tasks. An organizational level of analysis, in which the organization of individuals around a task shared with users regarding a portfolio of information-providing and action-initiating systems, permits the framing and investigation of questions of managerial interest.

In the following we suggest that future research in the area of software maintenance must incorporate more elaborate concepts of the maintenance 'user' and the maintainer. We also suggest that research on the impact of new technological developments on the portfolio and on the maintenance task is needed, and that new research approaches or methods may also be in order.

1. User characteristics

Much more knowledge about the user role in the world of maintenance is needed. In both this study and the previous Lientz and Swanson (1980) one, users are identified by the IS managers as the principal source of problems for maintainers. They are also the principal recipients of solutions from maintainers: users, we see, begin and end the maintenance cycle. The current study, which includes the notion that users are an important part of the equation merely scratches the surface of understanding their role in IS maintenance.

Classes of users need to be identified. The construct 'user' needs considerable elaboration before it can be usefully applied. The IS literature already distinguishes between computing-literate and naive users (McLean, 1979), direct and indirect users (Keen, 1976), and satisfied and dissatisfied users (Ives *et al.*, 1983). These distinctions, however, have not proven very powerful in explaining the relationship between IS and the user.

In future studies, demographics about users very similar to those we studied with respect to the IS staff—length of service, education, professionalism, training in computing—could be analyzed in relation to maintenance organizational problems. The notion of 'organizational distance' between IS and a user seems important here—consider, for example, the differences in supporting users located in the same department as IS compared with supporting users in other parts of a division, in a different division, or even in a different firm.

The current research illustrates that variation among users, as well as IS staff and application systems, is inevitable. Studying the fit between collections of users and collections of staff and application systems requires that we pay close attention to this variation as well as the central tendency within each collection of elements. Appropriate data-analysis techniques must be identified for this purpose.

Incorporating models of the user task into IS research, particularly where the task drives the need for information, seems absolutely fundamental. With respect to maintenance, this means incorporating the user's role in application use and maintenance into the overall model, as suggested by our Task Model (Figure 2.1).

This book has also argued that the policies and strategies of the host organization create a context for maintenance (see Chapter 4). This context and its impact on the organization of maintenance is no doubt mediated in part by the demands of IS users and should be studied in these terms. We have also argued (Chapter 1) that the application portfolio creates a context for organizational events by embodying and institutionalizing organizational knowledge, establishing the facts to which the organization attends, and structuring the processes by which it operates. The importance of the role of the IS staff in sustaining systems on which the organization depends in this way should not be underestimated.

At a minimum, user evaluation of maintenance service should be incorporated into maintenance studies. User assessments of maintenance problems, especially when juxtaposed with those of IS managers, might reveal quite different 'theories' of maintenance.

Particularly relevant and useful would be insights that would improve the predictability of requests for enhancements to systems. At present, much maintenance research and practice treat requests for changes as arising more or less from an unfathomable black box. It seems more likely, however, that patterns in user circumstances or in the interaction of user and systems might be used to predict at least some part of this arcane stream of requests.

2. Impact of new technology

A more detailed examination of the impact of new systems development technologies—particularly fourth-generation languages, programmer work-benches, and Computer-Aided Systems Engineering (CASE) tools—on the practice and management of maintenance is needed. It is important that this research examine not only the technical impacts of the new tools on the maintenance task but also the organizational and managerial implications of the tools and, most importantly, the way in which these new developments alter the IS–user relationship. This research can provide valuable guidance for the articulation of development policies.

The rapid growth of end-user computing raises several issues for maintainers that deserve study. One obvious issue is the maintenance of user-developed systems. However, other, more subtle issues are also raised by end-user computing. End-user computing has probably eliminated part of the maintenance 'burden' as end-users have taken over the job of developing extensions or enhancements for some systems. At the same time, it has made requests for enhancements and extensions less visible, less traceable, harder to control, and much more difficult to analyze. The division of responsibility for extensions and enhancements between users and IS needs much closer examination.

3. Professionalization of maintenance

The Software Maintenance Association is an association of professional application software maintainers. It sponsors an annual meeting, various symposia, and regular chapter meetings in 14 American cities. (Information can be obtained by writing: Software Maintenance Association, 56 Bay Street, #400, Staten Island, New York, 10301). This new association speaks to a growing professionalism among maintainers who are developing new norms and concepts regarding the practice and management of maintenance.

Research contrasting professional maintainers with 'developers doing maintenance work' might contribute to the debate on the motivating potential of maintenance (Couger and Colter, 1985). Among professional maintainers, moreover, we may also find differences—some may specialize in technical work, others in application domains. Maintainers, we may discover, are as varied as users.

4. Longitudinal research

Our final suggestion is methodological on the surface but systemic in intent. There is a need for more research on patterns of application system maintenance over time. Do older systems require more (Guimaraes, 1983) or less (Vessey and Weber, 1983) maintenance? Do all systems grow, or are there predictable exceptions? Do some parts of a system need more enhancements than others? How do characteristics of the user community for a system impact upon its life cycle? It is true, as we have argued here, that more mature portfolios are best served by a separate maintenance group in the long run?

Many questions surrounding system replacement arise from the current research. We have argued that as a portfolio matures, replacements are more likely. Replacements of basic transaction systems, and in particular those of basic accounting functions with new packages, are becoming increasingly common in IS departments. What policies should guide this replacement process? What characteristics of the existing system speak to the need to replace or not to replace? How does the replacement process differ from the usual development one?

To answer questions such as these it will be necessary to examine many systems over a considerable period of time. To explore such questions, however, it might be possible to reconstruct short periods of history for several systems in several locations or rough histories for a few systems over a lengthy period. This type of research requires solid co-operation from IS practitioners, but should be very revealing on important issues.

LESSONS FOR IS MANAGEMENT

Throughout this book we have harped on certain themes, which we repeat here for those readers who have skipped ahead or around or who are still in need of reinforcement. Our suggestions grow out of the case studies reported in this work, but are influenced by our experiences with other IS maintenance organizations, both as researchers and as practitioners.

We draw our lessons for managers of administrative information systems departments, wholly contained within a host organization and providing the bulk of that organization's information service support. While we are not specifically thinking of, for example, software houses offering maintenance services on a fee basis, or user organizations setting up a small maintenance unit to keep their user-developed code running, or units that maintain system software, some of what we say might also apply to those organizations.

1. Give it managerial attention

There is nothing like a little managerial attention when it comes to a business problem. Such attention provides a foundation for a maintenance philosophy (Chapter 4), it is a prerequisite for investments in maintenance tools and organizational techniques (Chapters 5 and 6), and it implies rewards for improved maintenance (Chapter 7). One of the best ways to direct managerial attention to maintenance is to put an experienced manager specifically in charge of it, giving it his or her undivided attention. This usually means centralizing maintenance and separating it from development. As outlined in Chaper 6, this has considerable productivity and quality benefits, but these benefits depend on a good manager seeing that they are both necessary and possible. Merely separating maintenance and putting a team-leader in charge of it will not achieve the benefits we believe many of our cases obtained by separating maintenance. Our advice is, give it one of your best managers.

2. Provide a vision for maintenance

Whether or not there is a good manager in charge of maintenance, there should be an IS department vision for maintenance. A clear philosophy for maintenance and specific goals for maintenance will go a long way toward guiding investment and other maintenance choices. For example, if the vision is 'Let's get completely rid of maintenance!' that might suggest doing all maintenance with outside contractors, or radically improving the quality of developed systems, or training users to do all enhancements. If the vision is 'Let's use maintenance to integrate our portfolio!' a different set of policies might result. Maintenance is not development gone awry; it is different from development. How it is different or, rather, what differences are to be emphasized, is up to the organization. Without the vision for maintenance, however, a concerted effort is unlikely.

3. Use information systems for maintenance

We have heard many jokes about IS being like the cobbler's children. Who has not seen an IS department that tracks all its projects with pencil and paper or, worse, with a black- or white-board? However, we all know that good information is important to good management, so we should be able to keep this short. As IS managers, you should develop systems to track three things: the application portfolio, the staff, and the users (see also Chapter 6 on measurement). You should track changes in complexity and growth of systems, monitor maintenance activity (researchers will take all these data off your hands periodically, with deep gratitude), and do life-cycle audits of systems to record demographics of the portfolio. You should also track skills, education, training, experiences, and career paths of the application staff and relate these to the application portfolio and cross reference application experience with user area experience. You can track similar characteristics for users, also cross referencing them with applications. When all this information has been gathered together, you must be sure to attend not only to the central tendencies of the data but also to the variation or cohort effects in it (see the discussion in Chapter 3).

Most importantly, you should collect information from and about the users and convince them to participate in life-cycle audits, too, even if you have to promise them something in return. Go beyond the formal information collected on users and really get to know them, remembering that it is the users who are the source of the bulk of maintenance problems, or so our IS managers tell us. If user knowledge is a problem, perhaps some training is in order. If user expectations are incorrect, perhaps some consciousness raising can be effected. If users are making unexpected demands for changes, perhaps some orientation for the IS department can help to make those demands more predictable.

4. Throw some money at maintenance

We suggest you invest in maintenance-oriented tools and techniques (see Chapter 5). Code analyzers, tools that extract documentation from code, fourth-generation languages, and test support packages can be purchased. Many more important investments, however, are internal human resource ones. Insisting that programmers develop and use re-usable code, for example, may increase development costs but will reduce those of maintenance, as re-usable code is easier to maintain, partly because it is of higher quality and partly because there is less of it. Creating maintenance-supporting documentation (which may mean updating the data-flow diagrams and fixing the data dictionary entries) may add to development costs, but it should save much in the maintenance part of the life cycle. Test harnesses, or extra code which supports de-install/re-install activities, also needs to be planned and built during development, at some extra cost, but will pay off down the line. Finally, be sure to invest in your own maintenance research, if you get the opportunity.

5. Insist on a clean turnover

The best investment you can make in maintenance may be in a clean turnover process. The fuzzy period that usually camouflages the termination of development can birth all manner of wickedness—untested end-of-year routines, sketchy documentation, rudimentary training of users and maintainers, mislaid test packages. A more formal turnover process promotes meaningful turnover criteria, which in turn require the developers to actually think about what the post-installation life of the systems is likely to include. Will the system be in and out of operation often? What are the likely areas of enhancement? What are the likely areas for corrective maintenance? What documentation will be the most useful? The real impact of a formal turnover process is on the development activities, which is where a large portion of maintenance problems originate.

A turnover process can sometimes be cloned from the life-cycle audit process, as many of the same questions are at issue. Maintenance escorts, as recommended by Lientz and Swanson (1980) also facilitate effective turnover. Training for maintainers by the development team is another possibility.

6. Design a maintenance career

Maintainers are a clever bunch. If they see that the stepping stone to top management is labeled 'development', the upwardly mobile ones will just naturally gravitate to the development projects. However, development, as we have argued in Chapter 5, is largely buffered from the day-to-day operations of the business. Developers are protected in the short run from the consequences of their own design choices and implementation strategies. Maintainers, on the other hand, live on the firing line. They get to know their users, their users' business, and the firm's business. They learn what works and what does not, and they often learn why. A demonstrated competence for maintenance should be an important rung on the ladder to IS management posts.

If the application portfolio includes strategic systems (and we believe that most portfolios either do or will) it is even more important that maintenance experience be required for all top IS managers.

CONCLUSION

If we were to sum up our point of view on maintaining systems in organizations in one short sentence it would be 'Maintenance to the forefront!' Maintenance is too important, particularly in organizations with mature portfolios, to be subordinated to systems development. It is also too complex and too difficult, especially if the organization is dependent on computing, to be allowed to coast along unattended. Maintenance is more than a set of techniques, it is an organizational issue, requiring an explicit strategy, a coherent domain of responsibility, professional management, and an excellent staff.

We have argued in this book that a broad view of maintenance, encompassing the portfolio of applications, the users, and the IS staff and the relations among and between these elements, provides the right foundation for managing maintenance. Without any one of these the view of maintenance narrows to merely a morale problem, a resource-allocation problem, or a documentation problem. None of these problems can be solved by itself. They must be attacked together, by focusing on maintenance as an organizational problem and by taking a broad view of it. However, such a view does more than help us solve some classic maintenance problems; it also positions us to deliver quality information services to the host organization.

As maintenance of the application portfolio moves to the forefront of the IS task, the role of the IS organization becomes clearer. We have shown, in the Relational Foundations Model (Figure 1.1) and in the Task Model (Figure 2.1), that sustaining operational information systems in the application portfolio, along with other portfolio-related work, is a task shared by IS and the users of these applications. That is, the application portfolio is at the heart of the relationship between IS and the host organization, and it is through this portfolio that we can see the long-term kernel of that relationship. It is maintenance.

REFERENCES

Couger, J. D.,and Colter, M. A. (1985) *Maintenance Programming: Improving Productivity Through Motivation*, Prentice-Hall, Englewood Cliffs, NJ.

Guimaraes, T. (1983) 'Managing application program maintenance expenditures', *Communications of the ACM*, **26**, 10, October, 739–46.

Ives, B., Olson, M., and Baroudi, J. (1983) 'The measurement of user information satisfaction', *Communications of the ACM*, **26**, 10, October, 785–93.

Keen, P. G. W. (1976) '"Interactive" computer systems for managers: a modest proposal', *Sloan Management Review*, **18**, 1, Fall, 1–17.

Lientz, B. P., and Swanson, E. B. (1980) *Software Maintenance Management*, Addison-Wesley, Reading, Mass.

McLean, E. R. (1979) 'End users as application developers', *MIS Quarterly*, **3**, 4, December, 37–46.

Vessey, I., and Weber, R. (1983) 'Some factors affecting program repair maintenance: an empirical study', *Communications of the ACM*, **26**, 2, February, 128–34.

APPENDIX
RESEARCH QUESTIONNAIRE

SOFTWARE MAINTENANCE QUESTIONNAIRE

PART I. THE I.S. ORGANIZATION

revised January 30, 1984

Computers and Information Systems Research Program
Graduate School of Management
University of California
Los Angeles, CA 90024

1. What is the current total annual dollar budget (all categories of expense) of the I.S. organization?

Equipment and Facilities			______
Data Processing Equipment		______	
Purchased	______		
Hardware ______			
Software ______			
Leased	______		
Services	______		
Data Communications Equipment		______	
Purchased	______		
Leased	______		
Services	______		
Facilities		______	
Supplies		______	
Personnel			______
Operations Wages		______	
Employee	______		
Contract	______		
Applications Systems and Programming Wages		______	
Employee	______		
Contract	______		
Other Staff Wages		______	
Education and Training Services		______	
Other			______
Total Budget, current			______

2. What was the annual dollar budget, <u>one year ago</u>?

Equipment and Facilities			____
Data Processing Equipment		____	
Purchased	____		
Hardware ____			
Software ____			
Leased	____		
Services	____		
Data Communications Equipment		____	
Purchased	____		
Leased	____		
Services	____		
Facilities		____	
Supplies		____	
Personnel			____
Operations Wages		____	
Employee	____		
Contract	____		
Applications Systems and Programming Wages		____	
Employee	____		
Contract	____		
Other Staff Wages		____	
Education and Training Services		____	
Other			____
Total Budget, previous year			____

3. What is the current total number of (full-time equivalent) application systems analysts and programmer employees (excluding contract personnel and managers)?

____ total application staff, current

What was the total number <u>one year ago</u>?

____ total application staff, last year

4. What is the number of first-level managers of the current applications staff? (A first-level manager is defined here as a manager to whom no other manager reports.)

    __________ first-level managers

5. What is the length of service (in the I.S. Organization) distribution of the current application staff? (Indicate the number in each category.)

    __________ 0-1 years
    __________ 1-3 years
    __________ 3-6 years
    __________ 6-10 years
    __________ more than 10 years

    __________ total application staff, current (This number should match the number in Question 3 above. References to total application staff in the questions to follow also refer to this number.)

6. What is the distribution of (immediate) prior job experience of the current application staff? (Indicate the number in each category.)

    __________ position in other I.S. organization within parent organization

    __________ other position within parent organization

    __________ position in other I.S. organization, not in parent organization

    __________ other position, not in parent organization

    __________ no prior position (student)

    __________ total application staff, current

7. What is the distribution of educational backgrounds (highest degrees obtained) of the applications staff? (Indicate the number in each category.)

 ________ Graduate college degree
 ________ Bachelors college degree
 ________ Two-year college degree
 ________ High school diploma or less

 ________ total application staff, current

How many of the current applications staff hold the Certificate of Data Processing (CDP)?

 ________ CDP holders

How many of the current applications staff are members of the following professional societies?

 ________ ACM (Association for Computing Machinery) members
 ________ DPMA (Data Processing Management Association) members
 ________ ASM (Association for Systems Management) members

8. What is the distribution of working-hour classroom education and training received by the applications staff during the past year? (Indicate the number in each category.)

   ____________ Four weeks or more of classroom education and training

   ____________ Less than four weeks, but at least two weeks

   ____________ Less than two weeks, but at least one week

   ____________ Less than one week, but at least one day

   ____________ Less than one day

   ____________ total application staff, current

9. What is the allocation of application staff effort to maintenance and new system development? (Indicate the number of staff in each category.) As used here, the term "maintenance" refers to all modifications made to an existing application system, including enhancements and extensions.

   _________ More than 2/3 of person's effort allocated to maintenance

   _________ No more than 2/3 of person's effort allocated to either maintenance or new system development

   _________ More than 2/3 of person's effort allocated to new system development

   _________ Total application staff, current

10. Are the maintenance staff (those allocating more than 2/3 effort to maintenance) and the new systems staff (those allocating more than 2/3 effort to new systems development) organized as separate departments in the I.S. organization?

_______ Yes
_______ No
_______ Does not apply (There exists no substantial maintenance and/or new systems staff.)

11. How frequently does the current application staff work directly (face to face) with the users (members of the using departments) of the applications? (Indicate the number of staff in each category.)

_______ Daily
_______ Not daily, but at least weekly
_______ Not weekly, but at least monthly
_______ Not monthly, but at least quarterly
_______ Less frequently than quarterly, or not at all

_______ Total application staff, current

12. Which of the following organizational techniques are established by the I.S. organization for application system maintenance? (Check all those which apply.)

_________ periodic maintenance audit

_________ user change request procedure

_________ change request review board

_________ operation and maintenance cost charge-back system

_________ maintenance escort (participation of maintainer in system development)

_________ acceptance review (in transferring software from development to maintenance)

_________ formal retest procedure (in implementing changes)

_________ scheduled maintenance (changes batched and implemented according to predetermined schedule)

_________ other(s) (please indicate:)

____

____

____

13. Which of the following work methods are established by the I.S. organization for application system development and maintenance? (Check all those which apply.)

_________ structured programming

_________ structured walk-through

_________ top-down design

_________ structured retrofit

_________ program development library

_________ checkpoint review

_________ benchmark testing

_________ test data generator

_________ programmer workbench (e.g., UNIX)

_________ application generator

_________ other(s) (please indicate:)

____

____

____

14. Which of the following documentation tools are established by the I.S. organization for application system development and maintenance? (Check all those which apply.)

    ________ data model diagram
    ________ data dictionary
    ________ user manual
    ________ HIPO diagram
    ________ Warnier diagram
    ________ pseudo-code
    ________ data-flow diagram
    ________ Jackson diagrams
    ________ PSL/A (Problem Statement Language/Analyzer)
    ________ system development journal
    ________ test history
    ________ system maintenance journal
    ________ automated code analyzer
    ________ operations error history
    ________ other(s) (please indicate:)

    ____
    ____
    ____

SOFTWARE MAINTENANCE QUESTIONNAIRE

PART II. THE APPLICATION SYSTEM PORTFOLIO

revised January 30, 1984

Computers and Information Systems Research Program
Graduate School of Management
University of California
Los Angeles, CA 90024

1. What is the total number of major systems in the current installed application system portfolio? (A system is defined as software developed, installed and maintained as an integrated unit. A major system is one in which significant I.S. resources have been invested.)

    ________ number of major installed systems, current

    What was the total number of major installed systems <u>one year ago</u>?

    ________ number of major installed systems, last year

2. Which is the size of the user population served by the current installed application system portfolio? (The user population is defined here as the total number of personnel in the user departments served.)

    ________________ user population size

3. What is the application domain of the current installed application system portfolio? (Identify the major installed systems by name and function.)

4. What is the age distribution (measured from date of original installation) of the current installed application system portfolio? (Indicate the number of major systems in each category.)

    ________ 0-1 years
    ________ 1-3 years
    ________ 3-6 years
    ________ 6-10 years
    ________ more than 10 years

    ________ total number of current major installed systems (This number should match the number in Question 1 above).

5. What is the size distribution of application systems in the current portfolio? (Complete the three sentences below.)

Twenty five percent (25%) of the major systems contain at least ______ thousand executable source statements; seventy five percent (75%) contain fewer.

Fifty percent (50%) of the major systems contain at least _____ thousand executable source statements; fifty percent (50%) contain fewer.

Seventy five percent (75%) of the major systems contain at least _____ thousand executable source statements; twenty five percent (25%) contain fewer.

6. What is the distribution of development backgrounds of the current installed application system portfolio? (Indicate the number of major systems in each category.)

__________ developed by the I.S. Organization

__________ developed by other I.S. organization in parent organization, adapted locally.

__________ developed by user organization in parent organization

__________ developed by outside firm, on custom-build contract.

__________ developed by outside firm, purchased as off-the-shelf parameterized package

__________ total number of current major installed systems

7. How many of the major systems in the current installed application system portfolio are known to be leading edge applications, in the sense of providing users with functions beyond those typically available to their counterparts in other organizations in the industry?

__________ leading edge applications, in terms of user functions provided

8. How many of the major systems in the current installed application system portfolio provide direct services to the customers or suppliers of the parent organization ? (A direct service is provided if the customer or supplier obtains information directly from the system, as for example, travel agents do with airline reservation systems.)

__________ provide direct services to customers or suppliers

9. Of the major systems in the current installed application system portfolio, how many rely on other major systems for their input data?

__________ rely on other major systems

How many are relied upon for input data by other major systems?

__________ relied upon by other major systems

10. What hardware and system software is employed to process the application system portfolio? (List the configurations and the number of major application systems supported by each.)

Hardware/system software configurations	Number of major application systems supported
______________	______
______________	______
______________	______
______________	______
______________	______
______________	______
______________	______

11. What programming languages are employed within the current installed application system portfolio? (Indicate the number of major application systems employing each.)

Language	Number of major systems employing
COBOL	______
Assembler	______
PL/1	______
RPG	______
FORTRAN	______
Other(s) (please indicate:)	
______________	______
______________	______
______________	______

12. Which of the following technologies are employed within the current installed application system portfolio? (Indicate the number of major application systems employing each.)

Technology	Number of major systems employing
data base management system	________
data dictionary	________
user query language	________
report generator, interactive	________
report generator, off-line	________
application generator, interactive	________
application generator, off-line	________
structured program code	________
graphics language	________
tutorial function	________
reusable program code	________
other(s) (please indicate:)	
____________	________
____________	________

13. What is the total number of major approved new systems currently under development, for future installation in the application system portfolio?

    __________ major new systems currently under development

    How many of these systems are scheduled for installation within the next year?

    __________ major new systems to be installed within next year

14. Of the total number of major approved new systems currently under development, how many of these are <u>replacement systems</u> (for systems currently in the application system portfolio)?

    __________ major replacement systems currently under development

    What is the age distribution (measured from date of original installation) of the systems to be replaced? (Indicate the number of major systems in each category.)

    __________ 1-3 years
    __________ 3-6 years
    __________ 6-10 years
    __________ more than 10 years

    __________ total number of systems to be replaced

15. In the case of the systems to be replaced in the current installed application system portfolio, what are the important reasons for replacement? (Check the appropriate category.)

No importance

Slight importance

Moderate importance

Substantial importance

Extreme importance

	5	4	3	2	1
a. Excessive burden to maintain					
b. Excessive burden to operate					
c. Excessive burden to use					
d. Existence of application package alternative					
e. Existence of application generator alternative					
f. Other (indicate:) ________________					

16. Overall, in your judgement, to what extent are (or have been) the following a problem in maintaining the current installed application system portfolio? (Check the appropriate category.)

	Major Problem	Somewhat Major Problem	Minor Problem	Somewhat Minor Problem	No Problem At All
	5	4	3	2	1
a. Turnover of maintenance personnel					
b. Quality of application system documentation					
c. Changes made to system hardware and software					
d. User demand for enhancements and extensions to application system					
e. Skills of maintenance programming personnel					
f. Quality of original programming of application system					
g. Number of maintenance programming personnel available					
h. Competing demands for maintenance programming personnel time					
i. Lack of user interest in application system					
j. Application system run failures					
k. Lack of user understanding of application system					

	Major Problem	Somewhat Major Problem	Minor Problem	Somewhat Minor Problem	No Problem At All
	5	4	3	2	1
l. Storage requirements of application system programs					
m. Processing time requirements of application system programs					
n. Motivation of maintenance programming personnel					
o. Forecasting of maintenance programming personnel requirements					
p. Maintenance programming productivity					
q. System hardware and software reliability					
r. Data integrity in application system					
s. Unrealistic user expectations					
t. Adherence to programming standards in maintenance					
u. Management support of application system					
v. Adequacy of application system design specifications					
w. Budgetary pressures					
x. Meeting scheduled commitments					
y. Inadequate training of user personnel					
z. Turnover in user organization					
Others (Please indicate:)					
____________________					
____________________					

INDEX